My Africa

By

Eveart 'E.B.' Boniface

This memoir is based on my best recollection of what I want to remember of what I can remember. In the interest of authenticity, apart from where it may cause embarrassment or land me in court, I have used the real names of real people. The events are real.

Please forgive me if I've spelt your name wrongly. If the name fits but the cap doesn't… it can't be you.

If however, it is your name, and the cap does fit…*Enjoy.*

Cover by Allison Johnson
features 15 year-old Bill Anderson descending Greycap in 1956.

Published by Eveart Boniface

ISBN 978-191069349-0

This is dedicated to Rhodesians

The people, some rich, mostly not, some dirt poor, who gave their all to establish the closest thing to civilised society ever to exist during the known history of Africa

Thanks and Acknowledgements

My old memory has needed reinforcement from time to time and for that I owe thanks to friends, various authors (acknowledged in footnotes), the internet and even Wikipedia. Of course, I have to thank my wife Eunice, for much more than help with my memory; she's put me right on numerous occasions, something she's very good at, as can be expected after more than 50 years of practice.

Of course there was a fair amount of editing required and for that I am very grateful to both friend and neighbour Jan Smallwood and of course Eunice.

Our eldest daughter, Charlene, has given up much of a very short visit from her home in Canada to sort out the computer-generated mess I made of the formatting.

Our son, Allan, supplied expert comment and photos of deep-level gold mining and our youngest daughter, Allison, has never ceased with encouragement, advice and instructions as well as designing the cover.

My appreciation also goes to all who have made this memoir possible; everyone who has touched my life and shaped my character, friends, relatives, teachers, bosses and colleagues. I'm glad to say my recollections are mostly good; I seemed to have outlived most of the bad. Sadly many of the good, from all communities, will never read this, among them are those who helped my parents when they really needed it.

Without a group of like-minded people this memoir would never have been completed. For that support, guidance and constructive criticism I owe thanks to tutor Brendon McCusker and my classmates.

EB.

Contents

Appendix

Family History

Illusrations

Chapter 1

1940

Yes, it's easy enough to kill a snake with a hefty stick, but, you might not see it and if you step on it, too bad, too late. The heavy-headed puff-adder's 20 mm fangs can easily pierce shoe leather.

When Owen, my Dad, was bitten by one of Brundett's large and well established snake population, he applied the standard Rhodesian remedy of the day. Speed was essential; he used his shave-sharp pruning knife to make a fang-deep, two-inch-long cut through each puncture. These he packed with potassium permanganate crystals. He was very ill, bed-ridden for a week. Years later, when I asked, as children do, he showed me the twin scars on his shin.

The cuts would have allowed some of the venom to bleed out, and the permanganate would help to prevent septicaemia, a common cause of death from wild animal bites. A powerful oxidizing chemical, it may also have reacted against the venom; most old-timers carried a small vial of it. Every chemist sold it.

The snakes were one of the disadvantages of Brundett, a smallholding and my 1940 birthplace, seven miles out on the old Enterprise Road. The other was the fact that we were tenants. Unfortunately, we would rent wherever we lived until after my father's death.

The thunder-box over a pit was the usual countryside self-contained sewage system; likewise a hand-cranked windlass to draw the well-water was normal out of town as was a woodstove for cooking and candles for lighting. What was unusual for a white family was our transport: most whites had a car of some sort, or at least a horse and cart; we had our Dad's bicycle.

That was partly because of his mistrust of any form of petrol-powered transport; he was an adult before the car existed on Britain's roads, but mostly, our money problems were down to alcohol.

Childhood wasn't bad. Sure we were poor, but hell… we had sunshine. There was always sunshine in Rhodesia, well almost always, especially in the winter when it wouldn't rain for six or seven months and sometimes more than a year. Eighteen months without even a drizzle wasn't so good.

When it did rain, it was a pleasure; an hour or so of clean tropical downpour to wash away humanity's debris followed by a warm drying sun; so different to the mucky, cold damp of England.

In 1940, most white children born in Salisbury (now Harare), Southern Rhodesia, were delivered in a prefabricated nursing home nicknamed the "Paper House" which was fully equipped with the mod cons of the day. I arrived at home, Brundett, only equipped as previously described.

The local doctor would have attended my birth but whether he was there at the time I don't know, the nearest phone would have been at a neighbour's place and it would have been on a party-line; the news-spread was immediate which, in a way was a good thing. It was the kind of community that survived on the goodwill of neighbours.

On the Enterprise Road, cars had a pair of asphalt strips to aim at; the tar inlaid into a wide, well-constructed gravel road. At the time, that country-wide road system was the best all-weather transport network in the whole of Africa and better than most of Europe.

My mother was 43 when I was born. Her generation was the ninth of her family in Africa, being descended from a French Huguenot, Jean Prieur du Plessis, a ship's doctor, who landed in Cape Town in 1688. Born in Poitiers in Poitou, France in 1638, he was said to be related to Armand du Plessis, better known as Cardinal Richelieu.

My father was 58 in 1940, well past the average life expectancy in the colony at the time. He was a nurseryman by trade, the youngest son of a Sussex shepherd, John Boniface.

Dad voted in the first Rhodesian election which took place in 1923 and the sparse female population provided the first woman Member of Parliament in the British Commonwealth, Ethel Tawse Jollie.

He survived the common tropical diseases, notably blackwater fever, the usually fatal complication of malaria. Many years later when I was about eleven, at 69, he was very ill with tick-fever. By the time he allowed us to call the doctor he was through the crisis.

"He's made it through the worst," the doctor said, "he'll be OK now". It wasn't surprising that life spans were short.

Of course I have no memory of Brundett because when I was one year old the place was sold and we had to find alternative accommodation. I know that at one stage we lived in my Burmester cousins' garage.

***

My education started in 1946 at David Livingstone School, half a mile from the shared house in Union Avenue, and named after the famous explorer, missionary and compassionate anti-slaver. As a child I was very impressed by the great man's goodness. When I was older, I was more sceptical of *the great and the good* so I was only slightly surprised to find that his benevolence didn't seem to apply to his own wife and children. There was no such thing as a national football team. We did scrape up a rugby team, cobbled together from school leavers, old codgers and ex-service men.

I was eight when I watched the Salisbury game and I have always believed that we defeated the All-Blacks in Salisbury in 1949. However I see that Wikipedia have the Salisbury match as a 3-3 draw, and it was in Bulawayo that we beat them 10-8.

Those two matches are always overlooked when the All Black-team are given press coverage. I could sense that it was a great achievement, but at that tender age I never had a clue about the game nor did I realise how embarrassing it would become for the New Zealanders.

Role models were mostly old men, who could tell thrilling stories of near misses while hunting big game. The soldiers returning from WW2 were mostly quiet, often lost in thought. Some would never recover fully from their wounds. The worst affected were the ones who had seen service or been captured in the Far East.

***

One early memory was being made to clean food colour off Spiro Woodhouse's garage wall, thus spoiling my beautiful artwork. I rubbed at the limewash, where my food-colouring paint had soaked in, until my fingers hurt. My creative talent for graffiti was stunted for ever.

It was hard to forgive that miserable old man. He had done a lot of hunting, but it took a while before he thrilled me again. Even his skill at producing music with an old wood saw and a violin bow left me cold. However, after he got involved in aircraft and took Neville and me for a flight, I liked him a lot more. Neville and I shared the passenger seat of a little two-seat monoplane.

I remember when I was very young I went over to their house where a friend of Spiro's was sitting outside on a little box cleaning some large calibre bullets. Spiro and this man were preparing to go elephant hunting. I think that man must have been Stroebel (later killed by an elephant; see Chapter 10). For a little boy this was fascinating. That's when my interest in firearms really began.

Spiro was a motor mechanic. On one occasion he had done some work on a Ford pick-up. My brother Neville, three years my elder, my pal, Bill Anderson and I were at the Woodhouses' house visiting Big Neville, their eldest child, who was older than us, being twelve or thirteen.

We were looking over that Ford when Big Neville claimed he could drive it, naturally we said that he should prove it. At first he declined, saying, "I'll be black and blue if my dad finds out."

"How could he find out? We would never tell.

We went all over the place in that truck, even visiting an isolated house in the northern outskirts of Salisbury where my "Aunty" Alice Foster was living at the time.

The route included quite a few miles of red dirt road. Bill and I had been in the back of the pick-up. Both of us, as well as the truck, returned well covered in a layer of powder-fine dust from the dry red earth.

We were wrong about his dad; we never told, but somehow he found out. Maybe the coating of red dust gave him a clue. However, Big Neville was right about the black and blue bit.

***

It was the Sinoia railway to the northern mining and agricultural areas that ran past our Union Ave. house. We usually walked along it to school and back, although that was a bit longer than by road and a practice banned by the school.

Bordered by the remnants of savannah grassland on either side, it was more interesting than the road. You could walk balancing on the rails as best you could or investigate whatever changes had occurred in the verges.

Every dry season the grass would burn. That was normal. The fire could be started by a lightning strike or even a broken bottle acting as a lens. However, human intervention was more likely; quite often we were involved.

If there was a large crowd of Africans equipped with long sticks ready to bag the rats as they fled the flames you could be sure the event had been planned.

Rats were, I was told, delicious, but I can't vouch for it. When we started the annual fire the few local Africans would soon appear equipped with sticks. I guess they must have kept the sticks handy.

The fire would expose all sorts of debris that had been hidden by the grass. Typical were the remains of stolen and stripped bicycles. We were strictly forbidden to take possession of anything we found. It would be stealing; so if it was important we simply reported it to the police. We decided on the importance of any find. The detritus was easy to find as it would usually smoulder for a while after the grass had been reduced to ash.

On one occasion a fire engine appeared which was very interesting for us, but we wondered why. The grass was going to burn as it did every year. No one had bothered before.

The firemen let it burn but I suppose it did give them an outing. There were very few house or building fires.

Within two weeks of the fire the ground would be covered with new green growth, whether it had rained or not. The conservation policy at the time was to prevent veld fires.

My dad, being an old-timer, would disagree, saying, "It's natural, it kills the pests, it's good for the soil and it supplies the animals with fresh pasture." Current thinking agrees with the old-timers.

Sometimes, on our walk to school, we would be joined by inmates of St. Joseph's Home for Boys in Baker Avenue.

When I saw two of those kids scrapping over the dregs in a discarded condensed milk tin I realised how fortunate I was.

St. Joseph's Home catered for boys from the children's home after they had reached the age of ten. The girls remained in the children's home. These kids included orphans and children in care.

Amongst our home-grown and pre-war births there would also be war-orphans; white children of Rhodesian troops killed in the wars as well as those left behind by the RAF pilots and crew who had trained at the wartime air bases.

Black children were never unwanted and would be absorbed into the extended family. The Africans had a very positive attitude to children. To them, children were assets. The man would claim the child of an unfaithful wife after casting the woman out and reclaiming the *lobolo* (bride price).

Later I met a few ex-St Joseph Home boys in my various work situations; all had responsible jobs and most were respected by their colleagues. Recently I met a successful UK businessman in the book-trade who was ex-St. Josephs.

***

In Rhodesia, railways were very useful as thoroughfares for both pedestrians and cyclists. To the north it passed between the jail and the police training camp and barracks. That rail line was our highway.

South along the rails would take us past the General Post Office (GPO) workshops and stores. These stores were not particularly secure and full of interesting things. Like a hand wound signal generator from an old-fashioned magneto phone.

You would wind the handle to alert the operator of a manual exchange, as often depicted in old movies.

Capable of putting out more than 75 volts (depending how fast you wound it), it worked a treat when we taped the bare wire ends to a plastic door handle. But we did that much later, after we had moved to the *pisê-de terre* (low-cost, earth-walled emergency housing) in the suburb of Rhodesville.

Built without foundations and with little reference to spirit level, plumb-bob or straight edge, the walls were of compacted earth simply rammed down between shuttering onto a concrete slab. Good strong rendering was essential for the integrity of the building and to support any wall cupboard the tenant was optimistic enough to install. Not many people tried that twice.

The early houses had rafters of eucalyptus poles and batten doors. None had gutters. The slab was cast directly onto a cleared quarter of an acre of ground. The building regulations had obviously been circumvented; it was a Government scheme.

They were, however, all detached, which probably helped to make for peaceful neighbours. Today, in 2015, some have exceeded their planned ten-year useful life by more than fifty years and, going by Google Earth, are looking good, although considerably altered. Our Tweed Road, unnamed at the time, even features on several websites today. The last two houses in that road were built later and are brick.

Among the interesting things in the GPO stores were coils of light gauge copper wire with an insulating enamel coating, as well as some obsolete telephone earphones. These had single earpieces, made of brass, with a ring on the back.

The ring was to hang it up after use. Later I used both an earpiece and some of the wire for a crystal set.

The crystal set design came out of a pile of old Hobby magazines I had bought at a fête. According to the author, prisoners-of-war had made this design to listen to the BBC while in German POW camps.

For a crystal they had used a rusty blue-steel razor blade and thin copper wire, coiled into a spring for the cat's whisker. It worked, but not like the door handle. It took ages of fiddling with the wire cat's whisker to get a very faint signal. Our transmitter was only two miles away. I wonder if the POWs could really hear BBC broadcasts in Germany. Maybe the degree of rust on the blade was important.

The signal improved considerably when I replaced the razor blade arrangement with a germanium diode, ex GPO, courtesy Neville (who was by then working in the GPO). It was even better after we moved to the pisê when I used the phone line as an aerial. The actual phone, which had been allocated to the previous tenants, had been moved with them.

Our fun with the phone generator came to an abrupt end when cousin Pat Cutler was visiting. That was the end for that super little toy.

Cousin Pat had kindly brought along some cream cakes for tea. Neville and I overheard her daughter, sweet young Francis, being persuaded to take the cakes through to us.. The cakes were tempting and I would really have liked one.

It was a difficult choice, our new electric door handle, or a cream cake.

The handle won.

As I said, our generator worked a treat. I had never heard such a scream before…it was only a joke.

Perhaps I should have been less enthusiastic when I wound the generator; perhaps I should have just given her a little shock.

I never got a cake.

Dad threw the generator into a lantana bush growing in head-high grass of the adjacent land.

We only recovered it after the annual grass fire. It no longer worked.

We had a lot of cousins but they didn't visit very often.

Pisê-de-Terre Wall
Not in Rhodesia but in the UK near Ottery St. Mary Devon; Sept 2 2014
My photo

Chapter 2

Frogs, Neville's Toe and a Bike

Across the Umtali-Beira road, where the railway line turned right to the station, we veered left over the Umtali-line to the local river, the Makabusi.

There was a little stream emerging from the storm-water drain outlets which were diagonally opposite our house on the corner of Union Ave and Eighth Street. It was little more than a ditch and we soon exhausted its playground potential. The Makabusi was different, it ran 37 miles from Cleveland Dam to where it joined the Hunyani River.

On the way to the Makabusi we passed The Young Men's Club, St. Joseph's Home for Boys, The Government Stationary Department and the GPO Depot. All played a part in our lives, if only because we were curious and inclined to trespass.

St. Joseph's Home was the only place that scared me. I thought it looked awfully like a prison. I was convinced that if something happened to my parents or if I got into too much trouble I would end up as an inmate. A belt of savannah grass separated these places from the rail line

Once at the Makabusi we could fish and generally explore. In the unfenced commonage, between the broadcasting station and the river, there were two resident donkeys which we would try to ride. I say try because they were remarkably uncooperative. The mild and gentle female would simply stand still or kneel down and we would tumble off. The male was more energetic. He would buck and kick.

The fishing was marginally more successful. Unfortunately, the only sizeable fish were a type of catfish known as barbel, these remarkable creatures could travel overland during heavy rain and survive buried in hardened mud when the river dried up.

There were, however, a fair number of tiddlers and even more *platannas*, a species of frog, which spent its whole life in the water. What nobody guessed at the time was that the *platanna* would become the pregnancy test frog.

Had we known this interesting fact, we could have put a few in a tank and tried. Apparently, if you added urine from a pregnant woman to the water the frogs would release spawn. The frogs and tank would have been easy to arrange, the urine may have been more difficult. No doubt we would've required a fair quantity.

Sadly, as we lacked this valuable knowledge, we regarded these things as a major smelly nuisance. You thought you had a fish and it would turn out to be one of those damn frogs. Admittedly we could use one or two for bait but any more were just a malodorous curse.

The smell came from a liquid they released when handled, a truly evil emission absolutely impossible to wash off.

WW 2 had only ceased two years before Southern Rhodesia was overwhelmed by an influx of British immigrants. From these kids we learnt valuable things, like which type of lock could be opened with a skeleton key and how to make the key; also how to pick a pin-tumbler lock.

The right type of immigrant was obviously valuable for the future cultural and economic development of the country.

Being short of money (people said poor) we were one of the few Rhodesian white families without a radio or car. It was a country where a car was regarded as essential. Public transport was all but non-existent and for some reason the rickshaws had disappeared shortly after the war. For Neville and me, a bicycle was a dream too far. But one Christmas, when I was about seven, we were greeted by a magnificent, if a little, just a little, rusty second-hand machine.

Newly fitted with mudguards and brakes, it was the gift from a family friend. She was "Aunty" Anne to us, but, I believe, the real aunt of a talented ballet dancer Merle Park, who would later become a Dame.

Neville and I were to share this bike.

Once, years later, after we moved to the pisê, Merle was brought to visit. I can't say at what stage in her career it was, but she had obviously achieved enough fame to be touted around by proud relatives; living proof of genetic superiority. She must have been 17 or so.

It wasn't that I was too young to be interested, but in the presence of a tall, elegant and beautiful female I was inflicted by puberty's tongue-tied, hormone-rich confusion. I carried on fixing my bike.

However, that was long after we were given that two-wheeled treasure and Neville was given the job of teaching me to ride. Exactly how much he knew about riding I never found out, but his system of instruction was simple. Each time I fell off he would thump me.

It took me just one day to learn to ride, or at least, after that first day I decided that I now knew enough and needed no further instruction.

Of course the mudguards were soon dispensed with, followed shortly after by the brakes. Braking could then be achieved by inserting your foot between the frame and the rear wheel. It was necessary to wear shoes for success. Most of the time we were barefoot, in which case an emergency stop was a simple matter of jumping off.

On one occasion Neville was riding with me on the crossbar. We were going down a rather steep hill on Argyle Road in Avondale. To Neville's credit we did manage to stop but the sole of his slipper was worn completely through. Why was he wearing a slipper? Well he needed to keep the bandage clean.

You see, a few days before he had been using an axe to chop firewood for some other project. He was using his bare foot to steady the firewood and he had thoughtlessly placed the tip of his big toe a bit too close to the arc of the axe.

I can remember the scene now. The axe on the ground, Neville clutching his foot, he was yelling a lot, I can't remember the words. He was hopping about on the other leg. I suppose the hopping was necessary for him to keep his balance. He need not have bothered, he soon fell over.

Naturally I ran to get the help which he obviously needed and, anyway, I didn't want him to see my face. He often disagreed with me about what was funny. He was like that, no sense of humour.

One day we were on that little bike, riding alongside the railway line. I was on the crossbar. Every 50 yards or so there would be a length of rail buried upright in the ground with about 18 inches exposed above ground; some sort of marker.

Neville would ride as close as he dared to these lumps of steel. Apparently he enjoyed seeing me wince in anticipation of the pain my bare feet would feel should contact be achieved.

Needless to say I obliged him by being a total wimp and making desperate efforts to protect my bare feet. In fact I was such a wimp that on the final occasion I over-reacted and swung my foot into the wheel between the spokes and the front forks. Neville was not pleased with the result. I think it was his first experience of going over the handlebars.

Landing on the combination of rock ballast and steel rails seemed to make a definite impression on him. He never tried that trick again. I had discovered that he could learn.

Of course my foot was sore and I got a thumping from Neville because it was my fault that we were banned from riding the bike until the spokes were fixed. I wasn't too unhappy. I was used to his lack of humour but I missed the use of the bike.

He only thumped me when no one else was around; if I retaliated I would lose. However, I realised that if I hit him with my parents present he wouldn't hit back, at least not at the time. So the next time I felt aggrieved, I did just that.

I was still smarting from a recent thumping. He was totally passive in a dream world, sitting down leaning forward with his chin sticking out. He was no threat to me at all. I clenched my fist and landed my very best punch on the side of his jaw. He burst into tears.

I was thrilled; it was the first time I had made him cry. My parents weren't thrilled. They couldn't accept that I had a reason to hit Neville without provocation and nothing I said could convince them otherwise. Needless to say I also ended up crying, but it was worth it.

The reason we didn't have the bike for long was partly my fault. I decided to visit Bill Anderson, who, at that time, lived on Trinity Road in Greendale, five miles out of town. They had a great place for children; four acres, with massive granite boulders to climb as well as a selection of trees.

It was very sandy soil so it was reasonably clean and it had plenty of ant-lions and camel-worms. The camel-worms you could fish out with a straw, but were not overly interesting. The ant-lions, on the other hand, you could feed. You simply dropped an ant into the little conical traps they made. It would struggle to climb the loose sand sides until a pair of jaws would appear to pull it down out of sight into the sandy bottom of the cone.

You could select a trap each and compete to see whose ant-lion disposed of its ant first. Of course you needed equally sized ants.

I am ashamed to admit we also indulged in another pastime in Bill's neighbourhood. It was thoughtlessly cruel and stupidly dangerous. At a nearby house there was a large and angry male baboon.

He was locked to a tree by a long chain. We thought it was fun to make him even angrier by throwing stones at him and generally teasing him.

His snarling charge at us would end in a spectacular somersault as the chain jerked tight, nearly dislocating his neck. We had no idea of a baboon's strength.

Had that chain broken, the seven-year-old he caught would have been lucky to survive. Baboons have been known to disembowel dogs.

I have since learnt how close to humans baboons are. They recognise a gun immediately and know the difference in the effective range of a catapult and a rifle. A car can be torn apart out of curiosity. They will push a juvenile monkey through the gap in burglar bars to open a door for the rest to enter. Once inside they will proceed to vandalise the contents.

A lookout will be posted outside. Just like delinquents anywhere.

Later in life, while on honeymoon at Victoria Falls, I saw one show grief and compassion for a dead companion.

When it came time to leave the Anderson house, I pedalled enthusiastically down the long sandy drive and turned onto Trinity Road's gravel; unaware that I was about to destroy our transport, our pride and joy.

Suddenly I realised that I needed more than the recently reinstalled back brakes.

It was immediately apparent that I was going to occupy the same bit of dirt road as a pre-war *Chevrolet* was about to use, its fat balloon tyres just skimming the tops of the corrugations.

The bike slid from under me across the washboard-surfaced gravel road. I managed to tuck up my legs out of harm's way. That trusty little bike was no match for those great lumps of rolling rubber.

Never mind the pain from the blood-oozing gravel-rash now covering my left thigh and extending well up under my shorts, I could already feel the thumping that would come when Neville saw the mangled, metallic mess, which had been our pride and joy.

Once again we were pedestrians.

Chapter 3

The Fungwe

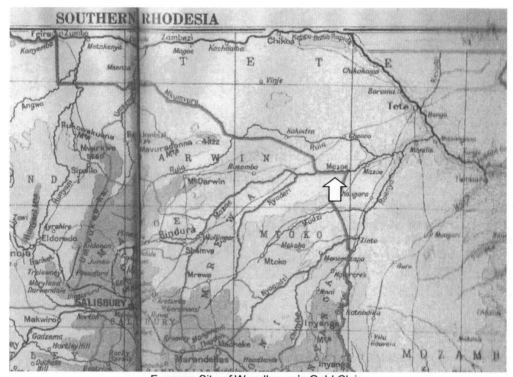

Fungwe; Site of Woodhouse's Gold Claim
Map extract from Philips School Atlas (circa 1948)

In the winter of 1950, when I was nine, the Woodhouses invited Neville and me to spend a long weekend at their mine. Old man Woodhouse was involved in a small-working. It was a gold-mining venture in an area on the Mazoe river just where it forms the border between Zimbabwe and Mozambique.

Known as Fungwe, sometimes The Fungwe, at 1200 to 2000ft (350 to 615 metres), it is in one of the lowest lying areas in the country. It is said to be one of the unhealthiest parts of the world.

Recently, in England, I heard a health expert say that the malaria mosquito would only bite within a very limited temperature range.

I assure you that particular expert has never been to The Fungwe. The few mosquitoes there during the dry season managed to bite regardless of the mid 30 degree noon-day heat or the near zero pre-dawn cold.

The mine was an excavation in the hillside adjacent to the river. The processing plant consisted of a small stamp mill and a James Table.

About the size of a billiard table, a James Table has a vibrating, ribbed surface. Water is used to flush the crushed ore produced by the stamp mill over the slightly sloping ribs.

This process separates the heavier material, the gold containing concentrate, from the remaining debris known as tailings or gangue. Mercury was used to separate the gold from the concentrate.

It was the first time I had come across that fun stuff, mercury. Impossible to pick up with your fingers, it would just roll away and disappear into the nearest crack, crevice, hole or hollow. It did, however, stick to some metals, notably gold and silver. If a pre-1947 coin, being silver, was dipped into mercury and then suspended in the flow of concentrate slurry, it would become covered in an amalgam of gold and mercury. It was an easy way to pilfer gold, common knowledge to the African workers.

Of course it should have been exciting, sleeping in the open in one of the wildest parts of Africa. The game was not that prolific. Leopards were probably the most common but there was no telling whether a lion would show up. Hyenas had been known to take a bite out of a sleeping man and they occurred throughout the country. Stories of snakes being found in a bed having cuddled up for the sleeper's body-warmth were legend.

Not that everyone slept in the open, in fact it was only Neville, Big Neville and me, who were "lucky" enough to sleep outside. I had no need for exciting nights nor did I want that kind of luck.

The large party of adults and little Butch Hulley, a child my age, managed to completely fill the two very small pole and dagga (mud) huts.

A tent was used as a groundsheet. We were a threesome, with Neville in the middle, all under a couple of blankets. Being on the outside could have been described as thrilling; I was petrified. Snakes didn't bother me but the thought of the bigger predators was very scary for me. No way would I show my fear, but I didn't sleep much.

Breakfast was maize meal porridge with goat's milk purchased from local tribesmen. The porridge was fine. After breakfast we all walked up river. When we came to some elephant tracks old Spiro Woodhouse estimated the size of the biggest as "Bloody huge" and checking the dung, said, "Yesterday."

A bit further on, someone said they saw a croc slide into the river on the other side. At that particular place the grass was too tall for me to see the far bank never mind a crocodile.

Big Neville impressed me with an expert demonstration of how the Africans blew their noses without a handkerchief. With one swift movement he blew into his fingers and flicked the mucus into the grass wiping his fingers on his pants.

A swift and hefty reprimand from his mother came just in time for me to stifle my applause.

Some nondescript little birds perched on exposed boulders in the river, constantly wagging their tails up and down. Big Nev kept referring to them as rock stuffers, the adults kept a stony silence.

He could have called them rock fuckers but that would have definitely got him into trouble in those days when children weren't allowed to know anything about sex. However, it was from the Woodhouse children that I gained the basic theory of sexual practice.

Every so often a mosquito would have a go at us but they were a rarity, even at night they weren't overwhelming. It would've been different in the rainy season when we would have been all but carried away.

We crossed at some rapids, being winter and the dry season, the flow was not too strong. On the Mozambique side we found our way along game trails, sometimes crawling through tunnels in the thick bush. Spiro went creeping, on all fours, into a tunnel in the bank just to have a look.

Returning to the Rhodesian side we crossed at a wide, shallow section. I heard one of the women complaining. She was ignored. She could stay behind or go back the way we came. It was her choice.

When we got back no one did much in the heat. After the evening meal we sat around the fire listening to stories of big game hunting experiences. As the pile of *Castle* beer empties grew, so too the adventures became more and more fantastic. After a while the only person believing or even listening was the raconteur himself.

Eventually the memories ran out. More beer and whisky was consumed but the past was lost in a mixed jumble of confused disagreement or slurred nodding confirmation.

The next morning I played with Butch in the knee-deep, quicksand-like tailings from the James Table. For some reason it was fun to struggle against the suction of wet mud.

In the afternoon Neville and I went down to the river to fish. About every 20 minutes or so the resident hippo would surface, look at us and make heavy breathing sounds. I was still hoping to catch something after Neville had left.

When it began to get dark the hippo surfaced and opened his enormous jaws in what I thought was a yawn. I was amazed at the size of that mouth.

I reckoned that, as a tall nine-year-old, I would only be a little too tall to stand in the opening.

I realise now that it was fortunate I decided to leave just then, having since discovered that the "yawn" was in fact a warning before a charge. Apparently hippos are famous for showing their displeasure with an intruding human by biting the offender in half.

That night we had just finished eating and were ready to go to bed when old Spiro went creeping around the surrounding bush with a rifle.

He said there was a leopard hanging around. We took him seriously. His bushcraft was legendary.

That night I slept even less. The African bush is full of many different sounds at night; I kept hearing all sorts of extra ones. I had no idea what a leopard would sound like but my imagination came up with a great variety of possibilities.

As it turned out I needn't have worried about the predators. The mosquitoes and the goat's milk were the real danger.

On the way back we stopped to look at a fish eagle perched high on top of a dead tree. The giant bird eyed us with suspicion. As soon as the car door opened he spread his enormous wings and was off.

The brown and black underside of his wings and belly contrasted with the white chest and head. Magnificent.

Skimming across the top of the corrugations of the dirt road at 50 mph, the necessary speed to avoid a bone-shaking experience, we kids were bored. We urged Spiro to go faster, eventually he obliged. The old side-valve V8 slowly crept up to the magic 60. We all cheered and Spiro eased the straining old Ford back to the smooth riding comfort of 50.

My arrival home was followed, shortly, by a policeman on a motorcycle. I wondered just exactly what I had done now.

I was indeed the subject, but no need for concern, he was simply a messenger to tell my parents that a bed was available to me for a minor operation. No-one in the house had a phone and the police were often used as messengers.

It was good news after a four-year wait, but it was the worst age for me. It was the sort of thing best done at birth or as a young man. A grown man would have been able to appreciate and join in the comments of the nurses. But they did put me in a grown-up men's ward. I felt really important.

Back at school I was excused physical training, (physical education had a different meaning in those days when the stick was a well-used teaching aid). The teacher inquired as to what the operation was; kind and gentle, sweet and soft, old Mrs. Tapson was at a loss for words when I replied, "I was circumcised."

A week later I was back in bed. A raging temperature, shivering, sweating and freezing, the doctor diagnosed malaria. Some said that the operation had "brought out" the malaria. I might have only been nine years old but I knew that mosquitoes were necessary to transmit malaria from one person to another and I knew that I had been well bitten in an area riddled with malaria.

To confirm the diagnosis the doctor pierced my thumb and squeezed a drop of blood onto a glass slide. This became a routine procedure. For some unknown reason he thought it was painless. I disagreed. To me the average injection was painless but not those thumb pricks.

The tablets had to be taken every four hours, day and night. Our alarm didn't work but my dad would wake every four hours and both parents were there to administer my medication, little yellow pills; a replacement for quinine tablets.

Sometimes they would float to the top of my mouth and I had trouble swallowing them.

Not to worry, ten minutes, later I would puke violently and bring up a vile yellow mess. The feeling of extreme malaise got worse.

The next day the doctor changed the medication to *Paludrine*, at that time the latest anti-malarial drug. I learnt to put the tablets at the back of my throat to get them down successfully.

There followed days of confused unhappiness and sometimes delirium. At one time I was convinced that the radio, a recent hand-down from Mrs. Ewing, was answering me when I asked the time.

I think my brain simply bridged the gap between my query and the next time check.

As I recovered I became bored. The only books in our bookshelf close to my reading age were a couple of Richmal Crompton's William books and Mark Twain's Tom Sawyer. The remaining little library consisted largely of westerns and murder mysteries. By the time I was on my feet again, Zane Grey, Sherlock Holmes and Agatha Christie were all part of my vocabulary.

My reading age was well up.

Back at school all strenuous activities were banned. Three or four weeks later, a relapse, the fever and chills were back with a vengeance. This time a combination of malaria and Malta fever (brucellosis) was diagnosed. The goat's milk got blamed for the Malta fever. Two very painful injections, probably of quinine, and some other pills supplemented the *Paludrine.*

The injections were given two days apart, one in each buttock. The second was administered just as the pain from the first one was subsiding; another two or three days sleeping on my stomach. They were, by far, the most painful injections I have ever had.

It was a full year before I was reasonably physically active again. In the meantime however, I did learn how to make gunpowder.

Chapter 4

Fireworks…Homemade

Cigarettes were cheap, which you would expect from the biggest exporter of tobacco in the world after the USA. Prices started from tuppence (less than one new penny) for eight or a pack of fifty better quality cigarettes for 1/9 (9 newpence). We tried smoking, but there were better things to do. For sixpence you could buy four ounces of potassium nitrate and thruppence would get an ounce or two of sulphur. Mix them together with crushed charcoal, after a bit of experimentation you had passable gunpowder; enough for several of our "bombs".

And that was one hell of a lot more fun than you would ever get from tobacco of any kind; even wacky-baccy.

We went to the public library to consult that American source of all knowledge *The Encyclopaedia Britannica* in an effort to improve our mix. However we could not duplicate the technique. It was Gareth McGuilligot, an older (about 15) neighbour of Irish descent, who knew all about gunpowder, possibly handed down through the family. He gave us tips on how to fine tune our mix. He also showed us how to make it go bang.

I don't know how Gareth gained his knowledge. Sadly, I believe he died in a potholing accident while at university in Britain.

The proportions in the encyclopaedia were; 75% nitrate, 15% charcoal and 10% sulphur by weight. We had no means of weighing the ingredients. In the end I settled for a 3:3:1 mix by volume of nitrate, charcoal and sulphur.

Neville would mix, test and adjust for ages to get the fastest burn. I would also test each batch but only change anything if it was obviously bad. I also learned that the test needed to be more than three feet away from the main batch.

With the gunpowder we mostly made explosions. Even our rockets exploded; unfortunately before they took off. For the "bombs" we would confine the powder in a piece of pipe, or similar. The difficult bit was the fuse.

Commercial dynamite fuse was ideal but not available to us. Then we had some luck. We discovered that the little building between the police golf course and their rifle range was, in fact, a storage magazine full of all sorts of pyrotechnics.

Initially we managed to fish some fuse out through a broken window which was great but there were more interesting things out of reach of the window. We could have tried picking the lock but the black art of lock-picking needs calm nerves, concentration and time; we weren't calm. Anyway our skill level wasn't up to that lock and there was a quicker way.

A friend of ours, Lawrence, one of the post-war immigrants, was planning a career in burglary; he could solve the problem. The door was secured with heavy-duty lockable bolts. Only one was locked. Lawrence used a short length of pipe to force the bolt past its padlock.

We emerged from that hut with our shirts stuffed full of goodies; rolls of military fuse, signal pistol cartridges and rolls of instantaneous (explosive) fuse known as cortex. Lawrence closed the door and forced the bolt back into the locked position.

Regrettably we didn't know what the cortex was or how to use it. We couldn't get it to catch fire so we threw it away.

It would have been so much fun if only we had known. I found out later all we needed to do was to tape one of our explosives to it as a detonator. We could've adapted it to make some really big bangs. I'm told that wrapped around a tree it would bring the tree down. What a shame to miss out on something so impressive.

We dismantled the signal cartridges and simply lit the contents. The powder propellant was excellent; we should have used it for our "bombs". The flare charges were even better; they burnt for ages, the brightest greens, reds, and oranges you ever did see, so much better than any firework which could be bought.

Come 5th November, I could afford to buy a full pound of nitrate. We scoured the photographic processors for "film tins," the little aluminium cans used for tropical packing of roll film, which we were now using to make "bombs."

Lawrence, who at fourteen was four years older than me and a year older than Neville, organised us on a production-line basis and in no time at all we had made 49 "bombs" and exhausted the powder.

We soon learnt which chemists would sell us both nitrate and sulphur and which would only sell one or the other. Some refused to serve us.

Our local chemist was as good as gold, quite happy to meet our requirements and very friendly. Well he was, until I was demonstrating some "bombs" to some schoolmates.

The demonstration would send a tin can 40 or 50 feet into the air. Unfortunately our formerly friendly chemist was also a witness; which was not surprising considering I had foolishly chosen his unfenced back yard as my demonstration area. After that he was decidedly unfriendly.

As we grew older we learnt a bit more. It was Bill Anderson who made the next breakthrough; an electrical firing device. To us children this was cutting-edge science. In fact what Bill did was really very simple. He took a length of lighting flex, connected a plug to one end and at the other end he bared the wires, separated the strands and cut away all but one strand. He then shorted the two wires together using the single strand of wire, which he set in the powder, insulated from the metal of the container. He then plugged it into the mains. It was brilliant! Switch on, and... instant bang!

However before the first "bomb," Bill demonstrated his brainwave. His parents were away somewhere and I had a sleepover at his place. We were about 12. I can't remember if his brothers were there or not, I think not. Anyway it was at night so we decided to use the boys' bedroom.

Bill set it up with the powder in a saucer. Being open it would, simply flash.

I had the honour of throwing the switch. It was an amazing feeling of power and control, absolutely instantaneous results. Technically it was a sound system, being only a single strand, the wire would fuse without tripping the circuit-breaker. Unfortunately, I never realised this, and I neglected to switch off.

Bill came forward and grabbed the exposed wires.

What happened next was spectacular; when the human body receives an electric shock the muscles involved contract immediately and with great power.

Thus a fist can be locked on to the conductor. Bill never had that problem. He was crouching at the time. His legs straightened with lightning speed. I am not sure if he did a backward somersault or not; neither is he, but he was absolutely spectacular.

When I saw his trembling form on the floor I was petrified. I thought I had killed him, my pal, my best friend. Then he started to speak; well shout actually.

From the words he used I knew straight away he was fine. The shaking was only anger. He was definitely annoyed. I was so relieved. What a good feeling.

Meanwhile my brother, Neville, had a brainwave of his own. We had been letting off some "bombs" underwater in the local stream. The military fuse worked just fine underwater but Neville came up with this new idea.

He used to do voluntary work in his school laboratory and had access to unusual chemicals. His scheme was simple. He came up with a mixture, which would ignite when wet. One of the chemicals was hydroscopic; it would absorb water from the atmosphere.

Anyway he made up the mixture and slipped it into his pocket. How smart was that?

A while later, after dark, he was in our unlit lean-to back veranda; suddenly he started screaming. Smoke was billowing from the pocket of his shorts, which he was trying to hold away from his body. My dad was fumbling with his knife, to cut through the welt of the pants. My mum just grabbed the welt and tore his pants off. His thigh was burnt to the bone.

I had to beg a lift to hospital from old Woodhouse who, at first, didn't want to appreciate the gravity of the situation. Once he realised the severity of the wound he was great.

Neville spent the next two weeks in hospital. The cratered and scarred tissue remained; a reminder of that incident until his death in 2011, shortly before his 73rd birthday.

Needless to say, our previously very tolerant parents, quite suddenly became totally intolerant of our interest in things that go bang. Anything involving fire or chemicals was strictly forbidden.

We had to work in secret.

I didn't ask Neville about his new mixture, I already knew enough.

One of the other tenants in our shared house, Mrs. Ewing, was rather kind to us. On one occasion she organized a party for us, mostly for Neville, Lawrence and Barry and the Johnson girls who lived nearby in Central Avenue. Barry was the son of tenants in the shared house next door where Lawrence and his divorced dad also lived.

Barry had an eighteen-year-old sister, blonde and sexy, but she wasn't at the party. I guess we were too young for her but I do remember her. Once I was sitting on the back step next door and she was in her ankle length dressing gown, hanging washing on the line. Each time she walked back towards me, every second step would flash the full length of a long and shapely leg; the whole way up to where her knickers should have been.

I sat there until she was quite finished.

As my contribution to the party I was delegated to extinguish the streetlights between our house and Central Avenue where the Johnson sisters and Moira Galloway lived. This was to enable the girls to be walked home in the dark. No sooner requested than done, easy job. with an air rifle.

Neville and Lawrence would sneak round at night to visit the two sisters. I would usually tag along. We would go up the sanitary (utility) lane and over the boundary wall at a spot where the broken glass topping had already been removed by some former ne'er-do-well.

All we did was talk to them through the burglar-bars at their bedroom window. I got the impression that their parents wouldn't welcome us in the house.

These visits were totally innocent. At least they were when I was present; innocence was guaranteed by the burglar-bars. However, on one occasion, Neville and Lawrence were invited inside. The parents had gone out. I wasn't with them.

They were in the bedroom when the parents returned. The only exit was the very small but unbarred toilet window. It was top hung and held open by a bar drilled with a series of holes, which would be dropped over a little spike to locate it as desired.

Neville had no problem making his exit.

For Lawrence it was that little spike which caused him difficulty. You have to imagine him sliding out feet first and face down but failing to lift his hips high enough.

He did make a big fuss.

Afraid of his father, with whom he lived, it was to my mother that a sheepish, worried and embarrassed youth turned. "I got caught up on a barbed wire fence," he lied.

My Mum washed the wound, assured him that it was minor and that the little tear in his scrotum was no threat to any future ambitions. She was wise enough not to ask him to elaborate on what was obviously a lie.

Chapter 5

My First Firearm

The top Martini is the one which is mentioned in the text.My photo

My education wasn't limited to gunpowder and bicycles. Another primary school friend of mine was Tómas Kennedy-Grant, the younger son of the main-man in the Presbyterian Church. Lying in his back yard on one occasion was a well-worn, vintage and more or less deactivated .303 Martini-Enfield; an ex-police carbine.

It was a gift from the next-door neighbour, a retired policeman. That Martini was one of the few things I coveted.

Tómas was a very decent, honest lad, a model of integrity. I now see from his website that he has become a lawyer, a QC no less, and now has a thriving legal practise in New Zealand.

He seemed to have unlimited access to everything "suitable." Apparently, toys were not particularly "suitable." His parents made no effort to encourage our friendship. I felt that I might not be quite "suitable." That was a feeling I got on a few occasions, especially in later years when I visited girls. However, Tómas's parents didn't ban me, unlike a few others. Regrettably I lost contact with him after primary school.

I had acquired, by swapping, a *Walt Disney* toy magic lantern on which cellophane cartoon filmstrip could be shown. It was, after all, a desirable toy, but in my eyes, it paled into insignificance compared to the Martini but still a fair swap. That Martini was a real gun.

We had to get the ex-policeman's blessing for the swap. I was overjoyed with my acquisition. Later Tómas did enquire as to the possibility of reversing the swap.

Fortunately his family's principles wouldn't allow me to be pressured, unlike some parents, who would create an unbelievable fuss if they felt that their child had made a bad deal. Those were the ones who could not accept that their offspring needed to learn about life and thought a child required perpetual spoon-feeding. Today one of those lanterns would probably fetch good money.

Perhaps it had nothing to do with a bad deal; maybe Tómas's parents had misgivings about me, a ten-year-old, owning a .303 carbine, albeit inoperable. How could they?

Having been purposely blocked at the breech with an empty cartridge case and cement, it took an entire long weekend to clear the barrel. Mud wasps had been using the rest of the barrel as a nursery. Gun barrels were a favourite place for them to entomb their larvae in mud together with a paralysed spider for food.

Thus we had a gun with a barrel of sorts. Although totally useless as a meaningful weapon, the barrel could pass a bullet. Unfortunately, there was another problem, a crucial part, known as the tumbler, was broken. Well that's what we thought, but looking at it now, I still have it; I can see that it's been deliberately shortened.

I traipsed around the four gunsmith shops with the broken bit. They would look at the tumbler, look at me and shake their heads. Until I got to old man Fereday's shop.

He scratched about in a box of old parts and produced exactly what I needed.

I was half-a-crown short of the seven shillings and six pence he demanded. I can't remember how I got the extra, but I did, and I soon had a working gun. You couldn't call it a rifle, the rifling having long since rusted away. Now I needed ammunition, standard military .303 bullets.

By scouring another playground of ours, the police range, I eventually found a live round. Now the test;

I had heard horror stories about the fearsome kick of a .303, so I sat on the doorstep of the side door to the garage and placed the butt under my armpit against the doorframe, pointing the carbine at the ground about six feet away.

Our macho mongrel, Mickey, was sleeping peacefully just out of the line of fire. Click! Anti-climax, the firing pin had struck the primer, but off centre.

So I turned the round by a few degrees and tried again. It was the third try that woke Mickey. It blasted a hand-sized hole in the ground about a foot from his head.

That was the first and only time I have been told off by a dog. As he stood up and stalked away, the look on his face told me exactly how stupid I was and how ashamed I should be. He had obviously lost all confidence in my competence with firearms. I was totally chastised.

It was Neville who came up with our first homemade round. Being experimental it was a blank.

Firstly he had to prime a used round. To extract the old primer we would fill the used case with water and hammer it into the soft thick bark of a nearby lucky-bean tree (erythrina abyssinica). It was difficult to avoid damage to both the case and the primer so the process needed to be repeated several times and the best examples selected.

The dent made by the firing pin was hammered out and the primer filled either with a mixture of potassium chlorate and sulphur or powdered match heads (the same chemicals mixed with glue and fillers).

Then it would be tapped gently back into the case. The case was filled with our homemade gunpowder and the end bent closed. The result was a bit untidy but as long as it went into the breech we were happy.

The first effort was reluctant to fire. Neville was trying with the muzzle resting on the ground when it went off.

I was standing facing him. Fortunately I was looking up when it did go off.

The explosion blew a cup-sized hole in the ground. Debris shot up, resulting in instant gravel rash on my cheeks. I had just learnt that blanks could be dangerous.

Some years later, after I had resolved the off-centre problem, I was given ten live rounds by a friend of Neville.

Bill Anderson and I took the gun down to the nearby stream, set up a plank against the bank as a target and I banged away. Bill refused all offers to have a go, preferring to stand well away.

The plank was untouched.

Chapter 6

Recreation

The house in Union Avenue was only a few blocks from Raylton Sports Club (the railway club). This Club's football field doubled as an open-air venue for professional boxing and wrestling matches. These only needed a quarter of the area and the organisers found it difficult or too expensive to secure the whole area.

The solution was to use a corner of the earth terraces as the two sides of a rectangle and make up the other two sides with steel seating stands. The resulting quadrangle was then surrounded by tarpaulins, which were laced together.

To prevent anyone from slipping in under the canvas or between the joints, police would patrol the makeshift wall. Should they see a suspicious bulge, it would get an almighty whack from a truncheon.

Of course we learnt to keep well clear of the tarpaulin sides once we had made it into the enclosure. The best places to slip in were along the sides opposite the terraces. The space under the stands formed ideal walkways. Once inside it was easy to worm up between empty seats.

When the giant, slow-motion South Africa heavyweight, Ewart Potgieter, fought there, we ended up in ringside seats. He fought a six-foot-six, equally slow American.

As they shambled around the ring, the American disappeared behind Potgieter, the bulk of the South African obscured his opponent completely. At 7ft $1^{1/}2$ inches and 326 lbs, Potgieter was a big and enormously strong man, however he lacked speed and had to abandon his boxing career when it was discovered that he had tunnel vision.

On that particular night we were chased by a policeman. As I ran around a corner on the earth terrace I slipped and tumbled down the steep back of the terrace, landing in the shadow of the leylandii boundary. Fortunately, this all happened before the cop made it to the corner, so I just kept still in the shadows until he was well past. After the fight I cycled to the hospital where a deep cut in my knee was dressed and I was given a tetanus shot.

Boxing matches were relatively uncommon; it was far more likely for the grounds to be a wrestling venue. In my day, although there were others, the two wrestlers who come to mind were South African Willie Liebenberg and an alleged American, "Sky High Lee".

I say alleged because he seemed to do all his fighting in Africa.

After a while the fights lost their entertainment value so we used to go just for the adventure of sneaking in.

One night someone had cut the lacing holding two tarpaulins together so an uncontrollable crowd simply walked in, ignoring the few policemen.

At the following fight the police presence was over whelming; nobody was going to sneak in that night. However the surrounding trees were festooned with bodies. The nearest white background screen (as used at cricket matches) was swaying dangerously on account of being top heavy with humanity.

Most were members of the coloured community (a Rhodesian term for mixed race not to be confused with Africans).

Survivors against prejudice from both black and white, they had the dark humour of the underdog as well as his determination to win by any means.

I climbed one of the screens but it was uncomfortable and too far from the ring. We knew when we were beaten so we left. I can't remember if we went elsewhere or just went home: defeated. We did try the same stunt with Boswell's Circus when they came to town but circus folk knew more tricks than we could ever dream up. We always had to pay.

***

It was in 1951, just after I had got involved with gunpowder, that I met a new friend, Peter Jenner. Peter had been born in India where his father had been in the Colonial Police. His family were among a number of white families who chose to live in Rhodesia after India became independent.

Peter was an only child, his mother was a teacher at our school and his dad was an estate agent. Both were very tolerant parents, he seemed to be able to get away with anything; certainly far more than I could manage.

They lived in Central Avenue, next but one north of Union Avenue where we lived. It was great to have a good friend so close. Peter came up with an alternative to gunpowder for making a bang. This was a soda siphon cartridge, one of those little CO_2 cylinders which were used at the time to carbonate water thus producing soda-water to be mixed with alcoholic drinks.

The procedure to explode these little CO_2 cylinders was simple. Peter would gather up an armful of dry grass, put the cartridge in the centre and light the grass. After a while the cartridge would explode with a most satisfying bang; easy.

However there was a limit to how many of these cartridges Peter could misappropriate from his dad's supply and anyway, gunpowder was more exciting. We had more control over the size of the bang when we used gunpowder. Perhaps control was the wrong word. Anyway there were other ways for us to amuse ourselves.

Peter's family moved to a magnificent house which his dad had had built right on the highest point of Avondale Ridge, adjacent to the local water supply reservoir. This was about the same time we moved into the pisê.

Our respective moves put us about seven miles apart; a hot cycle ride and an impractical couple of bus journeys, but we kept in contact and still had a lot of fun.

Peter's two acres of garden sloped down the west side of the ridge with a superb view of houses on the flat to West Road. Across West Road there was the uncultivated expanse of Pocket's Farm with the farmhouse in the distance.

This area was later developed as the Strathaven housing estate. Although there had obviously been a developed garden on the site of Peter's house in the past, it had long since reverted to nature. Now Peter's dad was having it landscaped.

The top terrace had been grassed and bordered with flowerbeds. It occurred to me that this terrace had the exact specification for a "foofy" slide. In the UK I think they are known as "aerial" or "zip" slides. To us they were "foofy" slides, a sloping cable with some sort of device to hold onto as you descended. Great fun.

At the high side of the terrace there was a large cedrela-toona tree, the size of an old oak; opposite it on the lower edge of the terrace was a smaller, but perfectly adequate, jacaranda. The site was ideal.

The next requirement was a cable and a sliding device, preferably a pulley cobbled to a piece of pipe for a handle. All proved impossible to obtain but my dad had about 30 yards of heavy gauge fencing wire. All I had to do was tell my dad that my friend's father needed it and our cable problem was solved.

We could have simply used a piece of pipe threaded over the wire to hold as we slid down but I knew that such an arrangement could get very hot. In the end I used two blocks of wood fastened together with a large and a small bolt with enough space between for the wire. The large bolt was needed as a handle.

We enlisted the aid of one of the garden labourers to help us string the wire between the trees and our "foofy" slide was operative.

The design lacked the safety arrangements of its modern equivalents or an automatic return device. We simply used a string to walk it back to the top. But that was fine; all those gismos would just have slowed it down.

The high end must have been 15 or 20 ft. high. At the lower end where it crossed a level area of lawn, the wire was about the height of a tall man's neck. It was also almost invisible. But that wasn't a problem; it was well above our heads. You just had to let go before you crashed into the jacaranda tree

Should a man of about six foot decide to run across that section, at the same time swinging his arm over his head, there is no doubt that his arm would tuck the wire under his chin. I imagine that the resulting experience would closely resemble being hanged. But why on earth should a man behave like that? We never thought of the possibility of someone bowling a cricket ball.

Peter's dad was a keen cricketer, and a six-footer, and indeed he was bowling to Peter. As I said, that wire was hard to see especially if you happened to be looking at a batsman 22 yards away.

I would never have dared to ask him what the experience was like, but apparently he gave a full and emphatic description to Peter. Our "foofy" slide simply disappeared. I didn't ask about it.

Then Peter was off to school in the UK, a hangover from his dad's service in India. Apparently it was usual for the Colonial Service personnel to reserve a place at an English school for their children from an early age, a concept foreign to Rhodesians.

Peter had already had a couple of years at school in England, during which time we had kept in contact by mail. Sadly I missed saying goodbye this time when he finally left and we lost contact.

Wherever he is, he has my sincere apology.

Chapter 7

Graffiti, Catapults and Cops

Two other friends were brothers, Tomek and Machek Makowski. They were Polish refugees, full of ideas learnt in England before they emigrated from the UK to Rhodesia. Notably they had a bad impression of the German nation and a much worse opinion of the Russians.

We were walking north along the old Sinoia railway. As we got to where it passed between the jail and the police housing estate, a mule wagon trundled along the road between the estate and us. We each had a catapult and it occurred to us that we might be able to speed up the progress of that wagon.

We were wrong. The mules totally ignored the barrage of catapult fire, simply plodding on. However, a female on the estate, someone's wife I guess, didn't ignore us and we were subjected to a verbal tirade which we treated with the same contempt the mules had shown to our catapults. We simply walked on ignoring the woman.

Soon we found ourselves accosted by a white police officer and two black constables. I'm sure we could have outrun the white guy but we had seen those black guys training, there was no point in running.

In the boss man's office we stood in front of his desk as he spoke to us at length. I was absolutely ashamed and contrite (I knew the drill). He then demanded the catapult. I produced mine from my bulging pocket.

The other two had theirs around their necks under their shirts. They never moved a muscle. They had also been there before and had had London experience; Rhodesia must have been like a nursery school.

There had been several other occasions when I had to listen to a very important man sitting behind a desk (any man with more power than sense is very important and should be feared). I am glad, however that it was not a magistrate doing the talking. On this occasion it was sufficient for us to look remorseful, apologise, listen to a lecture on how to behave in the future and promise to do the same.

When it came to magistrates, they always seemed to close with the same words, four, six or more, "strokes of the light cane."

I had no idea of what specified a light cane. I was however, somewhat of an expert on the headmaster's cane. I had no need to become more knowledgeable in that field.

The headmaster of David Livingstone School, my junior school, Mr. Lloyd, had been in the trenches of the First World War and had suffered lung damage from the gas used.

Perhaps he resented bad behaviour on the grounds that it devalued his personal sacrifice in that war. There can be little doubt that the gas poisoning suffered by those soldiers was a life sentence of pain. He was probably justified in feeling that a schoolboy's callous attitude was crass.

There were only three male teachers, the rest were all female. Perhaps that's why Lloyd took such a dim view of the little bit of graffiti written by George Thompson.

The result was that George received a heavy application of the stick.

Being a primary school the stick wasn't a 3ft. bamboo cane; that was something for next year, 1954, at senior school. At junior school Lloyd only used an 18inch ruler, but he could be enthusiastic. In my case, on one occasion, he broke the ruler, which was good for me because it was only the fourth stroke and he stopped. I'm sure he had planned on the maximum allowed, six. I can't remember the offence.

If you ignore the few words written by George, real graffiti was non-existent at that school, although the walls did get a bit disfigured from time to time. The activity was not a desire to cause damage, simply a necessary result of using a homemade toy.

The toy was made by pouring molten lead into a used .303 cartridge case and using a nail to make a hole in the lead before it solidified. The nail and case were then tied together by a loop of string.

To use it, a match head or two were crushed and the result was packed into the hole. The nail was then inserted and the contraption was swung against a wall. This made a most satisfying bang. It also left a dirty great black mark on the wall, but it wasn't graffiti. We didn't do it to make a mess. The big black stars were just a consequence of having fun.

There was another activity, which some might view as graffiti or vandalism, but that was never the intention. During the rainy season, there was always an abundant supply of clay, mostly black, but in some places, red, yellow or grey.

This clay had the consistency of plasticine. The stuff from a termite mound was particularly good for our purposes, namely a missile for a *kleilaaikie*.

The procedure was to roll the clay into a ball about the size of a billiard ball. It was then impaled on to the end of a flexible stick of two feet or so (the *kleilaaikie*). It could now be launched some distance at your target, which was probably a similarly equipped adversary. Sometimes we organised opposing "armies".

The principal of the *kleilaaikie* was exactly the same as the ball-throwers so popular with dog owners today. The clay splotches on the walls weren't vandalism, just practice.

George's graffiti was different. It was proper graffiti; large, clear and explicit. In a few words it stated exactly what George would like to do to, or with, Miss Dorrington, the art teacher.

Miss Dorrington was by far the most attractive teacher we had. A no-nonsense teacher, always smart and elegant, she was a honey, a real cracker. I really liked her.

Was the graffiti really that bad? George was simply expressing a perfectly normal male desire; assuming he didn't mean it as an insult. I'm sure most of the older boys, not to mention the male members of staff, could empathise with him. I did. Maybe the problem was just the "f" word.

I never found out what Miss Dorrington thought.

Chapter 8

Mickey and a New Neighbourhood

Mickey and My Brother, Neville (aged 10)
@144 Union Avenue/corner Eighth Street (Feb 1948)
Photo; by me aged 7. Camera; 127 Baby Brownie Special

We never planned on having a dog. When we lived at Brundette I believe we had been given a ridgeback pup, which we gave away when we had to move. I was told that we also had a cat which was an expert snake killer. I don't know how the cat did the job, but later when we had a cross-bred Staffordshire bull terrier I saw him seize a three foot snake and shake it so violently that it simple flew apart.

Mickey was a small dog, an absolute "Heinz 57 varieties" of a dog, the size and build of a fox terrier, brown with a white blaze on his chest.

He had been the Woodhouse's family pet. He became our dog because *he* decided to belong to us.

There was some resistance from both the Woodhouses and our parents, but Mickey won in the end. He liked to win. Of course we were pleased..

Like a short man he was full of attitude. He always had to prove himself. Fortunately he was a naturally good fighter because he was game for any challenge.

When we eventually became cyclists again, he was quite happy to sit astride the crossbar. He would use one hind leg to take the pressure off his sensitive area. Should another cyclist overtake, he would yap until we passed the offender.

Mickey had the same macho attitude towards fireworks. He would try to fight them so we had to hold him, especially when we lit our more powerful home-made variety. Nevertheless, he enjoyed them tremendously.

The first thing he did when we moved house was fight with the dominant dogs in the road. Unfortunately, the fight with the top dog, a large Irish terrier, was stopped before there was a clear winner. Apparently this meant they needed a rematch at every opportunity, as neither would accept the other as the boss dog.

Even in old age Mickey was always game for a walk, but coming home he would trail behind me by fifty or more yards; every step a struggle, in the end we had to have him put down.

I dug his grave and buried him under the avocado tree I had planted in the back yard of the pisê.

I was 11 in 1952 when we moved from our two rooms of the shared house in Union Ave to the pisê.

Two bedrooms, a veranda, a kitchen with running hot and cold water and a bathroom we didn't have to share with other tenants. It was luxury, Rhodesia's equivalent to a council estate.

By the time we moved in, mains sewers had reached the area so all that was left of the night-soil bucket system was a concrete slab in the back garden. The sanitary lane had become part of the garden. Not bad really, considering that I could remember when there were the remnants of a bucket system in the town centre.

The collection lorries would come round after midnight. They would be manned by "Zambesi Boys;" so-called because it was only a low status tribe from the Zambesi Valley who would do the work.

Without a name for the road, our new address was the plot and site number, "6419 site 4". Later it became 29 Tweed Road.

What I missed was the use of Mrs. Ewing's garage, which had been very handy for the homemade fireworks. The garage had been included in her tenancy. As she had no use for it she allowed us to use it.

Tweed Road certainly had its share of characters. There was the unfortunate 19- year-old retard who, a year or two later shot his cinema-cashier lady-friend. He was only saved from the gallows by a gifted advocate, a QC no less.

The lawyer's claim to fame was that he had never had a client hanged.

Unfortunately for the lawyer, his talents failed him when he was defending himself on a charge of illegally shooting a rhino. I can't remember the exact term, but four years comes to mind.

In this murder case, the cashier had dumped her child-mentality-lover after her husband found out that she had a toy-boy.

Then there was Johnny M. who proudly posed for a newspaper photo with the leopard he had just shot with his .22 rifle. The leopard was one of the most protected species and, in any event, a .22 was only legal for birds and vermin as it was not powerful enough to avoid unnecessary wounding. He should have known that getting caught was a guaranteed jail term.

In the early hours of one night I couldn't sleep, a dog was baying incessantly at the moon. There was the crack of a rifle and the noise stopped. I have no idea who fired the shot but I was most grateful. I always liked Johnny.

Down the road Old Man Laing was an excellent carpenter with short fingers. Legend was that he would cut off a finger joint to claim compensation whenever he needed a bit of cash.

Another fellow was famous for his speed at building motorboats. I think his name was Geldard. I was told that he had fallen out of a small open aircraft as his pilot friend performed aerobatics. The boats were his side-line; his full-time job was the maintenance carpenter at Lion Match Co.

Not to be forgotten was a cousin of ours, Cecil Jackson, who had been awarded the Military Cross in the war, a fact which was not widely known because he would never speak of it.

The Laing family were particular friends of Neville. There were three sons, all boxers, Rocky, Theo, Aldy and a vivacious daughter, Alice.

Rocky was one of the country's amateur champions; lightweight I think. Theo had been runner-up middleweight and Aldy was a promising novice fighter. Bubbly young Alice, with glossy black hair, was a younger image, just beginning to blossom, of a glamorous mother.

These were people I can remember from the thirty or so pisês of Tweed Road.

I never knew Alice well, but I do remember one incident. We were all teenagers and working. Alice owned a two-tone dark brown and tan *Morris Ten*, a model made when cars still had running boards and side opening bonnets.

My good friend, Jimmy Smith, was on his way home when he came across Alice.

"Hello, Alice, what's up?"

"Hello Jimmy, it starts but I can't accelerate. Can you help me please?"

Her car had broken down because the throttle linkage had snapped.

"Sure, don't worry I'll get you home". Without tools or spares but always resourceful, Jimmy had the answer. "You steer and change gear. I'll work the accelerator from here".

Jimmy stood on the running board, clinging on with one hand and working the accelerator with his other. Full marks go to Alice for staying on the road because Jimmy simply held the throttle fully open. As the car careered around the bend towards our house, I will always remember the grin on Jim's face; oblivious to any danger.

***

When I was still at school, circa 1953, Bill Anderson's family had moved from the pisês, in rough-tough-downmarket Queensdale, to their new house in the posh and genteel suburb of Highlands. That's where I all but electrocuted Bill.

I'm not absolutely sure if it was the same sleepover when Bill had that electric experience, but I think it might have been. Perhaps Bill's parents had just gone out. It was always interesting to team up with Bill when his parents were absent. Anyway, we decided to do the snake trick. It was guaranteed to work. It always did.

Bill's house was ideally situated for the fun. It sat diagonally on its plot facing the crossroads of Maiden and Victoria Drives, both of which were devoid of streetlights. The veranda had a clear view of the junction.

The trick was to pull a dummy snake across the road in the path of passing traffic. We made up our snake by threading a length of thick fencing wire through about five foot of hefty rubber hose. The wire enabled us to put some realistic curves in to our "snake".

We would pull it diagonally across the intersection in front of Bill's house. We crouched in the ditch, waiting.

The first car braked violently when he saw this thing give a spasmodic jerk. Soon there were cars at each entrance to the crossroads as well as a crowd of African cyclists and pedestrians lobbing anything they could find at our bit of hosepipe.

Of course if you throw something into the middle of a crossroad hard enough it will skid and skip across to the other side. In between lobbing missiles the participants had to dodge the efforts of the opposite side.

The crossroads were now centre-stage, well lit by the lights of the opposing cars. It could have been a movie scene of warring gangs.

There would be a surge of excitement and a hail of stones each time we gave a tug on the line. The cars were now beginning to form up in queues.

With the excitement growing we decided to leave by crawling through the storm water culvert and along the ditch. We made the veranda without being seen where we sat in darkness to watch the fun; very entertaining. It was only after the crowd heard our laughter that one brave soul took a closer look and made a lunging grab at the hosepipe.

As he held it up there was a round of applause and laughter followed by a few friendly waves at the darkness of Bill's house. We had obviously appealed to the Africans' sense of humour. I'm not sure if all the drivers in the mini traffic jam were quite as friendly.

As I said, this was our failsafe trick. On one occasion Jimmy Smith and I worked it on Samora Machel (Jameson) Avenue opposite the Tweed Road, Ray Amm Road junction, near our houses in Rhodesville. That time our snake was a broken fanbelt. The break was tapered which gave it the look of a snake with a long thin tail. To make the bends we tied it up in a network of black cotton. The result was excellent animation.

The first few cars swerved around it or tried to run it over but one stopped. The driver got carefully out of his vehicle and stealthily crept up behind our fanbelt. Even the combination of the sodium streetlights and his car headlights was insufficient to expose our "snake".

Our luck was in. It turned out that this guy was some kind of snake expert and was involved with the local press.

We watched him stalk our fanbelt and flinch with every tug of the line. Then he made his grab for the neck of our fanbelt and got tangled up in a web of black cotton.

We melted into the darkness laughing, but he kept his trophy and joined in the laughter. And our escapade did get a mention in the *Cabbages and Kings* column of *The Herald*, the national newspaper.

Chapter 9

Makaha

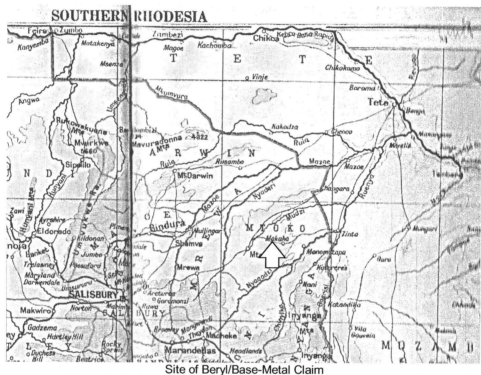

Site of Beryl/Base-Metal Claim
Map copied from Philips School Atlas (ninth edition for South Africa)

In 1956, when we were fifteen, Bill Anderson's step-grandfather died. He had been a prospector-come-smallworker. That is, one of the old-timers who used to spend their lives traipsing through the bush chasing rainbows in the hope of striking it rich. Some did, but the norm was a breadline existence.

They would look for anything which might make a profit, from gold to asbestos. Most of the modern productive gold mines were on the sites of ancient workings. These had been abandoned when the "ancients" had reached the water table and were unable to extract the water.

The country was, and still is, a treasure trove of minerals, both base and precious. The difficult part was to extract enough economically to be profitable. For the smallworker it was a hard, tough life of perpetual optimism.

At the time, Bill's grandfather was mining a deposit of beryl, (beryllium ore). Interestingly, emeralds are green beryl coloured by a trace of chromium. Other naturally tinted beryl crystals are aquamarine, morganite and golden beryl.

Regrettably, although the country was the world's largest producer of high-grade chrome and did, at a later date, produce both emeralds and diamonds, none had been found in the Makaha area where this mine was located. The Anderson's mine only produced the less valuable beryllium ore.

Bill's family inherited the workings in 1955 and Bill's father decided to invest in the mine. With more capital and the right management the prospects looked good.

Bill and his brother Michael had spent previous school holidays at the mine. In fact Bill had been there when the old man had his fatal heart attack, but for me it was the first of two occasions.

We travelled out in the 1940's *Ford* pick-up left in the estate. Bill and I sat in the back with most of the supplies including a box of dynamite. The detonators were in the cab in the glove compartment.

The first 80 miles of mostly strip roads took us to Mtoko. I remember the hotel, general store, garage and drinkable water on tap. I found out later there was a village hall as well.

The next 30 miles of dirt track went through tribal trust land on to crown land and the mine. In the African reserve we stopped at a white storekeeper's home-come-store for lunch.

Normally this land was for the exclusive occupation and use by Africans, however, if there wasn't an African available to operate an essential business then a white would be allowed to provide the requirements. He could never own either the land or whatever he built there. Clearly the trader was no better off than the average prospector, but like the prospector, it was his way of life.

For us kids it was a dream school holiday destination. Three teenage boys with a rifle each, in the bush for three weeks without adults, life was looking good. Having said that, an African labourer Bullouwah, who claimed that he could cook, was seconded from the mine to cook for us and presumably keep an eye on us.

During the first visit Bullouwah slept in a tent and we slept in the rectangular pole and dagga hut which had been Bill's grandfather's home. On the second visit he slept in the hut with us, apparently he was concerned about the lion spoor 50 metres or so from the hut's door.

The mine itself was nothing more than a large hole in the ground. To call it a small quarry would almost be flattering. However, the beryl was abundant.

The nearest neighbour, about half a mile away, was a Polish employee of Rio Tinto who was doing exploratory work for them. In the valley, about 500 feet below and a mile or so away, was a columbite and tantalite claim belonging to a big genial Afrikaaner by the name of Jordan.

He lived in a neat, whitewashed pole and dagga house. Note house, not hut. It had a cement floor, water on tap, several rooms and was rectangular, not round.

Bill's Grandfather's hut was also rectangular and it had a veranda. The mud (dagga) only came half way up the pole walls. This allowed enough light to read, once your eyes became accustomed to it, but kept it dark enough to deter the flies. The thatched roof overhung the walls by more than 3ft thus adding to the gloom, but helping to keep it cool.

In order to keep the wood-borer dust from the roof rafters being a nuisance, Bill decided we should use a tarpaulin as a makeshift ceiling.

When I heard rats scurrying across it that first night I was grateful for the idea. Only one ran across my face.

Of course we would have shot them, if we could. Most animals freeze when you shine a torch in their eyes at night. With those rats all we got was a glimpse of a pair of green eyes and they were gone. Eventually they gave way to us, or perhaps it was because we made sure that there was no trace of food inside the hut.

***

To the best of my knowledge, the bush dwellings in Rhodesia never adopted the Zulu flooring mix of cow dung and ox-blood common in early South Africa. I've always wondered just how the Zulus discovered that you could make such a fine floor with nothing more than blood and shit.

This was my first trip to the Anderson's Makaha mine. The routine was off-the-cuff we did exactly as we pleased. Typically we would get up and Bullouwah would cook breakfast before we embarked on the day's adventure.

Initially breakfast was bacon and eggs, that is, for the first two days, after which the bacon was used up. It would be pointless to carry a bigger supply without refrigeration. The same was true for fresh meat.

After that we ate a lot of boerewors (farmer's sausage). This South African specialty was highly spiced and would not spoil but did dry out and get tough to eat. Also it had another disadvantage, albeit minor, the spice was no deterrent to flies.

Our fly protection was improvised from an orange pocket, one of those mesh sacks used to transport oranges. It turned out to be totally ineffective. It was a little while before we realised just how ineffective it was. Anyway, Bullouwah assured us that he had extracted every last maggot from the fly-blown boerewors. We had no option but to believe him, we had to eat.

Our rifles would not have impressed any knowledgeable person, a .300 Sherwood (known in the UK as a rook rifle) a .22 rimfire and my .22 air rifle. When Jordan saw our weaponry he took pity on me and lent me an old single shot .22. It was an American Savage with a very heavy barrel and was one of the most accurate rifles I have used. Possibly it was originally made for target use.

Nevertheless, we were in Africa's big game country and we were going hunting. Not that we were stupid enough to shoot at big game with such underpowered weapons. Yes, I am aware that a shot from a powerful .300 such as a Remington magnum or 8 x 68 mm Mannlicher could bring down an elephant. The Sherwood may have had an 8 mm diameter bullet but it wasn't in that class. It might cope with a leopard in an emergency and it would be better than nothing against a lion, but not a sensible option.

Our bushcraft was sadly lacking. During the entire three weeks we only stumbled across two antelope. Stumbled is the right word. We almost walked into them; invisible until they sprang up and disappeared into the bush before we recovered enough from the fright to identify them properly let alone shoot at them. The only way I knew they were antelope and not deer was because wild deer don't exist in Africa.

On one occasion Bill and I went down into the Inyamsizi valley (a fair sized local river), where we found recent elephant spoor and a tree that they had pushed down. It was time to backtrack. To walk into an elephant would be unwise. This decision was reinforced before our next trip by news of the death in that area of a well experienced elephant hunter called Stroebel. He had been a friend and hunting companion of Spiro Woodhouse.

Spiro had identified the trampled remains. He said that the only complete and undamaged item was a boot containing a foot.

Obviously the elephant had been extremely agitated. During the next trip to the mine we were told by the local game ranger that, shortly before his death, Stroebel had warned some young men that the elephants in that area were nervous and aggressive. He said it was because Portuguese poachers, from bordering Mozambique, had been active there and had caused much wounding by the use of inadequate rifles. No-one blamed the elephants.

Michael had found a yellow flame lily *gloriosa superba* (Rhodesia's National flower). Normally red, none of us had ever seen a yellow one before. We followed Michael to have a look at this very special flower.

It was next to where the Polish Rio Tinto man was prospecting. He assured us that it would not be disturbed. I decided that I would ask my dad about it. As 52 years of his 61-year gardening career had been spent in Africa he had a good chance of knowing about it.

Our other main daytime activity was to walk the four miles or so to the nearest river for a wash. Flowing through mostly unpopulated sandveld, the water was clear and clean. The river was a tributary to the larger Inyamsizi.

Of course the large dominant koppie, Greycap, had to be climbed. Bill had actually climbed it on a previous visit so he had established a route, which he just had to show me.

This time he insisted that a very reluctant Bullouwah came along. Apart from a natural disinterest in doing anything overly strenuous and totally unnecessary, Bullouwah was adamant that "the mountain is bewitched."

However, perhaps because of Bill's persistence and possibly a sense of responsibility for the young white boys, he did come along. I have to admire him, for there were clearly times when he would much rather have done something less challenging.

Back on the ground Bullouwah's whole demeanour had changed, he had an air of confidence and a spring in his step.

I sensed that he now had greater status amongst his peers

On another occasion, on my first visit, being lazy, we had only taken the air rifle with us and we were on the way back. That was before there was a lion's paw mark the size of a dinner plate in dried mud just fifty metres from the hut.

This was not a stroll but a walk, which usually became a fast-walking competition between Bill and me. An ever increasing gap would separate a disinterested Michael tagging along behind us.

This time a deep throaty grunt of a growl came from the bush. This growling followed us all the way until we got within sight of the Jordan house.

Our walking was noticeably even faster than usual and Michael didn't fall behind. We knew that it would be a mistake to panic and run but it was hard to stay calm. We never found out what was responsible. The best guess was a leopard. We never left the rifles behind again.

Our established route to the river seemed to be unnecessarily long so Bill decided to find a short cut through the bush. He insisted that he had it figured out, sort of, we did find the river, or more accurately a river. It was a very attractive watercourse but too shallow, rocky and shady for comfortable bathing. A section we had never seen before.

We never returned along exactly the same route. I won't say we were actually lost. It just took a long time. We did make it back; a little later than we anticipated… well after dark and from an unexpected approach. That was the last short cut we tried.

Greycap
My photos

Bill Anderson creeping down the scariest part of Greycap.
To his left was a drop of 50 feet or so.

Chapter 10

Our Dad

Back home it was the first week of school and for my family it was the thirteenth month. Let me explain; for twelve months, while our Dad was on the blacklist, he was the nicest, kindest most pleasant man you could meet. He would be up at six, wake us with tea in bed, softly singing old music-hall songs, (born in 1882 the Music Hall was the pop scene of his youth). I couldn't recite a single nursery rhyme but I knew all about a *Bicycle Made For Two* and *Two Little Girls In Blue.*

"Two little girls in blue, lad
Two little girls in blue
One was your mother
I married the other
Two little girls in blue."

The blacklist was a control system for alcoholics. It was a criminal offence for anyone to supply a listed person with alcohol. A pub or bottle store could lose its licence. It may have been draconian, but it worked in our small community, or at least for us.

The twelve months of the blacklist were over and he was no longer banned from all licensed premises. It was once again legal for anyone to supply him with alcohol.

If I had been a mature wage earner with the knowledge and experience of life which comes with age, I'm sure I could have tackled my Dad's alcoholism in a more satisfactory way, but that could not and would not be.

In the pruning season he could supplement his meagre pre-war pension with a little cash. When we lived in the pisê he grew rose and bougainvillea cuttings for sale.

Now was the thirteenth month and Dad was off the list. He would only get up for opening time and not come home until after closing time. When his pension was spent, his bike used to be the first thing to be sold.

At 74 he no longer cycled because when he was 70 he had suffered a rupture, which he refused to have treated. With no bike to sell he would sell anything else he may have bought or been given during the previous twelve months. He was never violent or abusive. We would just end up totally impoverished. However, Neville was in his second year as a learner technician in the GPO, so we had some income for the month.

Dad's problem started long before I was born. When he arrived in Rhodesia, he was either teetotal or only an occasional social drinker. His first wife, Henrietta, died in 1923 leaving him with two children, Jack nine and Molly three.

For reasons, perhaps sensible to him but not logical to my generation, (he was after all, a Victorian) he took Molly back to England to be brought up by relatives.

Jack stayed with him in Rhodesia. He married my mother, Evelyn du Plessis, in 1926.

I have been told that Jack, who had been a top student and sportsman, suffered a brain tumour while a teenager and still at school. Certainly his life went badly wrong. An operation was not immediately successful and he was committed to a mental hospital.

Whatever the cause, Dad became an alcoholic. The problem got so bad in the early 1930s, that, experiencing delirium tremens and suffering from depression, he too, was committed to the mental hospital; probably in 1932.

That was when electric shock therapy was much in vogue and was administered without an anaesthetic. EST is still used for treating depression, but nowadays under anaesthetic. Dad said it saved him, presumably it brought him back to reality, but he lost his confidence and his job of 22 years. He refused to accept re-employment working under the man who had been his assistant. He was pensioned off.

While in the mental hospital he welcomed the time he could spend with Jack. He said Jack was perfectly normal. Perhaps the operation had just needed time to heal. But the decision had been made; Jack was committed for life; he died there in 1945.

The mental hospital was 300 miles away in Bulawayo; visiting was out of the question. Our parents were unable to attend his funeral. Obviously transport and money were a problem. However, other factors may have come into play. For my part, being not yet five when Jack died, and having had no contact with him, I was oblivious as to what was happening.

***

It was the first Friday night that I was back from the first trip to Makaha, when there was a knock on the door. We knew someone had brought Dad home. Neville and I argued about who should answer.

"You go."

"No you go!"

"I went last time. It's your turn."

"Alright," I gave in.

I'm sure Dad must have heard us. I opened the door.

It was the last time I saw him conscious. I never did ask him about that yellow flame lily.

The next night, Saturday 26th May 1956, I had just run my bath water when I heard Neville's voice. Neville had been at Roy Baines's house being made up to go to a fancy dress party with Roy. He was going as Princess Grace of Monaco. Roy would be Prince Rainier.

I could hear Neville through the bathroom door.

"There's been an accident, outside Roy's house. It's dad. He's badly hurt."

We had to get to the hospital. We needed a car.

We didn't have to ask, when Theo Laing heard the news he simply handed Neville his car keys.

"It's yours for as long as you need it."

At the hospital Dad was in a coma. He had never before had a broken bone. He had survived the worst tropical diseases as well as snakebite.

When the young men of the British Empire had been used up in the First World War the older generation was called on and Dad volunteered. But only after he had secured agreement from his employers to provide for his wife and child should he be disabled or killed.

He was demobbed after 137 days. The armistice had been signed. At the same time the 1918 Spanish flu was working its way around the world and had arrived in Rhodesia with devastating effect. With all the young men at the front and flu deaths amounting to ten per cent or more, normal life ground to a halt.

My parents told me the flu victims turned black before dying, as if there was overall bruising.

Some say this was a haemorrhagic disease, which caused the blood vessels to breakdown with subsequent death from internal bleeding. Others say the change in colour was due to oxygen starvation. I doubt oxygen starvation would result in the deep blue-black described by my parents.

Now, so many years later, Dad was a mass of bone fractures and internal injuries. All were the result of what was claimed to be a low speed car accident, just 200 yards from his house.

Of course we didn't know the extent of his injuries until after the autopsy. Body scanners were still science-fiction machines. Anyway, he was in the old white settler hospital.

The most modern equipment was in the enormous, recently built (early 1950s), state-of-the-art Harare Hospital (not the present Harare Hospital).

Said to be the best in Africa at the time; it was built to cope with the ever-multiplying African population; partly a consequence of improved infant mortality (typically ninety percent survivors in infancy compared to a mere ten or twelve percent before white settlement). The other reason was economic migration from Malawi and Mozambique.

"It's a miracle he's still alive. He's critical. Expect the worst."

Those might not have been the doctor's exact words, but that's what I remember and that's what he meant. I have always believed that the only reason my Dad made it to hospital alive was due to the arrival on the scene of Peter Wright's dad. He was a doctor and just happened to be passing on his way home. Peter Wright was in my class at school.

We spent the night and all day Sunday at his bedside. Sunday night we went home to eat and sleep. Neville was still in fancy dress.

I went to school as usual at eight on Monday. At nine I was called out. My Mum's friend, an unofficial aunt, Alice Foster, drove Mum and me to the hospital where we met Neville.

"Aunty" Alice was a sister of the "Aunty" Anne who had given us that trusty little fun bike. The bike I wrote off under a lumbering old Chevrolet when I was seven.

We waited at Dad's bedside Monday, Monday night and Tuesday until about 5 pm when we went home to eat. About 6-30 pm we got the news. Dad had died. It was 29th May 1956.

Dad had caught the last bus and was walking the 200 yards home when he was struck by the car. We were told that he wasn't intoxicated. It was also well before closing time.

The driver said it was a low speed collision. The traffic was light, almost non-existent, the early show at the Metro drive-in movie had yet to finish. No one came forward as a witness to the accident. The driver was a Hollander named Doedens, an employee of the international construction company, John Lang.

He seemed reluctant to disclose the name of his passenger, a young lady. It was several days before we knew her name, Miss de Graaf. She said that she hadn't seen anything.

At the inquest we listened to the long list of bone fractures and internal injuries. It's hard to believe that such extensive damage could result from a single low speed collision. I now believe there was a double or multiple impact at high speed. I can explain this theory by describing an accident I had many years later.

I was driving at speed when a large dog ran out immediately in front of the car. The first contact was made before it was possible to brake. The impact knocked the dog 30 or so yards ahead.

Although my brakes were hard on, the second impact occurred while the dog was still in the air. There was no indication at the scene that more than one impact had occurred. The damage to the car, a *Citroen DS20*, was insignificant. Of course the dog's injuries were fatal. I think a similar scenario would apply to Dad's accident.

There was another possible link, some years later in a newspaper report a driver was on a charge of culpable homicide. Evidence was given that this was the third death of a pedestrian involving that driver. The driver's name was Doedens.

I don't know if it was the same Doedens, and I don't know the outcome of the case.

***

The hearse was followed by nineteen cars, Jimmy counted them, last in the procession was the Anderson's *Hudson Super-Six*. In 1947, when it was new it certainly was super. It had all the bells, whistles and buttons which emphasised the prowess of the American motor industry of the day.

Now it was showing the stress of ownership by a large family addicted to the African bush. A family convinced that a *Land Rover* was unnecessary providing you had enough determination. The car still had the "elephant" dent in the roof, a proud scar of when an elephant had pushed a tree onto it while they were camping in the Zambesi valley. That part of the valley was soon to be covered by the 2,500 square miles of Lake Kariba.

I was amazed by the turn out, considering it could have been a pauper's burial had it not been for the kindness of Mr. Foster, Aunt Alice's husband. Mind you, had he not been so quick to come forward, I am sure other friends would have rallied round.

On route to the cemetery, a gang of Africans were digging a trench. They would have been on "job-and-knock," i.e. they would knock off as soon as the day's work allocation was completed.

To a man they stopped work and bowed bared heads. Dad may have been a stranger to my schoolmates' parents and the post-war immigrant generation, but he was well remembered by the Africans and the old-timers.

Amongst the mourners at the graveside there were two Indians and an African. They were unknown to me. The African I understood, but I was curious about the Indian presence. My mother explained that soon after Dad had become Park Curator, some members of the Indian community had requested a particular tree or shrub be planted in the park. This plant was of religious importance to them.

Dad procured the plant and had it planted in a suitable quiet spot in the Public Gardens where they would not be disturbed.

That had been so many years before, but their community had not forgotten.

The funeral had been on 6th June which just happened to be the Queen's official birthday. All the boys' schools in the country had a compulsory cadet corps. Ours was about 700 strong.

Every school cadet corps would field a best drill platoon of thirty for the occasion, except for our school, Churchill. Our hard-headed Afrikaner headmaster, "Jeeves" Hougaard was well into one-up-man-ship; we had to have two on parade. This meant that I ended up in one.

Although "best drill" looked a bit special with 17 inch World War1 bayonets on the rifles for the occasion, I was much more comfortable in the shooting team. Of course on the day I wasn't on parade, there was a gap where I should have been.

The next Monday afternoon, at the end of the weekly parade, second lieutenant Ferreira informed me that I wasn't on the Queen's Birthday Parade; a fact I already knew. He went on, "Stay behind, you're on fatigues."

Sod him! But I said nothing he should have known better, his brother was in my class.

Then second lieutenant Robinson arrived, "Why were you absent?"

"My Dad died."

"Why?"

"My Dad died." Robinson was an intelligent boy, but his ears didn't seem to work.

"Why?"

"My Dad died." I screamed and I broke; I could hold back the tears no longer. I dropped my head and sobbed softly. It was the first time I had cried.

"You're excused fatigues. Don't stay behind." Robinson had a word with Ferreira.

It didn't matter what they said, I didn't care, I wasn't going to stay anyway, regardless of what they thought they could do. But the tears didn't stop until after I had handed back my rifle and was on my way home. Surrounded by hundreds, no one spoke to me. I felt entirely alone.

Now, without Dad's pension, we were totally dependent on Neville's second year apprentice's wage and the goodwill of friends.

Chapter 11

Bees

During the second school holiday visit to the beryl mine we met one of the small-worker families in the area; the Watsons, a man and wife and nineteen-year-old son, Doug. They lived about two miles away, where they had a claim of some sort.

As Doug drove the family's *Land Rover*, we didn't have to walk to the river every time. However, Doug never washed in the river, he was always a spectator.

On one occasion, I guess he must have been bored, he decided to liven things up. We were downstream a bit, enjoying the water and sunshine.

Across the river about fifty metres away, fixed near the top of a tree, there was a large, square, paraffin tin, an African beehive.

Idiot Doug picked up the .22 rifle and fired into the hive. He then ran off laughing.

The bees, of course, were now unhappy and a swarm of angry individuals descended on us. Remember there was no need for costumes; we were starkers.

Doug was quickly followed by the naked forms of Bill and Michael clutching their clothing. I stayed on the rock, which formed the river bank, a perfect sunbathing spot.

Several bees buzzed around before settling on me, presumably to check my credentials as a friend. There was no doubt in my mind that I was a friend. I had no intention of upsetting the one buzzing around trying to escape my very curly locks.

Once an African bee has stung you, his barbed sting is embedded in you and is subsequently torn from the bee. This kills him but he's got a lot of back-up and his colleagues don't mind dying for the cause. I had no quarrel with the bees and I knew better than to pick one. I was very careful not to interfere with whatever they wanted to do. I was on their side. I hoped they knew that.

When the other bees had moved on I went down to the river and very carefully washed the trapped one out of my hair. I wasn't stung.

I don't think Bill or Michael got stung either, but Doug certainly did, several times. Speaking personally, I was quite pleased with his fat lips and swollen arm. Of course his stupidity could have turned out a lot worse for all of us. African bees can be bad news.

***

By now various things had changed. Bill's dad had bought out Jordan and installed a mine manager by the name of Major Hilton.

Amongst a community of colourful characters, Major Hilton was without doubt one of the most flamboyant. If you were to mention his name in almost any country pub, there would be someone with something to say, usually with a laugh, a rueful shake of the head and something like; "That bloody rogue! But you know you couldn't help liking him."

Unusually for an ex-soldier he was full of war stories. In fact his repertoire of tales went far beyond the war. Like the stories, he seemed to get involved in get-rich-quick schemes beyond the imagination of your average prospector.

Even more surprising, he did strike it rich. I was told that it was he who had staked a nickel deposit, which he sold on to a major mining company, probably Anglo American. This claim became the Trojan Nickel Mine.

It was said (but I cannot vouch for it), that he had approached another major mining company and they had turned him down without even looking at the claim. Apparently they judged the claim on Hilton's reputation instead of examining the site.

Another version suggests that Hilton was working for Anglo at the time, but I don't want to believe that; it would spoil other stories I've heard and discount his reputation as a wide-boy. Whatever the truth, all the tales were probably embellished with more succulent details in every telling anyway, all agreed that he was a likeable rogue.

Early in the 21st century the plant at Trojan Nickel was mothballed on a care and maintenance programme after being very productive for more than 40 years. However, now in 2015, it is operating again as the market has improved.

Major Hilton's wife was an attractive blonde. I'm not sure if they had one or two young daughters. I don't remember any other children. The family were settled in the ex-Jordan house.

Interestingly, I have been told since, that the Marquis of Winchester married a daughter of a Major Hilton from Rhodesia. From the description it sounded very much like the same man. I can't believe there could've been two.

As far as the mining project was concerned, Jordan was well into building a road, as arranged with Bill's Dad. This would link the beryl mine to the tantalite mine. It would save a seven-mile round trip. The essential tools for the job were Jordan's bulldozer and gelignite.

Bill having a wash at the river crossing
My photo

Massive granite boulders meant explosives were the only practical method to clear the way. Of course we had a natural interest in the proceedings, especially the use of gelignite.

The "dynamite boy," almost certainly in his 50s, (he was anything but a boy) would prime an explosive stick with a detonator and fuse. This would be pushed, detonator first, to the bottom of each of a series of one metre deep holes which had been drilled into the rock. The five or six-foot fuse was long enough to protrude two feet or so from the hole. The hole was then filled to the top with sticks of gelignite. This procedure was repeated for all the other holes and the fuses were lit.

Being 30 or 40 metres from the explosions was a totally new experience. It put my usual home-made bombs into perspective, now they seemed quite puny. It even dwarfed the city-block-rocking last one I made at the Union Avenue house. That was the last; not only because we moved house, but because I spent the following four days (Easter) in the bedroom. For me it was the worst punishment I had ever had.

I had never known my dad to be so angry. Although Lawrence and I had been entirely responsible, our whole gang was in trouble for it. Barry, from next door, had been at the movies but he still got the brunt of his dad's anger. The adults were well out of line.

View from Greycap summit.
The white patch on the hill across the valley is Jordan's mine.

The Two Sisters about five miles away.   My photos

But this rock-breaking scene was something else, great rumbling explosions rolled around the valley in ever fading echoes. The broken rock was simply pushed aside with the bulldozer. Trees were just uprooted or pushed over. The resulting road had a very steep gradient and sharp bends. It could be accurately described as challenging. Even for the *Land Rover*.

It so happened that our school holiday coincided with a national census. This meant that an official turned up in a *Bedford* truck with forms for the local white inhabitants to fill in for both themselves and their African employees. He was looking for a certain Maxton Meyer whose claim was on the banks of the Inyamsizi River.

We had never been there but we offered to show him the way because we knew which track he had to follow. Besides, he would need to negotiate the new road in his *Bedford* truck and we thought that would be interesting. We didn't tell him that there was an alternative route.

Bill, Michael and I travelled in the back with the African census official. The white official and Doug were in the cab with the African driver. Apart from the challenge of the route the trip was uneventful.

His African assistant with us was most concerned about the elephants in the area and didn't want to believe me that the .300 Sherwood rifle was not powerful enough for big game.

At the Meyer homestead we weren't invited inside, unusual because bush dwelling Afrikaaners are renowned for their hospitality; having said that, they are also highly suspicious of officials of any kind. While the census man was inside we went down to the river and simply enjoyed the clean well-wooded location; unspoilt by mass human habitation.

Doug told us about old Meyer and his wife. He also mentioned their teenage daughter. When we saw her at a later date, Doug's description seemed accurate enough; pretty, strong and fierce. My impression of Afrikaans girls was that they could usually be divided into two camps:

The first group; petite, friendly and very often blue-eyed blondes, right little crackers; the second lot were fierce, tough and aggressive, out to prove who knows what? Any natural beauty would be totally lost in the first impression. The Meyer girl was a mix, pretty enough, but not one to tangle with; definitely tough.

It would appear that the females of the family were in charge. We were told that if the labour got out of hand, it was Mrs. Meyer who would wade in with a sjambok (a rhino hide whip).

While we would have welcomed some female company we thought Miss Meyer could be passed by. It was rumoured that Mrs. Meyer could ring-bark an oak tree with her sjambok. A figure of speech of course, but the thought of an angry sjambok-wielding mother stopped my sap from rising.

When the census man left, after the third attempt to get up the new road, we noticed a trail of oil. It would seem that the new road needed further work. We never heard whether or not the *Bedford* made it back intact.

Chapter 12

School Holidays

The six weeks holidays over Christmas 1956 saw me selling men's clothes in Hepworths, a gentlemen's outfitters. Being very upmarket, we would take Africans to a back room, well, not actually a room, just the secluded passage where we had our tea; our changing room. White customers had a cubicle with a curtain.

Africans were our most numerous and most selective customers for expensive hats. A top-of-the-range hat seemed to be the essential status symbol to complement a bicycle. They weren't interested in the cheap unlined school-uniform trilbies; they wanted the expensive, fully-lined equivalent, products of *Christys, Battersby* or *Stetson*, (I see 2014 prices for these hats range from £80 to £200).

Proud of our quality, we sold the best and we had to be correct at all times; not always easy for me, I was once told off for saying "OK."

"In this establishment we don't use slang, we are not the *OK Bazaars*," the manager had informed me. Not that I needed to be told what we weren't; our prices were proof of what we were.

There was no call for schoolboy help after Christmas in the three-week May holiday, so I volunteered to help with the school fete. The fete was always extensive and very well-supported. It was an important fund-raiser.

If a project could get State Lottery approval, then the Lottery would match whatever was raised pound-for-pound. In the seven years since the school was built we already had a superb swimming pool installed on that basis.

That year (1957) they had organised a dog race, and our very deep-chested Staffordshire bull-terrier cross, also named Mickey, was entered in the second race.

At the start the punters asked me which dog would win; not thinking of School funds, I answered honestly and indicated Mickey. Apart from being young and strong he was enthusiastic, looked the part, and was used to running behind Neville's motor-bike.

We had Neville revving the bike just beyond the end of the track; there was no question as to the outcome of that race.

It was great fun, but a bit of a disaster as a fund-raiser.

***

Come August, Bill Anderson's parents suggested I try for a gatekeeper's job at the Agricultural Show. Fortunately I was lucky enough to get one.

For the gatekeeper job I had to be up at six and cycle the six miles to the showgrounds. In the evening the Andersons would load my bike together with two of their sons' cycles on top of their long-suffering *Hudson* and drop me within two miles of my house. This was possible because they also had showground jobs.

Bill, Michael, and I worked three shifts; their parents worked the evening shift, after their day jobs.

Because the heavy steel car access gate had a broken hinge, the entrance I manned was pedestrian only. It needed a combination of a special technique and muscle power to move it. The groundsman had shown me how, but it was obviously not practical to use the gate.

On the second day a police car came charging up the road and demanded to go through. I explained that the gate was broken and I couldn't oblige.

The cop was outraged. He wasn't taking this from a schoolboy. His passenger jumped out and seized the gate with angry determination. Clenched teeth, a red face and a near bust-gut, left the gate quite unmoved. I watched.

Now they both calmed down and asked me rather nicely if I could possibly give them a hand. I was strong and I knew the trick. So I walked over, put my shoulder to the gate, used my legs to lift and crab-walked sideways to open it. I am sure they resented the nonchalant contempt in my body language. They left without thanking me or helping me to close it, but they didn't come back that way. I felt good. Their display of irritation had made my day.

***

Being in the southern hemisphere, August was the tail end of winter. The mornings were crisp with cold. By midday it was uncomfortably hot, but at night the temperature dropped as fast as the tropical sun sunk behind a glowing red horizon. The talcum-powder-fine red dust got everywhere. A good soak in the bath and soft clean sheets in bed felt so very luxurious.

On the third day, as this lanky six foot of virgin testosterone was tearing a ticket, a sweet young female voice said "Hello." I looked up, to have the blood rush through my body at the sight of the dark flashing eyes of a gorgeous black-haired beauty.

I didn't then, and still don't know, the ancestry of Carmel Meyer but she could have passed for a Spanish film star. I had met her through Anne Green, a neighbour of Bill Anderson, and she kept surfacing in my mind. I had a crush on her.

There was no time to chat, anyway I was dumbstruck by my overdose of teenage male hormones on the boil. Then she was gone; slowly the hormones cooled down to simmer. I don't know if I've spelt her name correctly, I've never seen it in writing. If I had I would've remembered.

My simmering pulse was still hopeful of seeing Carmel again late on the last shift when, quite suddenly, an apparition was speaking. This petite white-suited blonde had stepped into my pool of light. She was asking a favour of me. A full-grown woman of maybe twenty-four wanted an escort through the black patches of dark which separated the mediocre streetlights of the show-grounds. *And* she was asking me.

I was back on the boil; never mind Carmel.

Some people thought that the show-grounds were spooky; it never worried me. Perhaps I would have felt differently had I given any thought to what my parents had said.

"They'll never build on the showgrounds. That's where they buried the African victims of the Spanish flu. Long trenches full of bodies. It had to be done and done quickly".

Anyway, I had forgotten about the flu dead; that was well before my time. The silent walls of black were eerie enough for believers of things spiritual and evil, but that didn't include me.

I guided this delightful, elegant peach of a woman through the menacing darkness for the half-mile or so to the north gate, wondering all the time just how to get her into my arms; fighting a near overwhelming urge to grab her.

I could have offered to take her hand. Perhaps I could have asked her for a kiss before we stepped into the light of her destination. I did neither. Not even when she thanked me.

My boys-only high school education had stunted those most important of social skills which men require to make it in a heterosexual world.

My wasted youth.

***

1957 was my last year at school and there was a turnaround in the family fortunes. Mum had come to the conclusion that she would never realise her dream of having her own house built.

With the government's decision to sell off the pisês to the current occupiers for a legal token payment of £1.00, Mum decided that she could sell the plot of land she had bought so long ago.

I presume she had bought it while she was in the Air Force during the war where she had worked covering and spraying aircraft.

With the sale at least she could have a little luxury in the winter of her life.

She bought her first fridge, a new 4-plate *Defy* cooker and she had the old *Belfast* sink and wooden drainer replaced with a new stainless steel unit. We also got new beds with spring mattresses. The old kapok mattresses were well lumpy, but better than the original coir; now sprung mattresses? Real luxury.

***

We still used the ex-Aunt-Esther hand-powered-bread kneading machine. This consisted of a large bucket to which a dough hook was fixed to rotate in the centre. The rotation was by a long, muscled-powered handle. It was only marginally easier than hand-kneading but, at about ten minutes, a lot quicker.

It had no effect on your hands. Hand-kneading was much better at cleaning your hands; stubborn longstanding well-ingrained dirt would be gone, even the under-fingernails-black. Both methods were good for your shoulder muscles.

Neville and I would take it in turns to knead the dough. When mum's deteriorating health got bad, I made the bread and did most of the cooking.

Now with the fridge we could use brewer's yeast instead of dried yeast for the bread. Having said that, dried yeast was less effort than the old potato yeast she used to make. For that you added two dessert spoons of sugar to water and grated potato and let it ferment in a strong well-sealed bottle. The first batch needed a few unwashed raisins to start it. It was ready after 24 hours. If it didn't "pop" like champagne it was a failure.

Mum also bought a new *VW Beetle* (the only *VW* sedan model at the time), which would become Neville's car, but her transport as and when she needed it. That was perfectly acceptable.

Being as it was a brand new car and therefore in perfect working order, I was allowed to have a major say in which car to buy.

To be fair to me she decided to buy me a car as well. It had to be cheap and therefore second-hand. Thus it had to be bought from a trusted friend, a motor mechanic who guaranteed the condition: and it was in excellent condition; but it wasn't my choice, I had no say.

My vehicle in any condition would've been something like an old *Riley RMA* or *RMB* or maybe a *Citroen Big 6.* Any one, of which, could have been within the £150 limit. The fuel consumption would have been worse, but not by much. I wouldn't have minded if I had to spend most of my time and money working on it. I was keen to learn.

The family friend's car-for-sale was a green, 1952 *Ford Anglia*, the box on wheels two-door model of the *Prefect*, a luxury export version of the *Popular*. It had the E-493A side-valve engine, a close relative to the *1928 Ford Model A*. The suspension was almost identical to the 1915 *Model T.* The windscreen wipers were operated by engine intake vacuum. That meant they operated at full speed when the car was stationary and the engine was idling. As you accelerated they slowed down to stop.

This was mechanical design which had either been long since abandoned by the rest of the motor manufacturing world, or never used in the first place.

The inadequate three-brush generator was a boon to the battery industry. Significantly, *Ford* also made batteries. It was a charging system which I doubt has ever been used by any other car company; another design dinosaur, and further compromised by being six volt. But it was cheap. The headlights were so lousy that the system had to be upgraded to include sealed-beams for the Canadian market.

Everything on my car worked as specified by *Ford*; *not very well.*

As I said, my choice would have been a banger of a *Riley* or *Citroen* or similar for the same money. There had also been a pre-war *Aston Martin* going cheap. Fixing it would have been all part of the fun but older and so-called wiser heads overruled my impetuous young dreams.

How I wish I had that *Aston* now.

***

My last day of school ended with four strokes of the cane, mostly because I refused to tell an incoming, jobs-worth of a teacher which boy had thrown the half-orange that missed me but nearly got the jobs-worth. It was the end of the period and the class was splitting for different subjects. I was in the group going to another room, which is also why the incoming teacher and I were strangers.

The fact that I swore at the person who grabbed my arm just as I was about to retaliate with the other half-orange didn't help. I didn't know I was swearing at the teacher but I'm glad he thought he was the target. I felt *fucking cunt* was an appropriate description.

My throw went high, well over Sinclair's head. Sinclair was, of course, the thrower who had just missed the teacher. I thought the hand grabbing me was Jimmy trying to snatch my half of the orange. How was I to know it was this new little prick of a teacher who had just walked in? The first half had only just missed the back of my neck. The new teacher was too short to be seen below the outgoing boys and, regrettably, also too short for the flying orange to make contact.

Had I begged for mercy from the Deputy Head, Cooper, who was authorised to use the cane, pointing out that it was my last day, I am sure that he would have laughed it off. He was a man with a wholesome take on life as he found it, and he had a sense of humour. But begging wasn't in my character. The crime was mine. I would take the punishment.

Chapter 13

Holiday and Employment

After my school leaving exams (the Cambridge Overseas Certificate) we embarked on a month-long holiday (Dec '57/Jan '58). Mostly we spent time visiting relatives in South Africa, from Durban to Cape Town.

Some distant cousins in George could hardly speak English, although all were Robertson by name. My schoolboy Afrikaans improved no end.

Not at all wealthy, their hospitality towards us knew no bounds; unlike a couple of stuck-up affluent ones who obviously had no time for their poor-relations. Then there was one low-life in Durban, who was politically confused; possibly the spouse of a cousin, he seemed to be a victim of the South African propaganda of the time and was still fighting the Boer War.

He seemed oblivious to the fact that our (his wife's and my) grandparent's home had been ransacked and burnt to the ground by rogue Boers on the night of 19 August 1901 (the Scheepers /van der Merve gang)[1]. True, Kitchener's scorched-earth activities in the Transvaal and Orange Free State with the resultant mass deaths of women and children were despicable, but they were nothing to do with the Cape Boers. However, the Cape was the closest the Transvaal and Free State Boers could get to Britain.

One relative, a third cousin, one of the Robertsons in George, was a great guy. He took me to the beach at a place called the Wilderness where we tried to swim in a sea which insisted on dumping us back on the beach. Eventually we gave up and swam in the adjacent lagoon.

Great guy that he was, he still got beady-eyed when he thought his teenage sister was too friendly towards me. He need not have worried; she was too young and I had no intention of getting involved with a relative. In Durban the surf was kinder and I learned to dive under the breakers to get out to deeper water. However, our time there coincided with a series of shark attacks, (shark nets had yet to be installed). I believe it was something like five deaths in three months. The anti-shark feeling was running high.

With the newspapers making the most of the situation, some nutcases wanted to go shark shooting. No one seemed to care that more than ten people died every week on the road travelling to or from Durban. People afraid to swim at the edges of the vast expanse of the Indian Ocean would think nothing of driving flat out on crowded roads, which boasted a remarkably high track record of death.

Back home at the beginning of February 1958 I started work. Like Neville, it was with the GPO as a learner technician, effectively an apprenticeship. The training was thorough and broad-based. After an introductory spell in each department we did the first of three sandwich courses.

---

[1] See page 117 *Commandant Gideon Scheepers and the search for his grave* ISBN 0-620-24534-4.

The first course covered line construction, cable jointing, phone and equipment fitting as well as basic electrical and telecom principles.

Initially, after college, work experience in the fitting section was driving around in a little *Bedford* van to fit phones or small exchanges. The work was mostly indoors with all the wrong kind of female contact; middle-aged, married and grumpy.

Working on line construction, it was a five-ton Bedford and outdoor fun-up-a-pole. Later, on cable jointing, it was a one-ton Bedford, more outdoor fun, but down a hole with much too much overtime.

More than once we had the help of the weather to add to the fun. The hole could get flooded and wipe out all the phone connections on that cable. On one occasion a temporary greased cloth tape cable seal of ours was under water for five weeks. In another downpour the two African labourers and I had held back a bulging, water-filled tarpaulin tent side just long enough for my journeyman to wipe the joint (seal the lead cable with a lead sleeve and molten plumbing solder). We all ended up standing knee-deep in muddy water.

Auto-Exchange Course 1959
Photo Tony Dennis

Under the circumstances, it was impossible to pressure test for leaks. Poor old Piet Botha, my journeyman, was worried for weeks until the water drained away and he could pressure test the joint. Although by that time the seal was well proven.

Working outdoors was my preference but it could be exhausting. Alternatively, it could be very pleasant and invigorating; especially on a cold winter's day, when we might start with a breakfast of eggs and boerewors, (that spicy-yard-long South African sausage) cooked on a shovel over a fire. All this before we went on to the second and most intensive course. It covered carrier and radio communication as well as automatic exchanges and more advanced electrical theory.

Chapter 14

Romance

With our transport options increased by my little Ford, the world was opening up. Jimmy and I decided to go to Mermaid's Pool. At that time it was an idyllic natural swimming pool 26 miles out on the Shamva Road.

I say at that time it was idyllic because later on, after it became licensed to sell alcohol, it degenerated for a while into the hang-out of the local drug-dumb low-life. People too confused to realise that swimming and broken beer bottles don't mix. However, that was in the future, but regrettably just when my children could benefit from an outstanding natural beauty spot.

Although later it was apparently brought back to respectability, I never got round to taking our children. There are photos on the internet.

Having just left an all-boys school, my circle of female friends was non-existent. Parents, particularly fathers, were quite often hostile. I don't know whether they overrated our seductive powers or simply thought we had the same moral values as they had; but I decided that I had to try for Carmel.

My testosterone level gave me the courage to roll up at her house to ask her to come with us to the pool. The folks were no problem, but she was ill in bed and refused to see me. I felt quite underrated, drained. Jimmy shrugged his shoulders, "Better luck next time, next girl."

We went to Mermaid's Pool anyway, just the two of us. It was a truly outstanding place to go swimming. The pool was about 70 metres in diameter fed by a clear water river flowing down 40 or 50 metres of a granite hill, the rock-slide. A "foofy" (aerial) slide traversed the diameter of the pool.

A notice informed us that the use of the rock-slide was at our own risk. The only charge was for entrance to the site.

First-aid was provided by the St. John's Brigade, and they were usually busy. The rock-slide was a major source of patients for them.

This was the first time I had been there since I was much younger and my tentative attempts on the edges of the slide had been painful. The highlight of that previous visit was breakfast of eggs and bacon cooked over a fire in a hubcap from the Evans's 1930s *Hudson Terraplane*.

It wasn't my fault that the frying pan had been left behind but I got the job of using sand to scour out the makeshift frying pan, the hubcap.

My reward was to have the first helping of breakfast. A mistake; I am sure that the subsequent helpings improved in flavour with every cook-up. My breakfast had a horrible motor-oily taste.

Now some ten years later, a brash teenager, I was ready for that slope of bumpy, slippery and super-hard granite.

The standard practice was to use a sledge made by inflating a large car or truck tyre inside a grain sack.

We didn't have a sledge but, as luck would have it, my cousin John Evans and his wife were there. Both had sledges which they were kind enough to lend us.

The technique was simple; you held the sledge against your chest; took a short run and dived forward onto the slide. Thus you went charging down over the slick, lumpy, water-worn granite.

Under the layer of water, the rock was covered with a greenish transparent slime, as slippery as ice. If you cocked-up; the sledge would flip up in front of you. You then followed the sledge, careering face-down over bumpy granite. It was, at best, a very bruising experience.

It was my first time ever. In my over enthusiastic run-up, I managed to belly-flop onto the rock behind the sledge. I felt every bump, crack and crevice.

Never mind the bruises or my cousin's concern, I immediately had another go just to get it right. Later I adopted a push-up stance without a sledge, a technique I had been told about. Akin to doing about a hundred push-ups it worked well as exercise. The risk of injury was a remarkably strong incentive to maintain the push-up stance.

If I ever have the affluence and opportunity I would buy that place and restore it to its natural state, purely for my own selfish pleasure. To me it's a superb bit of real estate in a country endowed with the world's best climate.

***

Still without female company, we were invited to the original farm of Christon Bank, seventeen or so miles out on the Mazoe Road. The farm was one of the pioneer or early settler land grants. The farmer, Mr Beachy-Head, was the son of the original owner. His mother-in-law was a friend of my mum. They had worked together in the air force and my parents had known his parents.

A knock-about on the tennis court was followed by a party. And there, amongst the guests, in full adolescent bloom, was pretty young Alison Scott.

A year or two younger than my seventeen, and already comely, she was promising to grow into a very attractive young woman.

The low-volume music from the stack of records on the classic radiogram was just the way I liked it; what I wanted to say to Alison was not for shouting. We *Rocked Around* Hayley's *Clock,* spun and wiggled to Presley's *Hound-Dog* and stumbled about to Crosby's *Tennessee Waltz,* on the spacious old farmhouse veranda.

Crosby's crooning gave me the chance to whisper in Alison's ear, "It's a super night; wouldn't a little walk be nice?"

Without missing a beat we took our stumbling waltz down the veranda steps into the darkness. The walk, under the bright sub-Saharan stars, was, as I had suggested, little; just as far as my car.

It was the first time I had been in such close contact with such a delightful and enthusiastic female. We did nothing more than kiss but it was an unbelievable head-lightening and throbbing-heart pleasure. I could only view any future developments with a thrill of eager anticipation.

Mr. Beachy-Head had already asked me to drop Alison off on my way home to save him the trouble. Of course I agreed and Alison added, "When you drop me off after the party, you'll know where my place is and you can come round anytime."

"Good idea, it will be a pleasure." As a matter of fact I thought it was an excellent idea. My hormones were on red alert.

Her house was one of those which were being developed as a township by Beachy-Head.

However, as we emerged from the car I was aware of Beachy-Head's bulky form in the background and I wondered if he had noticed just how nice our little walk had been.

Apparently he had, because now he brusquely insisted on delivering Alison to her door himself. Of course he felt a duty to protect her. I understood that, and, as he hardly knew me, he could only judge me by the young men he had known.

It was a pity, but overall I was well chuffed. We went out several times. I was intoxicated by her presence. Never did we go any further than enthusiastic cuddling, which might sound strange in this day and age. Looking back, I'm glad about that, I think a more physically intimate relationship would sour the sweetness of the memory.

Alison when I met her (left) and the woman she became (right).
Photos supplied by Alison

Her parents were some of the most pleasant and welcoming people I have ever met. They invariably invited me to dinner, and introduced me to wine as a complement to food. And there was Alison's older sister, Jennifer, attractive, tall and slim, with a definite promise of fun. She had a feel-good factor. The sort of person you couldn't help liking.

But nothing is perfect, Alison was a boarder and unavailable during term-time. And then there was Diana. I had suddenly discovered that a schoolmate had this very pretty sister. As a day scholar she would be available throughout the year, at least that's what I thought. So I dropped around a few times, intending to build up an acquaintance.

I had no idea that I had done anything to indicate that I had an interest in Diana, but it seems that she had me summed up and liked the idea. Apparently her mother had also summed me up; and *didn't* like whatever ideas I might have.

Absolutely nothing at all developed between us. In fact I hadn't even managed to have a chat with her, not a single word, before her mother had a chat with me, or more accurately *to* me.

On that occasion I listened to the vitriolic diatribe sitting in my car's driver's seat while her mother shouted through the open window.

"What brings you, a total stranger, uninvited, around here? We don't know you. We don't know your family. What are you intentions?"

"Who the hell do you think you are?" she continued, "We don't know you from a loaf of bread!"

Which, of course, was true, all of it, but I couldn't change that if she was intent on keeping it that way.

It's not possible to remember everything she was saying but from the tone of voice and the large number of uncomplimentary words, I gathered the distinct impression that I wasn't welcome there.

She was in mid-hysteric when I drove off.

What I didn't know was that she had recently lost her husband and was deeply traumatised. I felt bad when I found out many years later. I have always wished since that I could somehow have helped to ease her pain. To this day it troubles me that I upset her.

That unpleasant incident would have been avoided had I visited Wavell before I went to Diana's house.

I had no idea that there was any connection between Rosie, at Queen Elizabeth School, and Diana at Roosevelt School, five miles away. However I soon found out and could only be impressed by the speed and scope of the female grapevine.

It was the same evening as the rollicking from Diana's mother, that I discovered the link. I went round to visit Wavell and Rosie handed me a note. That note, from Diana, warned me not to go around. Too bad, too late.

Of course, Queen Elizabeth was also Alison's school and I was about to learn more about that schoolgirl grapevine the next time I met Alison.

That meeting began and ended with another chat. Once again I did the listening. It consisted mainly of instructions, not only on exactly what I could do but included a personal description of me using unpleasant, highly inaccurate and very enlightening adjectives. The informative mood was emphasised by her quiet, calm and measured delivery.

She did her best to let me down gently and without rancour. Alison Scott was, and still is, a very civilised person. She was the only girl I took out who met my Mum. Mum was an uncanny judge of character. She liked Alison.

That closed one of the most pleasurable chapters of my life, but not without leaving its mark. Not a scar, but a cherished and valued soft-spot of nostalgic affection.

Chapter 15

Beira at Easter 1959

It was common for Rhodesians to travel to Beira in Mozambique at any excuse. After all, it was the nearest beach and a magnificent one at that. Not to mention the cheap and plentiful Portuguese wine. Come Easter, we decided to make the 300-mile trip.

Jimmy Smith and Robin Stanford would travel with me in the *Anglia*. Eric Windel would go with Mike Jesson in his *VW Beetle*. Let me say now that Robin was not my favourite person. I had known him at junior school. Our personalities simply did not gel.

As far as I knew Robin was from India; attended junior school in Rhodesia; disappeared for a couple of years, presumably to a public school in the UK, and then reappeared as an eighteen-year-old.

His childhood certainly had similarities to Peter Jenner's. However, while Peter was easy-going and likeable, I found Robin's stocky-short-man-aggressive-trying-to-impress-attitude quite irritating. He was Jimmy's friend so I was determined to tolerate him.

Apart from Robin we had all been in the same class at school. Mike and Eric were old friends. They had left a few hours before us, so had made Beira in daylight and set up camp on the beach. We just got to the border, about half way, at dusk.

There was a small issue with Robin which meant that he needed a visa to enter Mozambique and that would take two weeks. He said it was because he had a British passport. No problem, we would drop Robin off before the border and pick him up on the other side. Robin was tough.

Most bush in Rhodesia is easy to walk through. Apparently the Mozambique border at Umtali was more challenging. So, on the other side we picked up a foul-mouthed, bloody and well scratched tough-guy.

It was now dark so I had to pick my way along the atrocious Mozambiquen roads by the light of the cheap and nasty six-volt Ford electrics. We made Beira just before dawn.

The next day the three of us slept into the afternoon. Meanwhile, Mike and Eric went to the local fish market where Mike bought a kilo or more of very ripe prawns for fish bait. He said, "The bigger the stink, the bigger the fish." He may or may not have been right.

However, Mike did have a very interesting sleeping bag. It was an army surplus body-bag which could be zipped completely closed. The next morning Mike woke up in a panic; totally enclosed with his stinking prawns for company…

Now some fifty years later Mike tells me that he is claustrophobic and he still has nightmares from that incident.

We never meant to be cruel, we just wanted to emphasise that he shouldn't have ignored our request to get rid of the prawns. He got the message, but he did moan a lot.

We spent the rest of the morning swimming. The gently sloping beach and slowly rolling waves of warm water caressed our bodies, lulling us into blissful ignorance. The tide came in and I suddenly realised that the shoreline was much further away than I had ever swum before. I have never been a strong swimmer but I did have incentive. I made it… just.

The next day, Sunday, we watched the Beira 100 road race. Various home-built specials, sports and racing cars would tear around the streets of Beira for 100 miles. Crowd control was non-existent. Most of the spectators seemed to be Rhodesian, as were the majority of the competitors. Amazingly nobody was injured, and I have no idea who won.

My involvement in sport in Mozambique has been limited to target shooting. The experience was one of overwhelming hospitality and total disorganisation. The Rhodesians took over the scoring and prize allocation; the Portuguese supplied the prizes, copious quantities of food, wine and goodwill. I imagine that motor-sport worked the same way.

Apart from football, the major Portuguese interest in sport was bull fighting. Unlike the Spanish, they never killed the bull, at least not in the ring. Naturally there was a bullring close to the Rhodesian border in the town of Macequece; a magnet to Rhodesian youth.

The organisers even provided a special bull for Rhodesian want-to-be-matadors, the ones suffering from bravado, one of the major side-effects associated with too much *vino*. The other major side-effect was big blue lumps on the head associated with police truncheons.

The innate hospitality of the Portuguese seemed to evaporate to be replaced by an insane lust for violence whenever the visitors lost their manners. I never went to a bullfight, but I've seen the big blue lumps on Bobby Jones, a friend of my brother Neville.

In the evening we went to the open-air dance-floor alongside the bar. Fully charged with rampant male desire we had ambitions to make out with any available females.

Some hope. No parents we knew would have let their daughters go camping with us, so why would anyone else be different, or even let the girls go by themselves? Sure there were girls; all with boyfriends, brothers or fathers obsessed with a duty to safeguard female purity. However, always optimistic, Robin and I did latch onto a couple of promising birds.

I'm unclear about the details with Robin but he definitely got the brush-off. In my case things were going quite well until the boyfriend turned up. Surprisingly he was almost as friendly as the girl. I looked at the girl, looked at the six-foot-four blacksmith from the car and locomotive spring factory in Umtali, and decided that I could be friends with that chap. I wasn't randy any more.

Robin, on the other hand, was fired-up and frustrated, so he picked a fight with Mickey Mitchell. Robin didn't know Mickey; we did, he was big and tough.

I was amazed by Robin's ferocity as he tore into Mickey. The poor fellow caught a thumping before he even knew the fight had started.

At that stage Mickey's much smaller pal, Scotty, decided to avenge the defeat. A miscalculation; Robin was still ferocious.

Robin had proved his point; which was, I presume, that for a little man, he had a high nuisance value. Something I already knew.

***

The following night, as sex wasn't going to happen, we abandoned our attempts at lechery and concentrated our efforts on the local *vino*. Except for Robin, who was once again raring to go, we knew it would be another fight.

The rest of us were absolutely happy; the *vino* was supplied in rather large flagons. Initially it was easy to support the flagon on a bent elbow and tip it down your throat, the fashionable way to drink it. That steadily became more and more difficult as the flagon became lighter. It also got easier to spill.

Robin didn't know Theo Laing. We told Robin that Theo was the one bloke not to tangle with. Of course that was a challenge to "The Nuisance". Theo was a friend of my family and had been very supportive when my father died. I didn't want Theo to associate me with Robin so I left the group. If Robin couldn't take good advice, it wasn't down to me to keep him out of trouble.

I was told that Theo did his utmost to avoid a fight. The more Theo tried not to fight, the more persistent Robin was. Eventually, Robin got his way. While his ferocity gave him a start it wasn't enough and he got his just desserts.

I was pleased with the result, not so much with Robin's appearance, but more his demeanour. He was ever so quiet, totally subdued. Not that he looked that bad, in fact I quite liked his black eyes and crooked nose. His whole face had a satisfactory appearance. It was nicely swollen.

Jimmy and I left Beira in the early hours of Monday morning, with Robin curled up on the back seat. At the border we threw a blanket over Robin. Jimmy and I processed our passports normally and collected the gate pass displaying a big "2" to indicate the number of persons allowed through the border.

The half-asleep early-shift gatekeeper on the Portuguese side hardly looked at the gate pass; he seemed to have enough trouble standing up to lift the barrier. Had he looked, I doubt he would have noticed Robin.

On the Rhodesian side his equivalent stood to attention, glanced at the pass, and gave us a very smart salute, which we of course, graciously acknowledged.

In Umtali we were having breakfast at a little café when Mike and Eric joined us. As we left, Mike, boastful of his *VW's* superiority over my little *Ford*, said he would catch up with us on the road. I was determined that was not going to happen.

Leaving Umtali we had a torturous climb to get through Christmas Pass on the outskirts of Umtali. Once that poor little *Anglia* was on the other side of the mountain pass, it was foot flat, hard against the floorboards. For the next 100 miles or so we bumped and bounced along those Rhodesian masochist's delight; strip roads..

Consisting of two 18 inch strips of undulating tarmac, not necessarily level with each other, they were set in a 22 foot wide gravel road. The law said that passing vehicles had the right to one strip each. Cyclists and motor cyclists had the right to one strip at all times; something that motorists were inclined to overlook.

Home-built Racers at Mashonaland 100, Belvedere Road Circuit
Circa 1952
Top row left: MG Special Top row right: Frazer Nash
Middle row left: Unknown Middle row right: Mike Apple Special
Bottom row left: As above Bottom row right: Riley/MG
My photos

Laid during the Great Depression of the early1930s, strip roads were one of the projects to give employment to jobless whites. The Africans were living off the land in their tribal areas, or were employed by whites who may or may not have been able to pay them. In any event they remained for food and shelter.

When I met Fred Maughan some years later, I discovered that he had worked on that road-building program.

"The clerks, accountants and other office types did the pick and shovel work. I was OK, as a bricklayer I was building culverts and bridges. It was just like any other job," he said, with a shrug of his shoulders.

However, driving that *Ford* on the strips was nothing like driving any other car anywhere else.

The bridges were narrow, only wide enough for a single vehicle. The barriers were usually made from old railway lines which were past safe usage as track due to metal fatigue. At 18 inches high, accepted wisdom in the case of a flooded river said, "If you can't see the railings, don't cross."

The approaches were usually down a long steep valley. When the valley sides were too steep the approach would be parallel to the river. This meant a sharp right angle turn onto the bridge followed by an equally sharp opposite turn on the other side.

With the *Ford* it was said. "You can't drive one of those things on the strips; you have to aim it." Every other vehicle behaved better on the strips. *VWs* were very good and the big *Citroens* were excellent. Both the space-age *DS* models of the day and those long, low, superbly sprung, Slough-built *Traction Avant* models were a pleasure to drive on rough roads.

The authorities in charge of vehicle safety accepted that it was impossible to get all the slop out of the Ford steering. The police would only impound your Ford if the steering wheel had more than 45 degrees of free movement. In order to get it back on the road legally, the play had to be below 30 degrees; even then, driving one of those *Fords* was different.

My method of coping with the slop in the steering was to keep up a right-handed shunting movement of the wheel hand with my elbow on the open window sill while my left hand was on standby for any surprises.

With the accelerator hard to the floor I aimed for home. That little side-valve engine was singing; never mind the heat we could feel coming through the bulkhead. Robin bounced around in a foetal position on the back, oblivious to the world.

Three hours, ten minutes and 172 miles after we left that café we were at my front door, an average speed of 54 mph. That might seem slow these days, but on those roads in that car, it was more exciting than an afternoon riding the giant roller coaster in Blackpool. We had dropped Robin off and were having tea and cake when Mike and Eric rolled up.

Chapter 16

Camping

We enjoyed camping. A favourite place was a superb camping-come-picnic spot at the intersection of the Shavanhohwe and Nyagui rivers. It was not official or organised, just a bit of countryside.

About 48 miles north of the capital, it was eight miles off-road, downstream from the bridge and a popular picnic spot with a sandy beach. We found it simply by going a little bit further north deeper into the bush. Both were in Tribal Trust Land.

Although the locals always welcomed us, whites needed permission from the District Commissioner to stay overnight there. Obviously not all whites could be trusted not to upset the inhabitants. As our spot was miles from any habitation and we were the only people there, we never asked. We weren't going to do anything stupid.

It was a clearing, just big enough for Mike's father's six-man tent and a relaxing camp-fire. The evergreen surrounding trees formed a shady canopy. In the dry winter the junction consisted of stretches of deeply pooled water connected by narrow fast flowing rapids.

Meandering through sparsely inhabited countryside the water was clean and clear, unlike the rivers to the south of the capital.

The city's water-supply-come-recycling-system was based on the rivers to the south. With abundant drinkable water on tap no-one gave a thought as to how that was achieved; as the general population would not like the thought of recycled water. It was not publicised and never denied. It was anyway perfectly safe and drinkable.

The annual rainfall was about 30 inches; all in five summer months of intermittent heavy downpours. It was not feasible to throw water away down the sewers; it had to be recovered. True, the early settlers had built the first reservoirs, Cleveland Dam, at the headwaters of the Makabusi River and Prince Edward Dam on the Hunyani River, well above any town effluent. That water needed a minimum of filtration, but that was in the early 1900s. By the 1950s the size of the city had grown considerably and with it the demand for water.

Rainfall alone could not meet demand. A much bigger reservoir was built, Lake MacIlwaine; crucially it was sited downstream of the sewage works. Needless to say, the filtration requirement was much greater.

On the other hand, our campsite, in sparsely populated countryside, had very little interference from humans. We mostly went there in winter so the nights were cold but the days were always sunny with clear blue skies. The water was never too cold to swim and we soon warmed up in the sun.

The fishing was poor, even Mike, who had the reputation of being able to catch fish where others failed, was unsuccessful this time. So we swam, and we messed about in Jimmy's home-built canoe.

Mike fell in almost every time we crossed the river. We also found some crocodile tracks in a sandbank upriver. Interesting, because the popular picnic spot seven or eight miles upstream, near the road, was believed to be croc-free and safe.

We ventured downstream several miles in search of a herd of hippo, which were reputed to be there. And they might well have been, but not at the same time as us.

The land area consists of giant granite hills separated by flat sandveld. I had been told that the largest hill, twice the size of the rest, was in fact 1100 ft above the surrounding countryside. Of course we had to climb it. To say "climb" was an exaggeration, we walked up the easy side. I suppose some people would find a difficult way up, but not us.

However, the best campsite was further down the Nyangui, at its confluence with the Mazoe River. This was ten or so miles beyond the little mining town of Shamva. Again we found a shady clearing for the tent.

When we went there Mike had no trouble landing a couple of good-sized tiger-fish from the Mazoe River. After he cooked them we decided that his duties should be limited to catching fish. Cooking was not his strong point at the time. I'm glad to say he has since had enough practice to become a very competent campfire cook.

Wavell, Jimmy and I didn't manage to do any fishing, we spent most of the time trying to fix Wavell's Morris Minor. Somehow, Wavell, the most careful driver in our group, had managed to hole his sump.

At least we didn't have to drain the oil or look for the plug. We found the plug and the surrounding bit of metal as soon as we dropped the pan. It had been knocked into the sump. The oil was down the road somewhere.

With great forethought Wavell had brought some aluminium solder along in his toolkit. We did manage to fix the plug in place but getting it oil-tight was ambition too far, even with thick and liberal quantities of soap as a sealant. Needless to say, the old gasket was now unserviceable.

We used all the available oil on the forecourt of the tiny Shamva Service Station, just proving that the repair wasn't oil-tight.

My little Anglia's sump was fine; it was the front spring that didn't like the boulder strewn dry riverbed, which suddenly appeared, twice, on the other side of a blind rise. The first time, when I bounced the car down over the rocks on our way to the site, the main leaf broke. I broke the leaf above it on the way back after buying oil; all down to a bad memory and the same boulder-strewn riverbed; the same mistake. "Shit!"

The spring could still support the car quite well, but it was a transverse arrangement and it was also used to locate the front wheels. This meant that the front axle could, and did, move from side to side.

It was the first and only time that a new friend and the fifth member of our party, Biff Bailey, came on a trip with us. He had travelled out in my vehicle and had already made it plain that he would never again travel with me as the driver. The friendship wasn't permanent.

"Not bloody likely," he had muttered. We didn't see much of him after that.

Biff travelled back with Wavell and Mike in the Morris. A bit paradoxical, as I had to tow the Morris the sixty or seventy miles back to Salisbury, with my car weaving from side to side on account of the broken spring.

It was remarkable how little directional control I had.

Mike and me in Jimmy's canoe.
Jimmy took the photo on Mike's camera.

Chapter 17

The *Ford Prefect* and the Drive-In Movies

Mike Jesson's *VW* needed tyres. By chance one of his work colleagues had just fitted new tyres to his *Ford Prefect* shortly before the second gear failed; bad news on a car with only three gears, but good news for Mike because his old *VW* used the same sixteen-inch tyres.

We agreed to club together to raise the twenty pounds asking price. Mike would swap tyres, we would fix the gears, sell the car and split the proceeds.

The gearbox only needed new bearings, everything else worked as well as could be expected from the down-market, outdated *Ford* mechanics. The upholstery was passable, my Mum made a new roof-lining from balloon-cloth and the rather tired paintwork got a quick re-spray with leftover black cellulose from a major repair on Wavell's *VW*.

Wavell had had a head-on with a truck on a narrow bridge. On the plus side, he discovered why the steering had been so strange. The bulkhead, to which the front suspension was bolted, had broken away from the floor-pan. The front wheel assembly was quite independent of the rest of the car, more or less just wedged in place. Sometimes tight, sometimes loose. Welding made a noticeable improvement.

I found out later that this failure was common enough on rough roads for the *VW* factory to put out a repair procedure. But that was some years after Wavell needed it.

The sudden opportunity to re-spray the *Ford Prefect* meant that masking was quickly done using grease instead of masking tape. This cleaned off quite easily from the glass and chrome but the raised plastic lettering of the number plate remained stubbornly black, all but unreadable.

***

Socially there were a series of parties. Rock-n-roll was the in thing and when we were bored there were always the drive-in movies. When we were all males in one car, we would pay for one; the others would slip around the back and climb over the fence. It was cheaper, and we saw the whole movie. When I took a girl I would pay for two and see little of the movie. You don't always get what you pay for.

It was a Sunday when we finished spraying the *Prefect* and it was also the first night at the massive new Mabelreign drive-in cinema; said to be the biggest in Africa. We had to go, never mind the black number plate.

We went that night and every following Sunday night for many months, just to see the first showing of the latest movie, only ever paying for one ticket. It became a habit.

Wavell did the driving as usual while the rest of us walked round the back where we found that a ten-foot fence encircled the whole property. Obviously the new company had less trust in the local inhabitants than the rival drive-in which was only part fenced by such high security.

The extra height meant a little extra effort from us, but we were soon inside to meet up with Wavell.

Half-way through the performance we noticed a couple of men were making a note of all the car number plates and their relative parking places. They seemed to be having difficulty with ours.

Presumably their purpose was to track any missing speakers. This drive-in's management did take security seriously, as Wavell was to find out at a later date.

The Mabelreign's ten-foot fence, with a barbed-wire return at the top, was only marginally more challenging than the little fence at the back of the Metro. One night at the Mabelreign we simply walked through a large gap in the fence, no doubt the work of some local hoodlums.

On another occasion there was only Wavell and Jimmy. I was visiting Jill Paterson. Mike and Eric were doing something else.

I had recently met Jill. Her family had come down from Kenya after Independence. She was pretty and I really did like her.

Jimmy decided that it was too much effort to go all the way round and over that ten-foot fence, so he climbed into the boot of Wavell's newly acquired *Ford Zephyr*.

It seems that they were about to join a couple of girls in the car parked alongside, when they were called to the manager's office.

"Let's see your tickets?" demanded the man.

Wavell dutifully reached into his pocket and pulled out a slack handful of tickets. Carefully selecting two of the right colour he handed them to the manager.

"These aren't current. They're not even the same month.

How many tickets did you buy?"

Wavell said nothing.

"One" said Jimmy.

"Why only one?"

"It's cheaper."

"Get out and stay out. Don't ever come here again!" fumed the official.

We did go back of course, and Wavell was still the driver, but initially we would use Mike or Jimmy's car. After a while we went back to using Wavell's *Zephyr*. Jimmy and I never got caught, but Wavell did.

One night Wavell and his brother Len decided to take two girls, possibly sisters Dawn and Linda Langley, to that drive-in. It was a while since he had been ejected, besides we had been back so many times we felt, or at least Wavell thought, the incident had been forgotten. Having three innocent passengers in the car, it was a bad time for Wavell to test the manager's memory, especially as he happened to be standing at the ticket office. Apparently he wasn't one to let bygones be bygones.

"I told you never to come back. Get out and stay out!" The angry fellow fumed.

Of course Len and the girls were mystified. Jimmy and I enjoyed Wavell's discomfort.

We never got caught at the other drive-in, the Metro. There, we usually stepped over the very low fence of the well-lit parking area provided for cars waiting for the first show to empty. Quite often we located our car in that area.

For some unknown reason on one particular night, Jimmy wouldn't climb the low fence but insisted on going further around along the back fence. It was still only a waist high barrier but backed up by an open foul-water ditch.

Jimmy led the way. It was Jimmy who discovered exactly where the foul-water ditch departed from the fence and led off into the adjacent field. He was also the first to realise that the ditch contained foul-water.

He never actually saw the ditch as it was obscured by long grass and it was dark. We could just make out his head and shoulders. He now also knew that the water was knee deep, and we could all tell it was foul. He smelled so bad we didn't let him into the car until it was time to leave.

Chapter 18

Cars, a Fire and a Fight

Your first car is always the one you remember best, not necessarily as the best. But your own opinion will probably be kinder than those of others. Certainly there was disagreement between Jimmy and me when it came to his *750 Renault* (the forerunner to the *Dauphine*). Jimmy thought it was a pocket-sized *Rolls Royce*.

I never argued with him, but would a *Roller* break down if it had been lent to a friend to take out a bird? Would the bonnet fly up as it approached a narrow bridge leaving you driving blind or would the engine catch fire under perfectly normal conditions? These were things I wouldn't expect from a *Roller*. On the other hand, I was absolutely certain that a *Rolls* and nearly every other car would stop when you stood on the brake pedal. Mind you, Jimmy did acknowledge that "The brakes aren't so good."

I remember that car very well.

It was a wildly gesticulating oncoming woman motorist who caused me to look round at the blazing engine compartment. As the remnants of petrol in the carburettor ran out, the car would have stopped anyway, but the fire would rage on; there would've been other material to fuel the blaze.

With his usual resourcefulness Jimmy didn't hesitate to whip off his overalls to use as a make-shift fire extinguisher.

A muttering Jimmy, standing in his underpants surveying a still smoking and charred engine bay, soon attracted a crowd. To give Jimmy credit, he did know exactly what had caused the fire, and he accepted it was his own fault. He explained what had happened to the onlookers.

"That bloody loose wire, I forgot about that and this crappy push-fit petrol pipe."

A loose live-wire with a bare end would swing about making sparks. He knew he should have sorted that out. He should also have fixed that lousy push-on connection on the outlet from the petrol pump which had a habit of coming loose even if it was "made-like-that" in the factory.

"Oh dear, oh dear. What are you going to do now?" smirked a giggling excuse-of-a-man.

A surly Jimmy turned slowly and looked the sniggering bright-spark up and down.

"Fix it. What the Hell do you think!" he snarled. It was about half an hour before we were mobile again. He drove home in his *Jockey Y-fronts* without bothering to replace his overalls.

Then there was that night when we wanted to leave a dance and that *Renault* refused to start. But that wasn't the fault of the car; that was down to some low-down jokers who crossed the plug leads.

Naughty… but soon-sorted; what we did to their *Ford Prefect* was much better, more imaginative, far less obvious, *and my idea*.

I took a tiny piece of paper and used a little dab of surplus grease to fix it between the points; something that would not be soon-sorted.

Eventually, once their car was going again, in the early-hours they found Jimmy's house and bombarded the metal roof with a hail of stones.

Now that the car-sabotaging pranks had escalated to a high nuisance level we had to respond in kind. So one night, about a week later, four of us went around to what we believed to be the ringleader's house in Greendale. Mike said it was the suspect's place. Mike's word was good enough for us.

A volley of missiles gave a good shake-up to the tiles.

Big Brian Walker charged out of the house followed by two cronies. We jumped into the *Renault* and were off with the three stalwarts in pursuit. We sped through the side roads into Coronation Avenue, across the tee-junction at Umtali Road and onto the forecourt of the *Total* garage, the one with the spectacular wavy roof.

Our pursuers were out of their car as soon as we were. Without a word we were at each other. Jimmy took on Brian. I went for the next out, Miles, but a short tubby fellow grabbed me from behind in a half-nelson and hung on for dear life.

Miles was about to land a heavy right fist on me. Fortunately for me, Mike was faster and put one on him, saving me the pain.

I fell backwards landing on a remarkably soft and comfortable Tubby. I lay there and proceeded to watch as if I was a spectator in a reclining armchair at the ringside.

Mike was busy with Miles in a very satisfactory fashion. Jimmy was sitting astride Brian, with his left hand in Brian's face and his right hand free to pound away. I was shouting, "Hit him, Jim!"

But Jimmy was screaming surrender, "I give up for Christ sake!"

Apparently Jimmy had been trying to push Brian's head back to get a good swipe at his throat. Unfortunately, Brian had his mouth open and Jimmy had been a bit careless with his fingers. Brian was now trying his best to gnaw his way through the bone of Jimmy's middle finger.

I was gutted. I felt that Jimmy could at least have got a couple of good clouts in before giving up; certainly before there was any real damage to his finger. Something Jimmy disputes to this day, claiming that his finger was close to amputation.

The fight over, we all called it quits and shook hands.

Our fourth companion, Wavell King, emerged from the shadows. Wavell's sense of fair play hadn't allowed him to join in; he felt that it would've been unfair, four against three, or maybe his sense of survival prevailed.

The African petrol attendants watched in bewildered amazement.

The next day Jimmy's finger was spherical, as big as a golf ball, a strange mixture of colours, mostly blue, white and red. It was like a massive, multi-coloured, translucent marble with a finger poking through it.

Having administered a cocktail of antibiotics, his doctor followed up with some after-care advice; "Next time, get bitten by a snake, it's easier to treat."

Let me give you some background to Wavell; he was the third of five children of George King, the Clerk and Chief Interpreter of the High Court; a man who could speak more than five African languages with absolute fluency.

Len was the oldest boy; of the two sisters I only met the younger one, Rosie. The other had moved to America, probably Texas. Sweet and pretty Rosie, was younger than Wavell, and liked by everyone.

Wavell, named after a relative, a British General of an earlier generation, Jimmy and I had been friends since the fourth year of junior school. Quiet and thoughtful Wavell was Mr. Dependable; we could call on him whenever we were in a jam for transport or whatever. When his brother's Oldsmobile 88 refused to take seven of us out to Lake McIlwaine, Wavell persuaded his dad's 1936 *Chevrolet* to start and we were off.

At the lake we enjoyed a super day out in his dad's speedboat, a vessel built by his dad from a set of American plans. His dad liked everything American, especially bourbon whiskey.

As an apprentice cable jointer, Wavell was sent to the UK to gain overseas experience.

He came back with shoulder-length hair, a new name, Ken, and a wife, Betty, who disliked Jimmy and me on sight. I found it very easy to feel the same way about her, but I did like her brother's music. His clarinet playing was superb. Well, she said her brother was Acker Bilk.

A few years later, Wavell was using a blowlamp in a cable trench which passed under a wall, when a labourer on the other side of the wall discarded a can-full of used cleaning benzine by throwing it into the trench.

I went to see Wavell in hospital, taking a pile of Playboy magazines. I had no idea whether or not he could even turn the pages, but I was hopeful, maybe there would be an obliging nurse available.

Chapter 19

Bad News Christmas

It was shortly before Christmas 1958 that I discovered Mum had cancer. I was at a girl's house to pick her up for a party. The mother introduced me to her husband as the son of the woman with cancer. His words were: "He lives opposite the Cockerill family, his mum is the one with cancer."

Neville and Annette (Neville's fiancée) had been told. One of them had told the neighbours, without a word to me. I don't know if the shock of the sudden disclosure showed on my face, but I realised that it was true. I couldn't speak and, fortunately, no-one followed up with concerned conversation.

My memory of that party is very vague, even that comely young dark-haired beauty's name is a blank; whatever her name, she went home with Wayne Blignaut. Good one Wayne. The news of my Mum's breast cancer had put me well out of sorts, not really up to charming a new female; no use to man or beast, certainly no match for that wench.

The doctors had said that, in view of Mum's history of major operations, they would never operate again, but come Christmas 1958 she was in hospital recuperating from a mastectomy. They hadn't considered cancer.

That Christmas, Wavell suggested that Jimmy Smith, Mike Jesson and I should visit his uncle, Buddy King, on his farm in the Eastern Highlands near Chipinga, about 250 miles away.

We decided that we would travel in two cars, the newly acquired *VWs* of Mike and Wavell. Both were the old 1950/51, split-back-window, crash-gear models; that's where the similarity ended. Mike's *Beetle* was very tidy with neat and clean bodywork. Wavell's car had seen better days, the paintwork was well worn and it had strange steering habits, but it was faster and a lot cheaper.

All those old *VWs* had very direct steering, Wavell's however, would be a bit lazy to respond; when it did it could get a little over-enthusiastic. There seemed to be no logical reason for this behaviour. Anyway, Wavell managed to cope and besides, I was travelling with Mike. Jimmy was travelling with Wavell. We reckoned that whatever the steering problem was, we would find out soon enough.

Of course we did; it was the broken bulkhead, (already mentioned in an earlier Chapter). Mike only had a provisional licence; I was the licensed supervisory driver. We were racing.

Wavell was leading us as we travelled on the strips about 60 miles out of Salisbury. An *Opel Estate* was immediately in front of us and seemed to be very reluctant to move over on to the left strip to allow us to pass. However, he had to move over for an oncoming car; as he stayed over for so long we assumed that he was aware of us and was waiting for us to pass.

Wrong! He was just nervous of the strips. As we drew level he plucked up enough courage to return to both strips, unaware of our presence. We had no option but to move onto the gravel, but as we were doing 65 mph we decided to pass him anyway.

There is a difference between my version of what happened next and Mike's story. But Mike did get a bang on the head.

After passing the *Opel*, as Mike tried to regain the strips, the back end started to drift. Mike did the right thing and steered into the slide. However, with the very light and direct steering of those early *Beetles* it was very easy to overcorrect. Mike did that too. So we were now sliding the other way.

That wasn't so bad. Well it wouldn't have been if the gravel hadn't built up into a ridge along the roadside. The sliding front wheels hit the gravel ridge, dug in, and over we went, onto the roof. As the car rolled over on my side, I simply rolled with it. Unfortunately for Mike, as we thumped down, just for an instant there was a gap between his head and the car's roof before gravity took effect; thus the lump on his head. It all happened in a fraction of a second. There was no time to swear. We crawled out through the windows. It was the first time I left a car that way. I switched the ignition off as I left.

In Mike's version he remembers rolling three times and ending in a maize (corn) field. I only remember one rollover, a grass field and Mike's head-lump. He agrees about the lump.

The *Opel* driver trembled his way over to us, "Oh my God! Anyone hurt? What are you going to do now?"

"No, we're OK." Mike patted the bottom of the *VW* affectionately, "She'll be alright. Germans make good cars. Give us a hand." We rolled the wreck back on to its wheels. Very sensibly Mike turned down my offer to drive. "I have to drive or I'll lose my nerve."

At the next police station, Rusapi, Jimmy and Wavell were waiting for us.

They burst into laughter when they saw the flat-topped *VW*. After filing the accident report we went on to Umtali.

At Umtali we branched off southwards towards Chipinga. The strip roads were always interesting; often like a roller coaster here amongst the foothills of the Chimanimani mountains they required total concentration.

A giant sign stated "DEADLY HAZARD."

Mike was driving, "What the hell does that mean? Shit!"

Suddenly we were aware of our speed; down a steep incline, left over a narrow bridge and immediately right up the other side. There was no time to think.

"Bloody hell!" I was amazed that we were still on the road. Mike was nonplussed. I think he was more surprised than me that we hadn't missed the bridge. It wasn't boring when Mike was driving. There were more "deadly hazards" but none as exciting as that first one. Mike became much more careful.

On the farm, life was very relaxed, at least for us. Buddy did take us out one night in search of impala (delicious meat, like top grade beef) but we found nothing. I don't think Buddy actually wanted us to do any shooting.

The following day Wavell suggested a visit to Ripisi Hot Springs about 40 miles away in the lowveld of the Sabi River valley. These springs were very remote and virtually unknown, which meant we were the only visitors, something I could appreciate.

The hot water was channelled into a clean, well-kept, tiled swimming-pool.

They were not the untidy Hot Springs Resort much closer to Umtali (now Mutare), in the area where, 30 or 40 years later, there would be a major diamond discovery. Nowadays this is, no doubt, a source of great personal income for Robert Mugabe, if not for the general population.

On the way the engine stopped. The lowveld heat had caused the petrol to vaporize in the *VW's* fuel line. The quick fix was to blow fuel through to fill the lines.

Those early *VWs* had a massive fuel-filler, opening directly into the tank. In order to blow effectively you had to use your entire lower face as a seal. This was fine, but having exhaled you now needed to take a deep breath. I discovered that it was a mistake to breathe in immediately over the filler. Especially true in the dry tropical heat of the Sabi Valley where petrol would vaporise so readily.

My knees folded and I sat down in the gravel to a round of laughter and ribbing. But it did work and I learned to breathe more carefully around petrol.

The following day we had an uneventful trip back to Salisbury. That evening, visiting Mum in hospital, I realised that Salisbury had been anything but uneventful. The hospital was full of casualties from an aircraft disaster at the ultra-safe Kentucky (Salisbury) airport.

On 26th December 1958, flight 736 of Union Aeromaritime de Transport had taken off into a heavy thunderstorm only to crash soon after becoming airborne. The Douglas DC-6B was on a flight to Paris via Brazzaville and Nice.

Three of the 63 passengers died, but many were injured. Mum said that some women, particularly the hostesses, had their nylon stockings melted into the skin of their legs.

***

The last time we went camping was shortly, just days, before my mother's death. Of course I knew that she was ill; her history of ill health and serious operations included an early form of heart by-pass. I must have been about nine at that time (circa 1950). I believe it was only the second such operation in the country and the first successful one. She spent nine months in hospital. Aunt Esther even contacted an undertaker. Aunt Esther enjoyed funerals. Mum never completely forgave her for that.

Within the four days of that last camping trip Mum had deteriorated from a seemingly viable person to near death. I returned home to find her heavily drugged with morphine to control the pain. The doctor said that she had between six and ten days to live. The district nurse came twice a day.

There seems to be a variety of cancers; in a few, a very few, there is almost no pain and death is mercifully quick. Regrettably most cause extreme pain and sometimes the pain is accompanied by a horrendous stench.

Vegetation, fish, and animals all have their own evil odour of disease and decomposition. Perhaps because of the association with my mother's death, the smell of cancer-rot is the worst of all for me.

There was little I could do but dribble water into her unconscious mouth and wait. She lasted the full ten days, dying on the 18th July 1959 at the age of 61. I used Neville's *VW* to fetch the district nurse.

All I can remember is the undertaker's black van; from then until after a headstone was installed I have no recollection connected closely to her death; nothing at all of the funeral.

We had been waiting for some time for a phone, having applied for one as a matter of urgency on medical grounds. Two weeks after the funeral the phone arrived. The fitter was sceptical, "Where's the patient then?"

"She's dead. You're too bloody late!" I was on the verge of violence.

I never want to be that close to cancer again. Death is always disturbing, but there can't be many scenarios worse than cancer.

Mum had never smoked, however the rumours of tobacco causing cancer wouldn't go away and it was common knowledge that a deadly insecticide could be made from boiled up cigarette butts. At the time I was enjoying smoking a pipe but common sense told me that whether those rumours were fact or not, smoking was a lose-lose way to spend money. For me it was time to be sensible. I have never smoked since.

Mum (circa 1946 aged 49)
Women's Auxiliary Air Force (RAF Rhodesia)
Family photo

Chapter 20

Jill and a Glimpse at the Future

We had got to know some girls who lived in a block of flats, Cumberland Court, in Baines Avenue, on the southwest Third Street corner, opposite Wavell's house.

One of the families, the Langleys, later moved out Northwood way. It was at one of their parties in Cumberland Court in early 1959, that I met another resident of the flats; sweet and pretty Jill Paterson. She was on a course at a local secretarial college. We started going out. When the BBC newsreader, Kate Silverton, first started broadcasting, she reminded me of Jill. At least, the teenage Jill I remember. I thought there was a remarkable likeness.

Jill was forbidden to ride pillion, so that restricted us to the nearby movies or theatre. However, she was once allowed to go for a short joyride.

Never mind a possible engine blow-up, I wanted Jill's little joyride to be the *Full Monty*, but not dangerously fast; so I took the revs up to near maximum in the low gears and in neutral, where the whole machine would achieve that spine-tingling harmonic peculiar to those 650 cc *Triumphs.* As the vibration reached resonance your lower body would glow with sensual pleasure; unforgettable.

She obviously enjoyed the experience, but I wouldn't even suggest a repeat against her mother's will. Besides, it was very unkind to the engine.

I needed a car, so I decided to fix the accident-damaged *Ford Prefect*, which I had bought with the intention of building a *Ford*-based Special, (a home-made sports car). Never mind building a Special, I needed transport and any kind of Ford was better than walking.

The first time I took Jill out in the car, I thought the door on her side had stuck. It took me a few minutes to realise that she was waiting for me to open it for her. By the next time she had figured out how to work the handle.

I don't know why, but I was always attracted to girls who were least likely to succumb to my efforts at seduction. Maybe it was the challenge; perhaps that's why I didn't mind much when that party-girl left with Wayne, in her case, maybe an alternative challenge was involved. Anyway it was a very pleasant, if innocent, episode with Jill, except for the ending; that was a body blow.

Jill never met my mum, although both her mother and Jill suggested a meeting, I had always postponed an introduction because Mum was so ill. One night, about a week before Mum's death, the goodnight kiss had resulted in a particularly passionate embrace. I left walking on air. The next day she phoned me at work and dumped me. Shit.

I don't think it was entirely Jill's doing, I feel sure she was heavily influenced by her mother. I can't blame the old girl, after all, what could I offer her daughter? All I had was obstinate aggression and an overdose of testosterone. But her timing was devastating; compassion was not her strong point.

The old woman had kept asking me what ambitions I had. Hell, it took me everything I had to keep a roof over my head and food in my belly. She seemed to think my only ambition in focus right then was to get into her daughter's knickers; apparently she thought her daughter would succumb to my advances.

It never occurred to me that she probably knew her daughter better than I did. That was another teenage error of mine. Another miss; I lost the plot. I wish I had realised it at the time, at least I could have tried. *Damn!*

My naivety was highlighted on another occasion with Jill. After excusing herself, she came back and cuddled up to me on the couch with her bare feet tucked up under her derriere. Although her skirt's waistband was fastened, the zip on the side was gaping wide, exposing bright red panties. What I did next has to be one of the most stupid things of my life.

What I should have done was take the gap. I should have slipped my hand through the opening for a little exploration. What I did do was completely impetuous, out-of-character and downright dumb, and I do owe her an apology.

I gave her a playful slap on the backside. Well I thought it was playful, but she seemed to think it was a bit too hearty. Come to think of it I have got quite big and heavy hands. That probably scuppered my chances completely.

On the other hand, if as it is said, which I doubt, you can predict the mature woman by the mother then, perhaps, I had a lucky escape.

Although I was always prepared (I kept a condom in my pocket, just in case, or perhaps hope), I accepted the propaganda of the day, that decent, well brought up girls were virgins until they got a ring on their finger. Jill was certainly decent and a ring was a long way off, so I put all ambition of seduction out of my mind.

***

For me it was a bad time; Jimmy and Wavell were on national service, Mike was married or nearly so. I didn't drink much, which was fortunate I suppose, considering how stupid I was riding a motorbike even when sober. I used to think that I survived by skill, now I'm convinced that I was incredibly lucky.

Had it been a year later and I had been in a pub at the same time that Tshombe's agents were recruiting for his mercenary army in the Congo, I probably would have joined; most of the time I was in a reckless state of mind. Fortunately it was only 1959 and I seldom went to a pub, neither was I aware of the fomenting politics of Africa.

In 1960, when Simon, a Malawian working in the GPO, told me that there was going to be "Much trouble in the Congo on the 1st July" I brushed it aside. What did a Malawian labourer know? How wrong I was. The planned civilised celebrations at the handover of political power from the Belgium Colonials to the African politicians cascaded into a terrifying orgy of rape and murder. Like all Mother Country Colonial Offices, Belgium's was out of touch with reality.

More fortunately, by the time M'butu was doing his recruiting a few years later, I had got over any nutcase ideas of mercenary glory. Fortunate because M'butu delayed paying his mercenaries until he no longer needed them; he then set his very large national army on to them.

Chased by the army, the mercenaries left in a hurry. Air Force contacts told me that one group, in a well shot up *Dakota DC3,* landed at Salisbury (Harare) Airport (not Kariba as reported in the press), having been flown out at tree-top level by one of their number. It was said that he was not a qualified pilot. Those sources said the plane was grounded at Salisbury airport.

Another group took refuge in Rwanda, where they remained until rescued by the Red Cross.

Others fought their way out. Some years later I met one of them, Wasserman. He had been sent to the Congo from Rhodesia as a heavy plant mechanic to carry out some urgent repairs. He had no intention of joining the mercenaries.

However, when he found himself trapped in a very nasty situation, he went to a mercenary group and asked them to get him out. The answer was; "Yes, but you have to join us and be prepared to fight."

He was given a machine-gun. He said they shot anyone in their way. He spoke of shooting children who attacked the mercenaries with AK 47s. "They were crazy. They would just keep coming, firing everywhere. I had to shoot."

High on drugs and told that their enemy's bullets would turn to water, these kids would charge, firing blindly, oblivious to the machine-gun fire. In retrospect I'm very glad I missed that scene.

Anyway, after Jill dumped me I reverted to the Ford Special plan.

***

The second GPO engineering course started shortly after my mother's death. I did manage to get to college on time each day, but there was no way I could stay in at night and do the studying the course required. I had to get out.

To say that my employers were disappointed with my results would be an understatement.

Having missed the chop by a hair's breadth and the intervention of one lecturer, I was rescheduled for the Mechanician Department.

The intervening lecturer, Mr. Ray Beaumont, wasn't being overly kind; he simply excelled in his profession. Unlike one of his colleague, "Podge" Lees, who was particularly good at gobbledygook, I could understand Ray's lectures without having to spend hours decoding Podge's confusion. I did well in Ray's subjects.

Meanwhile the politics of Africa were on the turn. Africa is simply too inherently well-endowed with mineral wealth to be ignored. Yet another scramble for Africa was about to begin, not with gunboat colonisation, but with cunning political chicanery and seductive talk of "freedom".

The foreign powers, notably the Soviet Union and China, generated the propaganda and supplied the weapons; the "Freedom Fighters" gave their lives. The existing colonial powers gave in to bleeding-heart ignorance and political and economic convenience. The new colonisers might be using a different strategy and it may not be complete in my lifetime, but I believe it will happen. Will the indigenous Africans benefit? Time will tell.

***

"What's he trying to say?" I asked a nearby older man after hearing Macmillan's "Winds of Change" speech in 1960. At nineteen I wasn't able to decipher political jargon, but it made me feel uneasy.

"The whites in Africa are dispensable. We're stuffed!" someone replied to my question.

"Doesn't he know that without whites, there's no hope for Africa?" a second chipped in.

"He doesn't agree with that. Statements like that would destroy his political career, even if he did agree," replied the first. "According to his Foreign Office, the black African is just like an Englishman but with a black skin, and very honest."

"Like Hell!" the second speaker nearly choked. "Doesn't he know that it's having the whites as a common enemy is what unites the tribes? Without us the tribes will be murdering each other. Heaven forbid they get modern weapons; *poor bastards!*"

Although I hoped this bloke was wrong, I don't think anyone could've guessed just how bad life would become for the poor of Africa under African rule.

When I left in 1978 I was convinced that Rhodesia's economy would flounder, but even I never thought that anyone could bring it down to the state of today's (2015) Zimbabwe.

Britain was insisting on dismantling the Federation of Rhodesia and Nyasaland. That union was the highly successful political and financial coupling of the three countries, Zimbabwe (Southern Rhodesia), Zambia (Northern Rhodesia) and Malawi (Nyasaland).

The white Federal Government had plans to enfranchise more Africans. Some already had limited voting rights and African tribal leaders did have a voice in parliament, but a whole generation were effectively city dwellers out of touch with traditional values. The break-up was counter- productive, the first step to UDI, the "Bush War" and the present poverty-stricken Zimbabwe. Today the beneficiaries seem to be the ruling political clique, and China.

In 1960 that particular "wind of change" was still to arrive. I should have seen it coming.

Chapter 21

Teenage Transport

Roundabout Jameson Avenue / Kingsway 1960
My photo from the roof of Livingstone House

The problem with a car from the bottom of the second-hand market is largely a lack of status. Never mind status, my objection was based on lack of performance. The affordable fix was simple, change to two wheels. For me a good choice was the predecessor to the *Triumph Bonneville*, a 650 *Triumph Tiger 110*.

The 110 designation was intended to give the impression that the machine would reach 110 mph. Perhaps it would under favourable conditions at sea level, but there was no chance at Salisbury's 5000ft. However, it was quick for its day.

I had learned to ride on my brother's 500 *Triumph* (the *Tiger 100*). Also a quick machine, but it was one of those trick models equipped with the horror of a sprung-hub on the rear wheel.

It was a device which could behave impeccably, most of the time, but would choose a random corner to deposit you on the tarmac.

The problem was simple to explain. When the wheel absorbed a bump, the rim would move off-centre with respect to the axle; this caused the wheel to be out of balance resulting in unpredictable and violent forces; obviously bad engineering.

Strangely, the German high-speed trains were fitted with wheels using a similar crazy principle where the steel tyre (rim) would bounce on rubber between the wheel and rim; it was thus possible to be off-centre and out-of-balance. Apparently it was a money-saving replacement for the Japanese suspension design.

In 1998 a wheel of this design failed; it was blamed for the Eschede train disaster, one of the worst rail accidents in Europe. The death-toll was one hundred and one.

Once I thought I would impress Eric Windell when he asked of Neville's machine "Does that thing go?"

"Of course, I'll show you."

We whizzed around the block. We were only wearing shorts and shirts…no shoes. I was deliberately scraping the tarmac at every corner when the hub decided to misbehave. Sitting on our bums on the tarmac was funny until Eric stood up and immediately collapsed in pain. The cause was a big toe which had had the end rubbed off against the tarmac. Eric stopped laughing. "You fucking stupid bastard!"

He must have meant me. I couldn't stop laughing.

Neville sold the sprung hub *Triumph* to an African. Foolishly he allowed the buyer to take the machine after only paying a deposit. Of course that was the last we saw of any cash or the African, but the bike turned up in the Vehicle Inspection Yard, having been taken off the road. Neville reclaimed it and sold it on to Jimmy, who now had to bring it back to roadworthiness. That wasn't so difficult. Although the silencers looked the part, they were more like megaphones, the baffles having been long since removed, so he borrowed my silencers for the test.

The biggest problem was to get some sort of performance out of the machine. Apparently the African had ridden everywhere in first gear without ever changing or even adding oil.

Maintenance work doesn't feature in African culture.

When Jimmy first reassembled the machine, having done a real classy re-spray job and an engine overhaul, the engine was too tight to kick-start. No problem, I could tow it with his *Renault.* Forty or fifty feet of rope would give him stopping distance. As it turned out it wasn't the bike that needed the stopping distance.

Once the engine started he roared up alongside me full of smiles and ecstatically happy; clad only in shorts, with a great loop of rope trailing behind the vehicles.

"Want a race?" he joked before he dropped back… into that loop of rope.

The next thing I felt a slight tug on the rope. Looking in the mirror I caught sight of a half-naked Jimmy in a reasonably elegant swallow-dive towards the tarmac.

I slammed my foot on the brake pedal and the "*Rolls Royce*" *Renault* came to a reluctant but dignified stop. The *Triumph* didn't; it slid and scraped its way across the tarmac to a halt just behind the Renault.

The next thing, angry with blood running down his face, Jimmy was at the car door.

"Why the fuck didn't you stop sooner. Look at the fucking bike; it's stuffed; all that fucking work buggered-up."

He was right, of course, the paint job was no longer classy and the tank was heavily dented. Nothing that I said could convince him that I had stopped as soon as I could.

Anyway, he got over it and he got the bike looking good again, but we never got the performance back to half of what it used to be. I think the camshafts must have been badly worn due to lack of oil.

My 650 had the industry-norm swinging arm rear suspension, so was much better behaved than a sprung hub. I could make the six miles from Rhodesville to the Post Office Engineering College, through the morning traffic, in six minutes. Of course the traffic at the only roundabout took skill, judgement and daring to negotiate, and the four sets of traffic lights needed to be more-or-less green. I also needed at least two feet between the lines of slow or stationary cars. The crash-bars were two feet wide.

Crash-bars were a legal requirement, but not helmets. Apparently, in Rhodesia, the legs of motorcyclists were more valuable than their brains. On one occasion, the gap in the lines of vehicles just starting on green at the Second Street lights, narrowed a bit between two cars. It looked a little tight. From the pillion Bob Macadam yelled, "You won't make it."

"We have to," was the only possible reply. We were travelling too fast to slow down. I heard the clunk! Bob heard two.

I slowed down to allow the previously immaculate, shiny red, late 1940s model *MG TF* to catch up.

The driver enquired, "Any damage?"

"Can't see any," I lied, looking directly at the ugly gouge in the glossy red beauty, and sped away. At college Bob pointed out that the red paint on the left of the crash-bar had an equal patch of white on the right side. The *Ford* on the right had been white. The gap had obviously not been quite wide enough. I must have passed though the exact centre: lucky!

During the lunch hour we would usually ride into town to walk up and down First Street; just checking out the female talent. On one occasion, Bob introduced me to two girls whom he knew from his family's stay as immigrants in Cranborne Hostel.

The Hostel was the old RAF barracks which were then being used as transient accommodation for immigrants when Britain's new post-war Labour Government was busy exporting their population surplus to ease the pressure on its war-torn housing stock.

One of the girls, a petite, talkative, slip of a girl, offered me chips from the pack of French-fries she was eating. I was glad to accept; I was always hungry. But I thought no more about it; I had no idea how tenacious, tough, capable and loyal that little seven-and-a-bit-stone teenager was. In time, I'm glad to say, I did find out.

Chapter 22

The Silver Lining and its Cloud

Come December 1959, my brother, Neville was preparing to marry. His fiancée, Annette, had arranged for us to accommodate the bridesmaids, her sisters Denise and Brenda, as well as their mother. Having the bridesmaids in the house was a most satisfactory arrangement. A silver lining you might say. The mother... well every silver lining has its cloud.

Jimmy and I took the girls out to the Shavanhohwe picnic spot and just had to take them to the top of that rock mountain. At 1100ft above the surrounding countryside it really was a mountain of granite in a range of barren grey rock foothills.

It was a day or two before the wedding. The girls (city-dwellers from Johannesburg) were wearing silly downtown shoes which weren't coping with the rough granite. Initially they declined the offers to wear our shoes so they simply went barefoot. They thought they would look like clowns in our big shoes.

I wondered just who they thought might see them, 40 miles out of sight of town.

By the time they accepted it was too late, which explains why they had that funny wedding walk. As they walked down the aisle you would think they were barefoot and the aisle was scattered with hot coals rather than confetti. A shame really, because the bridesmaids' outfits were absolutely stunning; to be appreciated, they needed to be worn with poise and elegance. Both were totally lacking that day. They did look silly. And they had an audience.

That Christmas was, for me, a very enjoyable festive season. Of course it could have been even better; I missed a beat or more here and there; I was still too inexperienced with women. The presence of the mother was a bit challenging, but so were two couples necking in Jimmy's tiny *Renault* 750.

After the wedding we took them firstly to the drive-in movies, where we opened the doors to give us a bit more space relying on the movie to distract any spectators. When the movie ended we found a quiet spot behind the old Coronation Park Dirt Track, (a motor-cycle and car racetrack, where Ray Amm started his racing career).

I knew the whole area well; it had been my favourite childhood playground. Later it would become The Makabusi Woodland Nature Reserve, (the modern spelling Makavusi).

Fearing their mother's reaction, the girls insisted on returning to the house. We made it by 3 am. Their worry was unnecessary; the old woman only got in at four; two hours before dawn, and she was well drunk. This was the woman who had sneered when she saw the crates of empties left over from Neville's bachelor party.

Alcohol exposed the real woman and I was about to get a better understanding of her daughters' anxieties. The house erupted in a fusillade of verbal abuse, but not at the girls; it was aimed at my brother Neville.

Of course he was away on honeymoon; I was in the firing line. I took the onslaught of pent-up hatred full-on.

She was overflowing with whatever made her angry and unhappy. She had only known me for a few days and I was taking the blame for every male misfit who had ever crossed her path or warmed her bed.

That drunken old witch kept going until well after daybreak. They say you have to earn respect. She was an expert in discarding it. I let her rant, determined not to spoil her misery.

No-one in my house got any sleep that night. My respect for her evaporated completely.

The next day we took the girls to Mermaid's Pool, found a quiet shady spot, spread out a blanket and went to sleep.

***

My final GPO course was on teleprinters (teletype machines to the Microsoft generation), a satisfactory outcome for me as it didn't require late nights of heavy study to interfere with my social life. This course was after Neville's wedding and I was now going out with Annette's sister Denise. Jimmy was similarly involved with the third sister, Brenda.

With all good things there's always a problem, and sometimes, as in this case, two; but never mind the mother; Johannesburg was 750 miles south. That was the major drawback.

At Easter, Neville and Annette decided that they should visit Annette's mother and sisters. Jimmy and I were pleased to have the opportunity to see the sisters again. Neville's driving was worse than mine and his newly acquired beetle-back *Volvo P544* wasn't nearly as smooth on the strips as his old *VW*.

As the car ducked, dived, pitched and bounced over those two lines of uneven tarmac, dipping culverts and narrow bridges, Jimmy and I spent much of the time in mid-air between the back-seat squab and the roof lining. The 750 miles took us eleven hours and twenty minutes, an average speed, including stops, of 66 mph; *on those roads, stupid?* definitely, but still a very good time.

We stayed with Annette's mum in the Johannesburg suburb of Hillbrow near the General Hospital where Denise worked as a nurse. Now in 2015, Hillbrow is a no-go area for strangers of any colour at any time of day or night. Then, in 1960, we walked about as freely as I would on any UK street today.

We spent a day at the Rand Easter Show, which probably would have been very impressive had the crowds been thinner, as it was, my entire show experience was like being in an enormous and totally overcrowded tube train; whatever was on show, I had no chance of seeing it. The following day we all went to a swimming pool-come-resort, which was enjoyable enough.

On our last day Denise took me to a large and well-kept public garden of indigenous plants, The Wilds. With a multitude of secluded nooks and crannies and very few visitors, the outing was more than enjoyable.

Unfortunately for Jimmy, Brenda was still at school, a Convent (of The Sacred Heart or something) and a boarder, so she had to go back early. I thought Jimmy would be a bit negative if not totally fed up.

He was surprisingly cheerful. I knew him. He was planning something.

That evening Neville dropped Denise and me off at the Brian Brooke Theatre to see a live performance of Irma la Douce as recommended by Denise. While I enjoyed the show, I only really appreciated it the second time around, back in Salisbury, when I went with Anne Torrey.

On the way we dropped Jimmy off in Jeppe. Once an up-market area it had largely degenerated into a slum, but it was still the location of Brenda's Convent. Jimmy asked to be let out just in front of a pair of massive wooden double-doors set in a high perimeter wall. Now I knew why he was so cheerful. Somehow he got over the wall, and once in the grounds the dormitory was no problem. Brenda let him in.

The tension must have been terrific, especially as Brenda wasn't the only girl awake and the nuns could sense something, so came to investigate, which meant Jimmy had to slip out via a window while the nuns prowled about. Of course he had to climb back in; he hadn't said goodnight to Brenda. He arrived back at the Hillbrow flat long after we were all in bed.

As most men discover, love or whatever it is with women, has a numbing effect on the brain. We were no exception; we decided to nip down to Johannesburg on my *Triumph* one weekend to see the girls.

The teleprinter course lecturer, Mr. Paul, and his assistant, Mr. Kennedy, were World War 2 veterans and had an excellent sense of values. When they heard my plan they laughed, wished me well, and let me off at Friday lunchtime.

John Leibenberg asked, "Have you got gloves?"

"No," I replied.

"Here, take mine," as he handed me his leather gauntlets.

"Thanks John."

I picked up Jimmy from his place of work and we were on our way. Jimmy had arranged for someone else to clock him out.

Just 80 miles into the journey a rattle developed in the primary chain-case. We removed the cover, a big mistake. The chain was only loose, easily fixed. But the damaged gasket was now useless, so it meant that the chain was without its oil-bath; not good.

We arrived at the Beit Bridge border crossing after dark and settled down on the veranda floor of the customs post, blocking the front door. We would be first when it opened.

Over the bridge on the south side of the Limpopo River we rode through the mountain pass known as Wylie's Poort. The boredom of a tunnel was still to come.

It was a beautiful and invigorating early morning ride. So sensually pleasant it made you wonder why anyone would want to zip through the anaesthesia of a tunnel. Now in South Africa, there were no more strip roads until we returned.

After mid-day we got to the seventh floor of the Hillbrow flat to be informed by the mother that she would not accommodate us. "You can't stay here."

I thought her attitude was rather uncivilised, considering that she had spent two weeks over Christmas in my house and her daughters had been out with us every night and on all our free days. Jimmy was totally unfazed, "OK, we'll sleep in the park. We've come to see the girls."

The Teleprinter Course
Mr. Kennedy, Me, Ian Logan, Bill Young, Des Preston, Dieter Reitz, Mr. Paul,
Bob Macadam, Ian Jackson, John Leibenberg, Alan Linnington, ? Harkness.
Photo Tony Dennis

.We went for a very dozy walk in a nearby park in the evening. In the park we each found a couple of secluded benches about 30 yards apart. Regrettably the 750-mile motorcycle ride had drained me of all my lecherous intentions. Rather than a pleasure, there was a numbness of the flesh.

The benches were backed against a terrace of several feet. Looking down from the bank was a silent group of spectators engrossed in Jimmy's lack of activity. I burst out laughing; I knew Jimmy was as knackered as I was. The spectators could've watched all night.

"Hey, Jimmy look behind you!" I yelled. The voyeurs dispersed.

It was an excuse to go back to the flat where the old-girl had by now remembered her manners and relented. I was so glad to get my head down.

***

Off at six in the morning we had covered 60 miles with 690 still to go, when the engine died. There was no spark; you could kick on the kick-start forever, the magneto points would stay stubbornly motionless.

I had stripped that engine so many times that I mistakenly thought that I'd had sight, sound and feel of every last piece. However, the four little roller-like bits that dropped into my hand as I took the timing cover off, were a total mystery. Jimmy and I gazed at the four little bits.

"Shit! What the hell are those?" Jimmy was as puzzled as I was by those little bits.

We soon found out. As soon as the timing gear was fully visible we could see immediately just where those things came from. Indeed we knew then exactly what they did.

They were the rivets which fixed the steel centre-boss to the fibre timing gear on the magneto. No wonder the magneto was stationary. "Damn. Bugger-it!"

There wasn't a spares supplier for nearly 700 miles on our return route.

The one stroke of luck we had was to break down at a lay-by, which featured a very convenient concrete workbench. Actually it was meant to be a picnic table.

It took about an hour to re-rivet the gear and get going again. We had had the sense to take a good selection of tools with us. Even as nineteen-year-olds, we weren't naïve enough to try a 1500 mile weekend trip without tools.

A bit of roadside straw, inserted through the spark plug-hole, came in handy to set the timing at my guess of three-eighths of an inch before-top-dead-centre.

The engine had never run better, the timing was spot on, but now the primary chain was showing the folly of no oil. It had stretched and was beginning to ride over the clutch sprocket. So we adjusted it. Fine… for a while, until the next time, and the next, and so on. However, as the road was mostly downhill to the border at Beit Bridge, a fall of some 5000 feet in less than 400 miles, we could coast a lot of the time.

The afternoon sun in the Limpopo River valley was unpleasantly hot. It raised a blister on my forehead the size of a large egg yolk. We were clear of the border by about 5.30 pm and it was beginning to get dark. Half-way home progress was slow. At the Lundi River petrol station we bought biscuits and Cokes as we had at every petrol station still open. It helped to keep us awake. After Lundi they were all closed. About another 200 miles and we would be home.

We took turns at being rider or passenger, waking each other as we dozed off. One passenger footrest broke off. We retrieved it to be welded back later. Luckily I had been using a four-inch long bolt with two nuts on it as the tommy-bar in the spanner. The bits worked well as a makeshift footrest.

Of course the chain problem was our main concern. It was getting steadily longer, and apart from the fact that the scope for adjustment was limited, there was always the possibility that it would break.

At Featherstone, with 80 miles or so still to go, the chain would grip no more; it was at its maximum adjustment. We dumped the bike in the roadside ditch and fell asleep, cuddling the engine for warmth.

It was freezing when we woke in the early hours. The bike had cooled down and the chain now had some grip, providing I kept the revs down.

Twenty-six hours after we left Johannesburg, I nursed that machine into the very busy 8 o'clock traffic of Salisbury; along Charter Road and through the "Cow's Guts," so called because the earliest settlers had given no thought to planning. The result was a contorted tangle of roads.

Fortunately, this was soon put right for the rest of the settlement and for the next 80 years by the work of an American planning expert employed by Rhodes.

After dropping Jimmy off at his house I had a lovely warm bath. I had to go in to college just to prove a point, so I started to hitch. I got a ride from young Fred Maughan who was passing in a 5 ton GPO Bedford. I met old Fred Maughan, his dad, later when I worked for Lion Match. He was the bricklayer who told me of his experiences working on the strip roads in the depression of the 1930s.

At college a practical demonstration was in progress. I woke up alone in the lunch hour. Everyone was amazed that anyone could sleep on the hard and unstable stools in the demo room. I was glad that no one had woken me, as I said, Messrs. Paul and Kennedy had a good grasp of common sense.

However, that weekend trip did nothing to cure my love-smitten brain, so come the first weekend in July (mid-winter) it was the Rhodes and Founders four-day holiday, I did it all again. This time on my own, Jimmy had got over Brenda. I took my time. I left after work on Friday, Monday and Tuesday being the holidays.

The troublesome *Triumph* electrics were playing up. They only affected the lighting; the ignition was on an excellent, separate magneto arrangement. The root of the problem lay in a design flaw, which made it almost impossible to keep oil from seeping into the generator. The problem was aggravated by my reluctance to buy a new battery; so I travelled hundreds of miles by moonlight, mostly on those strip roads. In spite of the cold it was very pleasant, a bright moonlight memory for future nostalgia.

I never met any other traffic from Fort Victoria to Beit Bridge, a distance of about 190 miles. In all the other times I have made that trip before and since, I only ever saw one kudu bull and years later a great many scorpions. The scorpions were in daylight and they went on for miles. All were travelling in a single-direction on a mass exodus. I'm glad to say I was in a car at the time.

This trip was the exception, as I rode through the Nuanetsi area, I passed two herds of impala. All were jumping high in the air while they were on the move. I stopped just to watch them in the moonlight. It made me feel strangely peaceful. Had my lights been working I probably would have missed them.

***

I made Beit Bridge well after dark, taking time to warm my frozen hands by holding them under the cold tap of the rest room and following up with a drink of the tap water. All tap water in Rhodesia was drinkable. Then I settled down under a tree next to a little fire to sleep, apparently alone.

It was after midnight when I woke to find a *Peugeot 404* had stopped just short of running me over. Looking around, the place seemed to be swamped with left-hand drive *Peugeots* and *Mercedes* with strange number plates. It was 1960 and unknown to me these were refugees fleeing the orgy of pillage, rape and murder directed against the whites which erupted when the Belgians relinquished control of their bit of the Congo. Only afterwards I remembered Malawian Simon's prediction of trouble in the Congo.

I thought violence was a strange reaction, because the Belgians had discouraged white settlement and been very positive in developing a black middle-class of traders, clerks and artisans.

This skilled and educated base should have been able to administer and run the country. Apparently not, it would seem that the atrocities of Belgium's Hitler equivalent, King Leopold, a hundred years before, was a still-festering sore. Now, 54 years after Independence, I wonder what excuse they have for the current savagery.

Fortunately, today's Europeans haven't embarked on a campaign of violence against the modern German nation in retribution for the misdeeds of Hitler.

There can be no question that the potential for a very affluent African nation was present. Both agricultural and mineral resources were abundant, so why did the Congolese embark on war between each other? I can only conclude that warfare and plunder are more appealing to the national character than hard work and industry. To the best of my knowledge, bloodshed has been the norm in the Congo since 1st July 1960.

Legend has it that the forest dwelling Pygmy tribes are petrified of the other Congolese, believing that the dominant tribes regard them as a desirable addition to that tribe's diet; *bush meat*. On the other hand the Shona of Rhodesia, who were said to originate from the Congo Basin, were appalled by the thought of cannibalism. "Would you eat your brother?" was the reply when I suggested to a Shona headman that a baboon could be eaten. Generally small in stature, perhaps they were also prey in the Congo.

***

Over the border, the early morning ride through Wylie's Poort was as pleasant as ever. I stopped the bike, gazed over the valley and revelled in the clean, cool, crisp air. Back on the flat scrubland of the Transvaal lowveld I found a farm advertising breakfast. Two big eggs, a generous helping of bacon and a couple of sausages did me a world of good.

Stopped at the only traffic light in Pietersburg, a policeman pulled up next to me.

"We slows down here when we comes by a town!" A thick guttural voice informed me.

I didn't think I had been speeding but instinct told me that it would be futile to argue.

"Ja meneer," seemed to be the sensible reply. It worked.

The roads in 1960s Johannesburg were narrow and congested with speeding traffic. I went skidding across an intersection on red, through a deafening blast of hooting cars. I had forgotten that my front brake had broken 650 miles before and the back brake wasn't man enough on those steep Johannesburg down-hills. I fixed it as soon as the shops opened on the Monday morning.

Once again Mrs Cassell, Denise's mother, was reluctant to remember her manners, but she did come round, and my weekend turned out well.

I took it easy on the way back, a nice relaxing ride suited my mood. It was just before sunset when I got through the border. Why not push it a bit and do the 300 miles to Salisbury? I wasn't feeling tired.

I had two panniers, one a steel box I had made, which was bolted to the bike. It contained my tools. The other, a commercial one, made of fabric, hung on a purpose-made frame.

It contained my entire wardrobe apart from what I was wearing. Unfortunately it was inclined to work itself off the frame, so I kept feeling for it from time-to-time.

About eighty miles from Beit Bridge the pannier was missing. My lights were working again so I made my way slowly back to the border, looking for the lost pannier, but my lights weren't man enough; no luck. At Beit Bridge I asked around, perhaps someone had found it and handed it in; again no luck. Not surprising; I hadn't even seen any other traffic.

'Hell! A warm bath and bed would be Heaven.' I worked out the very minimum I would need for petrol to get home.

At Peter's Motel I could afford a room with a bath, but not breakfast. I dropped my grubby dust-sodden clothes off onto the bathroom floor. What a great feeling of warmth and luxury, the warm water was like the hands of an expert masseur. I fell into bed, my naked body enclosed in an envelope of clean-sheet-pleasure.

Early next morning, sans breakfast, I reluctantly climbed back into dusty grubbiness and left on an easy ride home. With more than 300 miles to go and on a very tight budget I had to conserve petrol. Of course I was on the lookout for my lost pannier but hope was fading.

Eventually, when I thought I was past my u-turn of the night before, something ahead was shining brightly in the sun. My pannier was fabric and wouldn't shine like that. Wrong; the shine came from its sheet steel back.

Now that I had my entire wardrobe back I felt almost affluent. I had clean clothes for the morning.

Chapter 23

Speeding, *Irma La Douce* and Anne

L to R: Anne Torrey, Backstage Crew, Me
Salisbury Reps Publicity Photos 1959

It wasn't my fault I got caught speeding, at least it shouldn't have been. I should have seen that cop. In the past, when they used a measured distance and stop watches, I had managed to stop in the middle, just to blow my nose. This time it was a single job's-worth of a cop on a motorbike and I had no idea that he was behind me, he must have turned in from a side road.

I had gone home for some reason during the lunch-hour and was returning along Nigel Phillip Avenue when I decided to indulge in a turn of speed; after 250 miles of painfully running-in the recently overhauled engine, it would be a pleasure to feel a bit of speed.

The road and schools were deserted. School times were 8 am to 1 pm. The afternoons were used for sport. I suppose the rationale was that the kids were hard enough to teach in the morning, it would be impossible in the hot afternoons.

I took the bike up to near maximum and down again to a legal and sensible running-in speed, besides the road wasn't long enough for an extended run.

The rush of air was pleasantly cool regardless of the white sheepskin jacket I wore.

I was enjoying a feeling of quiescent goodwill from the indulgence when a clattering police *BSA Gold Flash* sped past and came to a screeching halt in front of me.

I hadn't realised that there was a policeman playing catch-up. He was visibly shaking.

"I'm going to bump you. I was doing eighty-five and you were pulling away from me," he blurted out immediately.

I couldn't argue about the speed as my speedometer was faulty, only indicating the mileage, and I had indeed been going fast. I said nothing; just hoping that he wouldn't check my tax disc. It was three months out-of-date. Fortunately he was totally overwhelmed by my speeding; he seemed too shaken to check anything else.

It took a long time for the case to come to court, probably because the evidence against me was weak and thus needed, and obviously got, considerable creative work to make it suitable for a prosecution.

By the time I got the summons the second 1500-mile round trip to see Denise in Johannesburg was just a memory and my enthusiasm for long distance love had run its course. The most loving letter is no substitute for physical contact. In the mean time I was trying to save up to pay the inevitable speeding fine.

During the wait for the court case I bumped into Anne Torrey. I had gone to a workshop on the old Belvedere airport site where we had both been working on some backstage sets. I can't remember what took me there that day, but Anne was the only other person there and the place was locked.

I've wondered since how we both made the same mistake of believing that that Sunday was a work day when it obviously wasn't. However, I'm glad we did. Anne was an absolute honey, just a bit over five feet; a petite and pretty little pack of dynamite. I was well smitten by her.

She had a *Vespa* or *Lambretta*, you know, one of those scooter things. The only dealings I had with a scooter involved a *Corgi*, a nasty little fold-up wartime leftover, apparently the paratroopers used them; but anyway horrible.

That Sunday I was thrilled to see her again.

"Where's everyone?" she wanted to know.

I shrugged, "Dunno, it's all locked up. There's nothing we can do here, jump on, I'll show you where I got done for speeding."

It was always quiet on Sundays. We sped through the empty streets to the other side of town. The site was Nigel Phillip Avenue, past Roosevelt Girls High School and across the road, my old school, the male equivalent, Churchill School. I was going to impress. I opened the throttle wide.

Those two storm water dips in the road were always fun. Hit them fast enough and the bike would take off. It did and I did. I was off the saddle. Only my hands were in contact with the bike.

Anne slid up my back, her thighs were right under my armpits.

Having a warm female piggy-back behind me, off the saddle, several feet above the tarmac at 80 mph, was an especially exhilarating feeling of sensual pleasure mixed with sheer undiluted terror. We must have passed over the second dip. Somehow we landed intact.

"That was brilliant!" She yelled in my ear.

"Yes, wasn't it!" I yelled in reply, deciding that we would go back a different way. We went on past the wavy-roofed Total Garage, where Jimmy had his finger bitten to near amputation by Brian Walker, and found a place for refreshment.

We got talking about theatre. The Brian Brooke production of Irma La Douce had arrived from Johannesburg. I had already seen it in Johannesburg with Denise, but hadn't been overly impressed.

"I'd love to see it." Anne informed me.

Never mind being the second time around, and sod the speeding fine, it was my opportunity to ask Anne out. We fixed the date for a performance shortly before my court appearance.

I dropped her off back at the workshop where she'd left her scooter.

You may have gathered Anne loved two wheels, the bigger the better, she was a true adrenaline junkie. We had already spent a day together on a previous occasion, mostly just riding about. Firstly 13 or so miles out on the Prince Edward Dam road to the micro-midget track then 26 miles out in the opposite direction to the Mazoe Dam.

Carved out of the sandveld bush on someone's farm (possibly Peter Platt's) this dirt-track was the venue for both motorcycles and tiny home-made racing cars powered by motorcycle engines.

It was set in virgin land dotted with large anthills as big as small houses. Some of these termite mounds had been hewn into terraces to form seating. The races were a bit like present-day go-carting, but far more spectacular with acrobatic crashes in every race.

Anne asked to be dropped off at Chikurubi Farm, where her parents were visiting. This was when Chikurubi was still a model farm. Half-a-mile of high-grade two-lane gravel driveway bordered by an avenue of overhanging trees led to the old-style Rhodesian farmhouse. I had been there before as a schoolboy with Jimmy, who had permission to fish in one of the three farm dams, which had been stocked with both bass and bream (tilapia).

When it was sold off in the late 1960s or early 1970s, the Government bought the largest part as a prison farm. It had the potential to be a world-class rehabilitation facility.

Now in Mugabe's Zimbabwe it's a horrendous hell-hole of high security, where Kevin Woods spent 20 years, five of which were on death row.[2]

Anne invited me inside, but I was grubby not only with road dust but also had the trademark, oily right boot of the 1950's *Triumph* rider.

I was more than a bit unkempt. It was getting dark, so I used the excuse of having no lights to leave. I wished I hadn't; I've got a feeling that had I met

----

[2] * *The Kevin Woods Story; ISBN 978-1-920143-14-5.*

Chikurubi's owners, I would have more to add interest to my writing so many years later.

I enjoyed that performance of Irma enormously. Heather Lloyd-Jones in the lead was absolutely superb. It was a totally pleasurable evening. Of course having Anne for company was a powerful ingredient.

The next day it was my show...in court and I had spent the money I had saved for the fine.

The policeman had had his speedometer tested, he wanted to be thorough. It had been found to be 1 mph fast at sixty. He was being creative when he said that he had clocked me three times at sixty; I had probably reached more than ninety but at no time did I travel at a steady 60mph. I could have pointed out that he must therefore be lying. However I figured that the truth wouldn't work as a defence. Neither did lying.

The magistrate was quite correct when he informed me; "I find your account to be a complete fabrication."

I thought it was quite nice that he hadn't called me a liar. As I say, I could have said the same about the prosecution's case, but decided that it might be counter-productive to call the policeman a liar. I had a feeling that an approach like that would only make the situation worse.

I was found guilty of doing 59 mph in a 30 zone.

"Fifteen pounds or fifteen days."

I respectfully asked for time to pay. It was fifteen days to payday; he allowed me fourteen. The bastard.

Fifteen pounds. I had exactly fifteen pounds, it was half of my month's salary, and I needed it to feed me until payday. I had no option but to pay.

Having had a few disagreements with Neville and Annette, I wasn't going to ask for their charity. I was having one meal a day at the Young Men's Club, although I was still living in our house.

At the Club I had to persuade the warden (that's what they called the manager) to give me my meals on credit until the end of the month.

The Club was a non-profit making hostel set up by the worldwide Toc H organisation. The initials referred to Talbot House, a soldiers club in The First World War. Initially built to help returning soldiers from WW1, the Rhodesian Club was later open to any young white man in need of cheap accommodation.

I already knew the Club well because it was opposite the Union Avenue house where I spent my early years so it was an easy choice when I needed somewhere to live. In the Club I came across a ledger listing residents who had volunteered, but not returned from World War 2.

The list was long enough to include the entire occupancy of the Club.

In the meantime, unable to buy petrol, I walked or hitched the 6-mile round trip every night from Tweed Road to the Club for my daily meal. For the same reason the 15 miles to Anne's house was out of the question. Anyway, I was told she had taken up with some other guy.

I never thought to phone her and tell her how much I had enjoyed her company. Pity, I'm sure she would have appreciated a call.

I gave up on Anne.

Chapter 24

The Special and a Special Slip of a Girl

Now I was no longer attached to a female I got serious about *The Special* (the DIY sports car project). It wasn't long before I had chiselled through all the spot welds holding the body of the old *Ford Prefect* to the chassis and rolled the seven hundred-plus pounds of sheet steel and glass to one side. That exposed the primitive mechanics in all their naked glory. They looked even better after being cleaned.

I bought five sheets of twenty gauge aluminium, a bundle of three-quarter-inch steel conduit, and borrowed Jimmy's arc welder. Jimmy worked for the Electricity Supply Commission where Duncan Davidson, the charge-hand in the winding shop, was employed to repair power transformers. Arc welders were a natural by-product of the recycling process; they were Duncan's sideline.

Of course, an industrious electrician would make one for himself as Jimmy did as an apprentice and I did some years later, when I worked there for nine months. The equivalent, at that time, would have cost more than a month's salary to buy. I still have, and use, mine.

The Rhodesian conduit was softer than the British equivalent and was easy to bend over your knee. I bent up a framework of conduit and welded it to the chassis. The steering column required lowering, that only took the elongation of two mounting holes and a bit of packing. I obtained a lower radiator from a car-breaker.

I used pop rivets to attach the aluminium to the conduit frame. Wavell had borrowed an old pop riveter on my behalf. The engine was standard apart from the exhaust manifold. I made that up from surplus tubular guardrails which I found neatly wrapped and packed away at work. They just happened to be the right diameter tube and conveniently bent.

Having cut all the various parts of the manifold to size I had to arrange to get locked into the machine-come-welding workshop during the lunch-break to complete the job. That area was kept locked at lunchtime to prevent just such private work.

It was also the first time ever I had done any brazing, but it worked out OK. I didn't arc weld it because my arc welding skills weren't up to the standard required.

The headlights were from a *Light 15 Citroen*. They were handsome chrome-plated separate units and once I had fitted double-filament bulbs were legal with bright and dip. The original had an electromagnet on the off-side reflector to tilt it for dip, while the near-side remained on bright. They must have come off a very old *Citroen*.

I bought new taillights. They were meant for trailers but they worked in very well, really looking the part. Of course it wasn't as easy as it sounds; it took much more time than it should have, and life had to go on.

***

That little slip of a girl who had fed me chips on the street corner was Eunice. Our paths just kept crossing.

After the meeting on First Street she was at Marie Simonson's party, where Johnny O. had invited me outside for a fight. I had no idea what the grievance was but when I agreed, he backed down.

I think he thought everyone knew that he was a tough guy and a policeman to boot; therefore I should have been intimidated. I had an advantage, I knew none of that, but he thought I did. He knew nothing about me and I must have seemed confident; actually I was just fed up at watching this lumpy braggart playing to the crowd. I'm glad he backed down though.

However, two weeks later he got me. He was the sergeant in the police car when I was stopped for my pillion passenger riding side-saddle. I recognised the voice that told an apologetic constable to "Bump him!" Johnny didn't show his face.

"Sorry, my sergeant says I have to bump you". Apparently I was also lacking number-plate, tail and brake lights. I got done for the lot.

The pillion-passenger?...A tall angular female; who, in my opinion, was better forgotten. However, she had apparently once won a beauty contest; exactly why and how had me baffled. She had conned me into going to a spiritualist meeting. I thought I was on a promise. It turned out to be an expensive disappointment.

She did have a couple of good points however, even side-saddle, she sat on the pillion as if she belonged there; like Anne did. I was totally unaware of having a passenger and her good-looking legs were probably why that constable was so insistent that she should sit astride the pillion in such a tight skirt while the other occupants of the police car gawped at her.

The third time my path crossed Eunice's was at another party in a building behind the little rock kopje next to that Total service station with the wavy roof. Eunice had left a stole behind. I had just got as far as establishing her address when she returned to claim it; damn! I wasn't too put out but I did want some female company and it would have been a good excuse to call.

Finally we were both at a party at Dawn and Linda Langley's new house in Northwood. I had travelled with Dieter Reitz in his home-built *Riley* Special. Dieter and I had often spoken about building a home-made sports car; a special, but he hadn't liked the idea of wrecking a perfectly good *Riley RMA*. It was dated but it was basically an up-market car. It certainly had more class than any of the cheaper cars of that time. However, he had his opinion changed for him one night.

He lived on his step-father's farm where the family tobacco grading business was located. It was 26 miles out on the Umtali road, very close to the *Jamaica Inn*. Dieter was driving home that night with his mum and brother when a drunken cyclist appeared in the headlights' beam. His evasive action was to go roll-about into the bush; three times over before it stopped on its roof. Fortunately their injuries weren't too serious. However, the traditional-built bodywork was wrecked.

Those *Rileys* were fine examples of British coachwork; but a wooden framework covered with steel and aluminium panels was never suitable for tumbling around the African veldt.

Rhodesian panel-beaters were as good as the best anywhere when it involved all steel bodywork, but anything with a wooden frame was regarded as a time-consuming nightmare.

For a commercial organisation, economical repair was out of the question, so it was then down to Dieter's ingenuity.

Initially, while his *Riley* was laid up on the farm, Dieter had the use of his stepfather's *A55 Austin*, which was a great help, particularly when he needed to shop for materials and equipment. In fact it was just such a lunchtime shopping trip that brought an end to the happy arrangement.

I was with him at the time. We were on our way to buy welding rods for his special project. He wasn't going fast and we had right-of-way on Sir James McDonald Avenue. An elderly Mr. Satterthwaite, a salesman for Cairns, the *Vauxhall* agency, was travelling at a steady 30 mph down Coventry Road. He saw the car behind us and knew he had the space and time to cross in front of it. What he didn't see was our *Austin A55*, he had neither time nor space to cross ahead of us.

We all realised that both cars needed the same bit of road at the same time. He looked as frightened as I was. I don't know why he was so worried; he didn't have a brand-new golden monster of a *Vauxhall Cresta* about to wipe him out. I would have jumped into Dieter's lap but there wasn't time. The next instant the Austin was spinning down the road on its driver-side door handle.

Although the first point of contact was on my door, the maximum force took effect on the back of the *Austin* because of our forward speed; thus the mind-blowing spin. For a moment or so I was stuck to the seat like washing in a spin-drier.

Once again I was climbing out of a car through the window. It's amazing how urgently I always want to get out of an upturned car. I remember feeling the same way when we turned over in Mike's *VW*, and again a few years later when Jimmy rolled his *Zephyr.*

Dieter's stepfather wasn't at all upset about the wrecked *Austin* as he was planning on selling it and the insurance payout saved him the trouble. Dieter, on the other hand, needed transport so now he was in a hurry to get his *Riley* back on the road.

The result was an open six-seater sheet-metal box-on-wheels. It did however, have doors, windscreen and mudguards; also a lever for the instant conversion of the front bench seat into a double bed. But using it didn't always work out the way Dieter had in mind. Apparently the sudden appearance of a double bed could compromise the planned seduction. In truth I'm not sure if it ever worked as a bed of sexual pleasure; but the thought was there.

I was at that party in the Langley's new Northwood house when I once again came across that slip of a girl, Eunice. This time I hung on to her and offered her a lift home in Dieter's special.

"Dieter won't mind," I insisted.

That night Dieter's car became a bit more than a six-seater when several partygoers piled into it for a lift home. Eunice was on my lap for the whole ten or twelve miles. That was the beginning of the next fifty plus years.

***

Having sold the *Triumph*, my special became a priority. It was a rush to get the car mobile. With Jimmy and Wavell pitching in we got it going in the third week of December 1960; one midnight.

Mudguards would have to wait. Doors were an unnecessary complication; I simply left a gap to swing your legs in or out. A bit of bodywork next to the seats, like the arm of a chair, stopped you sliding out sideways. I was relying on the ample amount of flexible piping I had used in the twin exhaust system for silencing.

I wanted to take Eunice out in it. Anyway, her sister was being married at the end of the week and I couldn't expect to use her mum's car in the evening, so it needed to be on the road.

When we got it going at midnight, we took it around the block and on to the Gremlin drive-in restaurant for the trial run. It was immediately apparent that my silencing arrangement wouldn't work. My home-made-free-flow manifold and twin exhausts made it sound like a full-blown racing car.

If I was to use it the next afternoon I had to get silencers sorted out. So the next morning I fitted a pair of motorcycle silencers which brought the sound down to a soft and pleasant rumble.

No need for me to dwell on Diana's wedding, if you've been to one…Of course I'm sure that some weddings can be interesting, but I was not directly involved. To me it was just a bit of a party. The evening was mine. Now with the special on the road I suggested we go to the Mabelreign drive-in cinema.

We hadn't been there long when the thunder started and the stars disappeared behind thick layers of cloud. Never mind the privacy issue, watching a movie from a car without a windscreen, doors, mudguards or top in a tropical downpour wouldn't be a good idea. The twelve-mile drive back to Eunice's house had to be the sensible option; well, that's what we thought.

The coming storm looked fearsome, and it was, that I can vouch for, but not at the drive-in. It never touched the cinema. But how was I to know that? Dieter, who happened to be there that night, told me the following Monday.

The way back went past the Blue Gardenia drive-in restaurant; surely we had time for a coffee; wrong! As we left the restaurant the storm broke, within minutes the road was covered with two inches of water.

I knew that if you drive through water without mudguards there would be spray; I never realised that it would come off the front wheels like a fire-hose. I also hadn't worked out that my no-door design was exactly in line with that jet of water. I was further surprised by the effect of the unguarded rear wheels; Catherine-wheel-like water-sprays poured down the backs of our necks.

I pulled into the pisê on the way back, where we changed into dry clothes and waited for the storm to subside.

I suppose it was a bit strange, taking the Coopers' daughter home in a set of my oversized clothing after a night out at a drive-in movie. Whatever they thought, nothing romantic or otherwise happened. I did offer to help her change into my clothing; however, she somehow managed without my help.

She wasn't at all put out by the drenching; I knew I had found the girl for me.

Eunice was delivered in 1943 London's Croydon, by a plumber, her Dad; that was the year Hitler started sending the V1s to London. Those were the petrol powered flying bombs nicknamed *Doodlebugs.*

Croydon, being on their flight-path, became a drop-zone for many that fell short. Apparently it was known as Doodlebug Alley; at least that's the nickname which I heard on a recent TV documentary. Of course that may just be the creative reporting of a latter-day journalist.

I have no idea what effect the war had on Eunice's personality, she can't remember anything of her life in England before they left in1947. I have met many survivors of the intense bombing of that war including Dieter, who was from Berlin; all have always shown tremendous fortitude and had unusually strong characters.

Time would prove that Eunice has all the good points of a South Londoner, but I couldn't even guess that by simply meeting this five foot two, demure, pragmatic, slip of a girl.

As soon as she could, at seventeen, she had passed her driver's licence and within a month she was called on to recover her Dad's truck. It had broken down at Odzi, twenty miles from Umtali. This meant towing it over 150 miles on roads which made many grown men blanch; a round trip of over 300 miles.

Eunice was fun, but she didn't flaunt her charms; a neat treat in a modest box that had to be unwrapped to be appreciated. Well worth the time and trouble, durable too, after fifty-one years and four children she still weighs in at seven-and-a half stone.

The slip of a girl

Sixteen Year Old Eunice on Beira Beach before I knew her (1959)
Photos by John Arnott on her camera

My Special

Chapter 25

Call-up, Kariba and Victoria Falls by Thumb

By now *The Special* was on the road equipped with a windscreen and a hood sewn up by Eunice. It was a fun vehicle, but there were teething problems, like the light switch, which burnt out one very dark night. What made that night particularly interesting was that it happened when we were visiting the Mazoe Dam, some 25 miles out on an unlit road.

I drove back following the broken white centre line. It was just possible to make out the markings by looking at the road immediately next to the driver's door. When I veered too far to the left the bumpy shoulder put me right. Fortunately the other traffic was negligible and once we got within the city limits the street lighting was very good.

Aware that *The Special* needed more work to make it street legal, I took it to the Government's Vehicle Inspection Depot, not for a test, just for friendly advice. A laughing inspector said mudguards were a must as well as a barrier between the cabin and the back axle. He also weighed it. At 1100 pounds it was light enough to be a pleasure to drive.

"Can I use it like this?" I queried.

"You might as well, we'll catch you soon enough!" was the grinning reply. He was wrong, although a lone policeman did stop me once.

"Where's your front number-plate?" he demanded.

"There." I said, pointing at the front cowling, where young Norman Eley had volunteered to do an excellent bit of sign-writing.

"We use motorcycles, not low-flying aircraft. Get it fixed!"

"Yes Sir, will do." I lied, it seemed the appropriate response.

Within a few months of first taking Eunice out, I received my call-up papers for National Service. I was lucky not to have been drafted before. Every white and mixed-race male got drafted in Rhodesia, most as soon as they left school.

I was particularly lucky because I was called into the Air Force, at least I thought so at the time. In retrospect I think the Army would have suited my character better. In the Air Force there was an attitude barrier between the regulars and the national servicemen. Many regulars had an inflated opinion of their self-importance.

For us (national servicemen) it was great because it was an absolute skive. The Air Force lacked the technique of being able to make recruits totally miserable in order to bond them in a common hatred of their immediate superiors. The officers would probably have liked to impose a strict disciplinarian regime, but that would have required a large input of effort from the NCOs concerned; something in short supply in that force. They simply weren't energetic enough.

There were other advantages; out-of-hours, time was our own. In the Army, the new recruits were confined to barracks for the first six weeks and only allowed out with permission after that. The Air Force base was on the outskirts of Salisbury and only eight miles from Eunice's house where I spent most of my time, although I had to sleep on the base.

At that time the initial call up was just four and a half months, followed by three weeks a year for the next three years. The big downside was the pay; ten shillings a day. All employers held the jobs open. Most made up the wages to their employee's normal remuneration and some even paid their men in full. Mine did neither, so I took as much leave as I could to gain a bit of cash, but timing my leave to allow me three days to myself before returning to work.

I used the *Ford Special* a few times while I was on call-up, however it had developed a bearing knock so I decide to sell it. A couple of young neighbours bought it and managed to get it impounded within days which is, of course, what happens when you make a nuisance of yourself in something which isn't exactly street legal. Another serviceman was selling an old *Ford Prefect* for thirty pounds. I bought it. I had transport again.

When my four and a half months of basic training ended I took advantage of the extra days leave to visit the Victoria Falls. My Dad had lived so long in Rhodesia, but had never managed to see the Falls. I had to go. I would travel firstly to Kariba, which I had not seen since the visit with Neville in 1958, when the annual flooding reached an unprecedented level sweeping away both the road and the high level footbridge.

On that visit only a Blondin cable, hundreds of feet above any possible flood, connected the two river-banks. The cofferdams, although built higher than any previous recorded flood level, had been submerged. This caused the work site to be abandoned until the water subsided. Now in 1961 the wall was complete. It held back a surface area of 2,500 square miles (6470 square kilometres)) and 180 cubic kilometres of water. The surface area of the completely full Aswan Dam is bigger at 2,700 square miles but the capacity is less at 111 cubic kilometres.

Kariba's 420 foot (130 metre) high wall doubles as a 1,900 foot (585 metre) highway across the Zambesi, which I would cross over to travel to the Falls via Mazabuka and Livingstone. I would return via Hwange and Bulawayo, about 1500 miles in all. It would have been a big ask for that little thirty-pound *Ford*. I decided to hitch-hike.

The first two rides took me about sixty miles, both from tobacco farmers and both with very strong, definite, but opposite political opinions on the forthcoming constitutional referendum.

Several vehicles sped past completely ignoring my thumb. In frustration I gave the two- fingered salute to a dark blue *Studebaker* from the 1950s, which cruised by. It stopped a hundred yards on and an elderly man clambered out. I was working on an apology when he shouted, "Hurry up. I don't have all day!"

He was non-committal all the way to Kariba, I think he might have wanted to complain about my rude gesture, but his wife was quite friendly. I sensed that she was on my side, the decision maker, the boss.

One of the fellows on call-up in the Air Force was Noel Smith, also a GPO employee, who had been stationed at Kariba. I had promised to look him up if I ever went there. Of course I didn't know his address or where the GPO works were, so I followed some phone lines to the exchange.

Being automatic it was unmanned and as it was now almost dark I decided to settle down on the veranda. I hadn't even unpacked my sleeping bag when an irate engineer arrived in a cloud of dust.

"What the hell are you doing?"

"I'm looking for Noel Smith, I believe he works here."

"He was transferred ages ago."

"Well if it's all the same to you I'll just kip down here."

"You can't sleep here. Get in." I climbed into the *Land Rover.*"

After we arrived at his house, and as I told my story, Jack Barnard mellowed. His very pleasant wife provided a most welcome dinner and twelve-year-old Mike, his eldest child, gave up his bed on my behalf.[3]

Kariba Dam Wall (the vehicles crossing indicate scale)
My photo from the Rhodesian side 1961

In the morning the family left on a visit to Salisbury, cramming me into their car as far as the dam wall, where I was picked up by an Austrian family in a *VW Kombi* and taken across into Zambia (Northern Rhodesia at the time) and on a hundred miles or so to Mazabuka.

---

[3] Mike later became an apprentice in Salisbury's Electricity Department while I was working there. Later he joined the Rhodesian branch of the UK's *Reyrolle Co.,* the manufacturers of the "*Rolls Royce*" of switchgear. I heard very favourable comments about him from *Reyrolle's* Rhodesian M.D. "Bob" Strickland.

There I bought something to eat and a razor. Made for the African market and called a *Minerva* or similar, it certainly removed hair, some below skin level. I can only describe it as user-unfriendly.

My next lift was from a crab-tracking, ex-army *Willys Jeep*. The wheels were so far out of line that, even with such a short wheelbase, it could barely straddle the strips. The front wheels were rolling along the right edge of the tarmac strips with the rear wheels on the left edges. The driver was a cheerful young man apparently oblivious to the waywardness of his vehicle. However, the open-air travelling was very pleasant in the warmth of the Zambian winter, albeit very dusty whenever we were passed by the occasional traffic. The *Willys* dropped me off in Livingstone just seven miles from the Falls; almost immediately I was picked up by a Danish guy in an *Austin Healy Sprite.*

"Do you have a camera?" he asked.

"Yes," tapping my pocket where I had stuffed my childhood's *Baby Brownie* as a last minute afterthought. He looked at the bulging pocket with disdain.

"Shit!" was his disgusted comment, "all this way and that's your camera?"

The road took us to the border bridge and my first sight of the Falls themselves. The spray had been visible for miles before that. Despite his obvious disappointment with my camera, my benefactor stopped on the bridge supposedly for my sake but he obviously enjoyed the view. He was right, this magnificent awe-inspiring place deserved the best photography could offer. I decided another camera and I would be back. What a place for a honeymoon.

I rented a one-roomed chalet in a bleak and deserted camping ground, bought some tinned food and I ate directly out of the tin. I slept well enough in the borrowed sleeping bag on the lumpy coir mattress, but it was nice to get up in the morning, and even better to wander down to the falls for a closer look at this ruggedly beautiful wild and wonderful freak of nature. The pleasure was simply to be there.

I wondered down through the rain forest. It was a tiny remnant of what was said to have covered most of sub Saharan Africa a thousand years ago. This fragment, together with a small sector on the Mozambique border amongst the Chimanimani Mountains, were all that had survived in Rhodesia through the ever-changing climate and population, both human and animal. On the mountainous section of the Mozambique border, the high rainfall nurtured the thick tropical vegetation.

Here at the Victoria Falls it was the spray from the cascading water that enabled the forest to thrive. In the summer, when the river was high, visitors would wear raincoats or be soaked while walking through the forest. Then the spray would often obliterate the best view, however, looking at recent (2013) photos, the river looks horribly low; more climate change?

In a tree a large, glossy-black, chicken-sized hornbill was being raucous; his grotesque yellow beak bigger than his head. At the chasm's edge, I gazed down at the foaming rapids nearly 300 feet below. It was too early to see the rainbow that forms in the spray. That would have to wait for my next visit, as would a stroll along the Razor's Edge and a climb down to The Boiling Pot on the Zambian side, when once again I would stand in silent awe.

Victoria Falls Chalet (Hitch-Hiking 1961)I was the only campsite occupant.
My photo

From the Zambian Side (1964 on honeymoon)
My photo

In spite of the thunderous roar of the torrent of falling water, somehow it was pleasantly quiescent; I was the only human there early that morning.

I felt tranquil, it was so very peaceful to be totally alone here.

Never again, on my subsequent visits, would I have that degree of serenity, future visits would be plagued by casino gamblers, disco dancers and golfers. Only then did I realise how privileged I was on that first trip.

About nine I started to hitch, soon to be picked up by a couple of thirsty Road Dept. workers in a *Bedford* truck. Why they were thirsty I don't know. I thought that the amount of beer they were drinking was enough to quench even the worst thirst. They dropped me on the road some miles past the coal mining town of Hwange. I should have asked to be dropped in the town as the odd car just couldn't be bothered to stop.

Eventually some sort of salesman stopped on his way to a trade fair in Bulawayo. But he wasn't in a hurry as he also needed refreshment and so we spent some time at a *pole-and-dagga* outpost, which sold beer and had two elephant skulls flanking the entrance. The result was that we arrived in Bulawayo after dark.

I wasn't comfortable about dossing down within the city limits so decided to try and make it back to Salisbury. Some national servicemen took me as far as Heany Junction, the turn-off to their barracks, just 18 miles out of town.

By that time there was no hope of me making the 280 or so miles back to Salisbury before morning. Three or four pairs of headlights appeared through the dark only to disappear again as fading taillights, oblivious to my thumb. So I crossed over the roadside ditch and laid out Jimmy's sleeping bag on a stubble-covered termite mound.

Unlike ants, termites don't attack you unless you actually invade their nest. Doubtless there were other creepy-crawlies about, but I would worry about them when they worried me. The only ones which really concerned me were scorpions but it didn't look like their kind of countryside being almost devoid of rocks. Anyway, it was getting cold and they wouldn't move until the sun warmed them up. Of course I could be unlucky and put my sleeping bag on top of one. I didn't think about that.

It was a very cold and uncomfortable night on the roadside. Thankfully the first car that emerged through the early light of dawn stopped. It was a *Citroen DS 19* or *20*, a rarity in Rhodesia at the time but they became very popular after sanctions destroyed Britain's motor trade with Rhodesia. French *Citroens* and *Peugeots*, Japanese *Datsuns* and German *BMWs* took over former *Austin* and *Ford* factories.

What an impressive car, the *DS Citroen,* it coasted over some of the roughest dirt road deviations at motorway speeds, as if we were in armchairs in a luxury lounge. One day I was going to own one of these, that was a definite. When I eventually did I wasn't disappointed. Of the more than thirty cars I've owned; mostly wrecks but a few were new or nearly new, my *DS* was by far the best. The *Citroen* dropped me off in Salisbury city centre.

I made the last three miles in a *VW Combi* driven by a Swiss who was most concerned that my army-style kitbag wasn't suitable for hiking, apparently it would put drivers off. Maybe he had had an unpleasant experience with a soldier, but in Rhodesia it was probably an asset.

Certainly later during the Bush War it would have been. He was very insistent that I should get a knapsack. The fact that I had just covered 1500 miles didn't seem to register with him. I didn't tell him that my backpacking days were over.

I only had 200 yards to walk home.

Chapter 28

Mechanical Muscle and Some Stink

"Alright, I'll move out!" I was already eating my one meal a day at the Young Men's Club.

As mentioned previously, the Club was a non-profit hostel run by the international Toc H organisation, originally for returning soldiers from the First World War; subsequently the Club took in financially challenged young white men.

Initially Annette didn't like my cooking and resented cooking for me, anyway other tensions built up, I suppose I was a pain to live with, being young and a bit headstrong. So I became a resident of the Club.

I liked my new housing; three meals a day, inclusive in-house laundry, room cleaner and a telly lounge, it was great. It wouldn't suit everyone however. The normal arrangement was three to a room, women weren't allowed upstairs and two men wanting to share a room were regarded as suspect; homosexuality was both illegal and socially unacceptable.

When I moved in occupancy was low, so initially there was only me and Des Cox in the room. Des was the Club's long-term resident. He had been there eight years, since he left school at sixteen and started work as a fitter and turner apprentice. His dad was a diamond driller, a short, lean and pleasant man, a really nice guy with a steel hook where one of his hands should have been.

His job was boring holes in the ground for water extraction and mineral exploration. It took him all over the country, sometimes to the most remote of places, so Des' home had never been in any one place. After a while we became good friends.

Des was engaged to Anne from Harmony House on the corner of McChlery and Derry Avenues. It was a hostel specifically built for single Afrikaans girls living away from home, probably by their Church; nice and handy to the Club, just across the vacant land where the old Sinoia railway had been. The line was rerouted a few years after we moved from Union Avenue to the *pisê* but the scar was still there.

That railway had been part of my early childhood playground before we moved to the *pisê*. Our old shared house was across the road from the Club. By now, 1961, the next-door house, Lawrence's ex-lodgings, had been demolished to make way for a six storey block of flats. The houses had been renumbered, 144 had become 164.

Apparently Des had set his heart on Anne after extensive and intensive research amongst several other residents of Harmony House. He was short, fiery and good-looking with a natural and easy charm. He had a way with women. I think he owned that old 1940s *Nash* coupe parked under the jacaranda trees out the front. It never moved, but was said to be very useful, bus shelters being almost non-existent in Rhodesia.

Our room was at the end of the west corridor overlooking the passably pleasant front garden; the window was level with the top of a superb flamboyant tree in the club grounds and the jacaranda lined Union Avenue.

Although the jacarandas were pretty enough when in purple flower, I didn't think they could compete with the flaming red and deep green of the flamboyants. I know that the flamboyants are more difficult and time-consuming to propagate, but in my opinion, well worth the trouble. Come to think of it, quite a few householders would've been proud to have that hostel garden.

The entrance to our room was directly opposite a set of doorless ablutions. Why were they doorless? Because someone, said to be George H, the son of a preacher, had sold the doors, all six from the upstairs showers and toilets. There was always a market for second-hand doors in Rhodesia. Our room's door had its own problem it couldn't be shut on account of being in the locked position while the door was open. The key of course was missing. Come winter I fixed our non-closing door with a single swipe of a hammer; it then closed sweetly.

To the best of my knowledge, apart from each person's cupboard, there wasn't a lockable door in the whole building. We did have a burglar once. He was lucky to escape. Can't count the TV being swiped as a burglary, it was more the action of a sneak thief. It wasn't missed until the next day; mind you, had he been caught, I'm sure he would have been unhappy in the care of 40 or so of the inhabitants.

The three meals a day were fine, but each was predictable by the day of the week. If required, sandwiches would be provided instead of lunch. In my case the GPO workshops were only a few hundred yards away so I walked back for a midday meal.

After I had been there about two years, a new housekeeper/cook was engaged. Mrs Pretorius was Cordon Bleu trained. The meals were brilliant. The manager agreed but was unhappy about the bills. Suddenly the dining hall was always full. It was amazing how many people were coming to the Club just to eat.

I still had that thirty-pound *Prefect*, and late one night when I parked, some fellows from the Club were changing a wheel. When I woke to wheel-changing noises soon after going to bed, I thought they were still at it. Cursing their incompetence, I rolled over and went back to sleep.

In the morning I found out how wrong I was. The only good tyre I had was missing. Across the road a *Vauxhall* was on bricks with all four wheels missing, likewise another *Vauxhall* in McChlery Avenue was also plundered. My *Prefect* wasn't supported at all; the bastards had just dropped it onto the ground.

At least with the spare I could still drive the car, never mind that the remaining tyres were all completely bald. In the past I had driven down to two layers of canvas. I suppose there was something to be said for having tyres which weren't worth stealing.

In conversation with another diner, Mike Torrington, I mentioned that I wouldn't mind owning a *Vincent* motorcycle. Although by then out of production, it was the fastest road machine at the time and would be for many years to come.

As it happened Mike knew a fellow with one. Chris Foreshore had a very desirable model, a 1000 cc *Black Shadow*. Chris ran a welding business in Macheke, 60 miles away. Mike gave me his number and I arranged to meet him at the Micro-Midget track when he came to race.

I gave £60 and the *Matchless 500* single I had bought in pieces from Bob McAdam in exchange for the *Vincent*. Although in pieces the 500 was all there and in reasonable condition.

***

The *Vincent* proved to be too temperamental for everyday transport. The front cylinder spark plug would oil up unless I could go fast enough to burn off the carbon. The centrifugal clutch was a gear-change nightmare. 0 to 70 in first within three seconds was expected and usually no problem, but then she might stick resolutely in first.

However, from time to time, as the clutch was released, she would quite likely self-change too early into second and amble off at her own pace. Never mind the foreplay, get her going and she was hell on wheels. Of course I had to try her out for speed.

1,000 ccs of Mechanical Muscle
My photo

Eunice and the *Black Shadow*
Neville's photo

The best I could get on the Bulawayo Road was 117 mph. Trying to improve on that, I was changing the main jets on the carburettors when our new room-mate, a Dutch lad, by the name of Jan Wouters, came by.

"What are you doing?"

"I'm just trying to get more speed out of her."

"When you try it out can I come too?"

"Sure, why not?"

This time I went out on Mazoe Road, "The New Golden-Stairs" Road. I opened her up as we were alongside the pig farm. Anyone who travelled that road knew exactly where the pig farm was. 100 mph came easily, but there she stayed, as obdurate as any human.

There was a shimmy. I turned my head to look at the rear wheel.

"What was that?"

"Dunno Jan."

The next moment I was having a totally new experience. The front wheel was slamming from lock-to-lock. I hung on, tucking my elbows into my hips and using every bit of adrenaline in my system to try and quell this beast. It made absolutely no impression. I was swung from side to side along with the front wheel like a rat in a pit-bull's jaws.

The bike yo-yoed to-and-from the tarmac as the forks slammed from side-to-side. Each time we were about to be dashed to pieces on the blacktop, a mighty last-minute yank would pull us back in the opposite direction threatening oblivion on the other side. I was dreading the trail of flesh and blood that I was convinced would be the outcome of this new experience.

Of course I should have tightened up the steering damper before we started. There was nothing I could do now; I was fully occupied. I wondered what would happen if Jan was thrown off the pillion.

It's said that when you're frightened enough your past flashes before you, not for me; I was looking to the future; hoping I would survive to appreciate the nurses. If they were young and pretty it would be a bonus, but survival would be good enough.

However, for some reason we didn't come off. Eventually we rolled to an exhausted and trembling stop. It had been the most frightening experience of my life. I don't know how Jan held on at the back. I guess he somehow found some extra strength. He never rode pillion with me again.

Our course was marked by a series of S-shaped black tracks. The valve had been torn out of the front wheel's tube in total contempt of the security-bolt. British manufacturers installed these devices on high-powered motorcycles to lock the tyre in place and safeguard the valve. The rear wheel had three to stop it slipping within the rim during acceleration.

"Shit! What were you doing?" demanded a white-faced Jan.

I was shaking as well. I didn't reply. I had no answer. Right then we had a transport problem.

Being designed in the days of common sense, it was a simple matter to remove the front wheel without tools of any sort. So that's what I did and we hitched a ride to the nearest phone box, which was conveniently next to a garage. I would be able to use their air supply.

I phoned Jimmy Smith to beg the loan of tyre levers and a tube from his bike. His tube was 18 inch; mine was 19. Never mind, I fitted it anyway and we rode carefully back to the Club.

In the meantime I had sold the *Prefect* and bought Reg Brophy's *Vauxhall Velox*. He had spent money on the engine and a re-spray but it needed new tyres. His price was more than fair so I fitted new tyres, polished up the paint and I now had a really nice car. Its only fault was a remarkable ability to get stuck in little more than a hint of mud. One rainy Christmas, on a dinner-dance evening at *The Highlands Park Hotel,* there was considerably more than a hint of mud.

There must have been fifteen or twenty in our group alone and it was a busy night. To cope with the extra cars the management had enlarged the car-park by clearing some of their overgrown land. I pulled up on this newly cleared patch and immediately felt the car settle on to its belly.

"Shit Eunice, we're stuck!"

"Don't swear. How do you know?"

"Didn't you feel the car sink? And that's not all; I know what we're in, I can smell it. Can't you? We've parked on top of the septic-tank soak-away."

"Oh, sewage; it's the soak-pit! But that should be sealed off. I know because my dad's a plumber and he builds lots of them."

"Ah! But your dad didn't build this one. This place is out of town and beyond the reach of the building inspectors. We're deep in shit."

"I thought I said not to swear. What are you going to do now?"

"I wasn't swearing and we're going to get out very carefully."

"Just say we're stuck in mud," I continued, "don't say in what kind of mud. We'll need a tow-rope and as much help as we can get. Wait until the end of the night when everyone's tanked-up and hopefully they won't notice the detail when we ask for a shove. With luck it'll all be very jolly and they'll have a lot of fun."

I stayed sober. At the end of the evening I quietly asked around for a tow-rope.

"Try the manager, the Hotel must have a rope they can lend you," my friend Basil Chard suggested. I did just that.

"Not my problem if you park in mud," was the response when I approached the manager.

I spoke quietly in his ear. "It fucking well will be your problem when the Government Health Inspector finds out that you expect your customers to park in your sewage. My car's up to its axles in your hotel's shit-hole. I need a tow rope."

I got the rope.

It took two cars in tandem and a lot of jolly laughing joking stalwarts, ankle-deep in muck, to get the car back onto firm ground. Spray from the spinning wheels would not have helped. Eunice and I sat quietly in the car.

Once on firm ground again I thanked everyone profusely and we drove off to rousing cheers of goodwill. I hoped that they wouldn't be too disappointed when they sobered-up and their sense of smell returned.

I spent the next morning hosing down the *Vauxhall* and my shoes. My suit was in a big plastic bag ready for the dry cleaners. Eunice and I hadn't got too mucky. There had been a hard crust of earth on the surface which the car had broken through but which had managed to support us on our very careful negotiation to and from the front seats. I have no idea how our valiant helpers felt. I had a fair insight as to how they had fared, but I never heard any complaints, perhaps they were just baffled as to how they got in such a mess, only remembering how much fun they had the previous night.

Chapter 27

Different Digs

I was now living at Mrs Pretorius's house in Hillside. She had decided to turn it into a boarding house and had persuaded me to become the first tenant. Initially the arrangement was excellent, but as she still had a commitment to the Young Men's Club her sister moved in as manager.

Mrs Pretorius was a refined, well-spoken and dignified gentlewoman; "as pure as the driven snow," someone said. I had never seen snow of any kind, driven or otherwise, but I knew what they meant. Her sister was none of these things.

Soon two new lodgers arrived: men friends of the sister.

Having grown up on the rough edge of white Rhodesian society, I could type these two immediately; polite and friendly on the surface, in reality, devious and cunning strangers to integrity. They would be described by many Rhodesians as "a waste-of-human-skin;" unwelcome in any decent community.

It wasn't long before Mrs P. took over and her sister disappeared, together with her dubious fellow travellers. She didn't elaborate on the sudden departure of her sister. However, there was a rumour that another resident had noticed the back view of one of her male friends through his old *Ford Consul's* windscreen. Apparently upright on his knees, he had a female leg under each armpit.

My impression of "driven snow" melted a bit when I was presented with a choice of a room-mate or higher rent. I decided to leave. I couldn't match Mrs P's cooking but I was already eating a lot of meals at Eunice's house and they were every bit as good. If I had to fill in with my own cooking they would be even more welcome.

I thought a flat would be the answer. As there was an over-supply of housing I had the choice of three within my budget. The best was a good-sized one-bedroom apartment in *Banbury Court*, a Moffat Street block, between the shady, evergreen, oak-sized *cedrela-tuna* lined Baines and Montague Avenues.

The block was "L"-shaped with the car-parking in the elbow of the L. Each flat had its own parking bay. The main entrance was via Moffat Street, always impressive when its borders of purple flowering *jacarandas* were in bloom. Access from the car-park was by the open steel fire escape. The car-park was overlooked by balconies which gave access to the flats.

The flat was unfurnished, and I hadn't even thought about furniture so a cooker and fridge were the first essentials. I had my own bed from the *pisê* and a small bedside cabinet, but that was my lot.

A suburban housewife was advertising both a 3-plate *Fuchsware* stove and a very small *Kelvinator* fridge for £70.00, which wiped out my savings. Eunice's Dad was good enough to transport them from the Mabelreign house to my flat.

I had never come across the South African *Fuchsware* make before, but it was well designed, nicely finished and very robust. We used it trouble-free for the first 15 years of our marriage, until I sold it when I left Rhodesia to join Eunice in the UK in 1979. The *Kelvinator* behaved just as well.

Of course I needed a table and chairs, so I had a word with Mr. French, the woodwork master at my old school, Churchill. He kindly let me use the school woodwork shop at weekends, where I made a dining table and four chairs, using the common African hardwood, mukwa (muninga in the UK). For the top I used mukwa-faced blockboard, sealing the edges with mukwa veneer.

Cutlery was a pair each of cheap, *OK Bazaar*, stainless steel knives, forks and spoons supplemented by the vintage remains of a *Joseph Rodgers* Sheffield steel carving knife, valuable because it took and kept a superb edge. It dated from the days when German open razors boasted; "*Made in Germany from Sheffield steel*" The *OK Bazaar* knives resolutely defied sharpening. They had nothing to do with Sheffield.

My working hours were 8 to 4 on weekdays and 8 to 1 on Saturdays. The outdoor crews worked 8 to 5 and had the weekend free. I resented working Saturdays and did my best to fill my time with homework. So one cold Saturday morning, when I felt a need to warm up, I decided to do a bit of forge-work, I thought I could look busy by making a kitchen knife.

Percy Hulley, the boss, seemed to have a lot of paperwork to do on those mornings, as result places like the forge, in the gas welding shop, were good places to look busy working on the assumption that if the boss asked whether anyone had seen you the person would simply say, "busy in the welding shop". And indeed I was busy.

On the welding bench there was an old magneto-phone generator, the type you wound a handle to wake the operator. It was one of the originals with a bank of horseshoe magnets; identical to the one my dad had thrown away after we connected it to the door handle and I gave cousin Frances that shock. They were obsolete but police liked them for interrogating prisoners. My ex-South African Police friend assures me that they were "the best."

In his words, "We would sit him on a wooden chair, cuff each wrist to the adjacent upright and connect a lead to each pair of cuffs behind him. He would be unaware of the generator or the operator. When the suspect had difficulty with his answers, I would give a nod to the operator who would flick the handle. I only ever had to give two flicks and the suspect couldn't stop talking. It didn't hurt, left no marks, did no damage, was quick and worked every time."

Having personally experienced the muscle spasm induced by the output from one of those machines, I think the "didn't hurt" assumption was a little optimistic. Although he was speaking of the apartheid period, I am quite sure the practice hasn't been abandoned by South Africa's new Government. Most likely it would be supplemented with practices which do hurt, if only for the enjoyment of the interrogator.

I knew that those old-time magnets were made from high carbon silicon steel; it should make a fine knife. In a matter of minutes I had one off and into the forge.

In section the magnet was about 20 by 7 millimetres. Straightened out it measured 200 mm, which stretched to 230 in the forging.

As I hammered it out, it took on a pleasing scimitar shape and I decided that it was going to be too good for a kitchen knife. It took many odd hours of grinding and polishing to tidy it up. After four months of intermittent work I had the finished knife.

After hardening and tempering, I needed a hilt and handle. For the hilt I wanted brass.

"I've got some German silver." "Mr Mac" Maglashen volunteered.

"What's that?"

"A copper, iron, nickel and zinc alloy." "Mr Mac" liked to be precise, that's why some called him, "*Enos,*" (as an ex-Birmingham toolmaker had said; "'E knows everything!")

"It's like brass but harder, tougher and doesn't tarnish enough to notice; a sort of stainless brass."

"Thanks, that's great." I gratefully accepted a small sheet of 6 mm brassy material from which I hacksawed, filed, bent and polished the hilt. For the handle I used two pieces of Rhodesian teak glued together to sandwich the handle end of the blade in pre-cut recesses. The adhesive was our in-house epoxy resin known as *Knight's Sticktight* on account it was produced by Gerry Knight, a gifted chemical engineer working for the GPO.

I found Gerry intriguing. He worked from a little laboratory-come workshop doing a variety of interesting things with resins and plastics. Over 40 years later I was to meet his son, also Gerry, working for Cambridge Capacitors in Romsey. When I saw the son, I immediately thought, 'I know that man. That's Gerry, no he can't be, he's far too young.' Later I heard a call for "Gerry Knight" on the intercom.

Of course I went to introduce myself and enquire of his father. Sadly his father was terminally ill, but I was pleased to have made the contact.

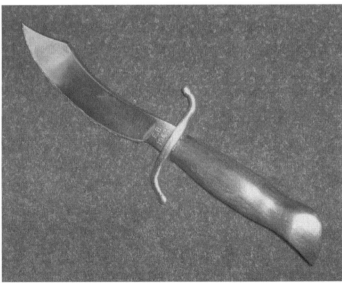

The Horse-Shoe-Magnet Knife
My photo

Chapter 28

A Near Miss and an Intruder

It was early in 1963 and we were planning to get married in February '64. In a foolish attempt to save money I had already replaced both the *Vincent* and *Vauxhall,* with a 150cc *James.* Selling the *Vincent* was a poor decision.

This *infra-dig James* transport was horribly boring and totally reliable, although one night I came close to wiping-out both that little motorcycle and myself.

Level-crossing barriers were a rarity in Rhodesia, in fact I can only remember one and I don't know if it existed in the '60s. Flashing lights were more common but most crossings simply had a signpost; it was up to you to use your eyes and decide for yourself whether or not to compete with a train for that little bit of land.

The Widdecombe Road crossing, on the way home from Eunice's, did have flashing red lights and they were very busy that night as was the train's whistle, but I could see nothing except darkness in the void beyond the bright street lights. Up the line was black; the exact colour of a goods train. Surely the giant *Garrett* steam-locomotive's headlight would be visible for miles up the line?

As a matter of fact it was visible, but shrouded from the side; suddenly I could also hear a tremendous amount of clanking and screeching steel and then I saw the light, high above my right shoulder. The mass of clanking, screeching steel was almost on top of me. Those *Garrets* are big and the threat of my elimination was very clear.

You do get a fright under those circumstances. The scream of the whistle was deafening. I know exactly how the driver felt; my own heart nearly stopped, but I wasn't angry. I bet he was. I bet he was using up his entire vocabulary of swearwords on me in an emotional mix of relief and anger. I was just very... very relieved. It was so... so close. I checked my watch; 11.30 and decided never to be near that crossing again at that time.

There was another silly mistake I made on that bike. I allowed it to run out of petrol. Again it was on the way home from Eunice's. 100 yards or so from the Braeside service station the engine stopped. I managed to coast up to a petrol pump. My problem, however, was financial. I only had a single penny.

"Fill the tank and you can have my shirt." I tried to negotiate with the attendant.

"Ikona funa hemp, a'funa scumba." He rejected my shirt and demanded my leather jacket.

"Tula eweh! Fuga one penny."(Fuck you! Put in a penny's petrol.)

"Munji oili?" This smartarse knew it was normal to mix oil in with 2-stroke petrol.

"Azikoh indowh oil, petrol kepela." (Never mind the oil, only petrol.)

Shaking his head he complied.

I had no idea how far along the remaining three miles a penny's petrol would take me, but I was prepared to walk the rest. As it transpired, I managed to nurse that little *James* all the way home.

The next morning there was absolutely no chance of co-operation from that little 2-stroke.

However, just then Keith Nortjie came by. He owed me a favour, at least he felt he did, from that early-hours incident on a previous night.

I had been in my flat for several months but knew none of the other residents apart from the German caretaker couple. Keith could be described as a chance encounter that night; anyway he was very happy about it. In fact, so happy that he not only ran me down to the nearest petrol station, he also paid for the fuel. Which pleased me, nothing had improved overnight. I was still broke.

The reason for his happiness occurred a few days before at about three in the morning. I got up for a drink of water when I heard a commotion outside. So I climbed onto the sink to look through the little window above the door. I caught a glimpse of a small white figure clad only in pyjama shorts running across the car-park.

"He's wasting his time. He'll never catch him," I muttered to myself, presuming he had been chasing a burglar. I was wrong about catching the burglar.

Just as I was climbing back into bed I heard, "Help! Help! Call the police."

I didn't have a phone, but I had an evil-looking knife. That hollow-ground, shaving-sharp mini-scimitar I had made from a horseshoe magnet. I picked it up and started for the door.

Then I had second thoughts. The police would arrive and, at best, my knife would be confiscated regardless of what happened: at worst the result would be deeply unpleasant. I put the knife back. I ran out into that bitter winter night in my lightweight summer pyjamas, armed only with enthusiasm and an overdose of adrenaline. I felt no cold; my bare feet felt no pain. I ran down the steel steps across the car park and through the dark gap between the blocks of flats in the direction I'd seen the shorts disappear.

A couple were screaming from the balcony of a nearby second-floor apartment, "Help him! Help him!"

Keith was the shorts; he was on his back in the gravel of the Montague Avenue verge. Sitting astride him was a big and well wrapped-up black man with a firm two-handed grip of Keith's throat.

Apparently Keith had brought him down with a flying rugby tackle, but the black fellow wasn't well versed in the rules of rugby and didn't know that was supposed to be game-over.

I pummelled the African about the head and particularly on the nape of his neck. He was obviously stunned and rolled off Keith. I grabbed his wrists and pinned him to the ground.

As Keith recovered he said, "I was blacking-out! I didn't hear you come! I'll get my handcuffs, I'm a policeman."

By now a group in various states of dress had gathered. One middle-aged idiot in a dressing-gown would pace about then take a swipe at the black man. "You fucking black bastard!"

"Piss off you old prick! You're only hitting my hand! Wait for the police."

Every time dressing-gown man tried to hit the burglar, his target managed to block the blow and the fist would strike my hand.

I was in danger of losing my grip.

That could have been disastrous; it transpired that the burglar had a dagger-style paper knife in his pocket.

Our captive started talking, claiming that he was only delivering papers.

"Let him go, he's the paper-boy," from dressing-gown idiot.

"With gloves on?" I queried, another swipe.

Fortunately Keith returned with a pair of handcuffs and cuffed our prisoner securely to some nearby ironwork.

Suddenly I realised it was mid-winter and freezing. The gravel beneath my feet was the sharp-edged, glass-hard, crushed-granite-and-quartz-mix of the Rhodesian stone quarries. It hurt.

Shivering, I picked my way back to my flat and sat on the side of the bath with my tender, half-numb, half-frozen feet in water; as hot as I could bear. I became aware that my right fist was swollen and as painful as it looked. I couldn't say whether it was down to dressing-gown-man or the burglar's head. But I decided to have it checked out. It was anyway time to get up.

The casualty department of the old whites and mixed-races[4] hospital was only a few hundred yards away across North Avenue. I ambled over.

The nurses always ask how you managed to hurt yourself, so I told my story.

"Oh! You're the bloke. We know all about it, Keith's fiancée works with us. She told us how they woke up to find a burglar going through their possessions, how Keith had caught him and how someone had arrived just in time."

So Keith was the name of the fellow in the pyjama shorts.

The results of the X-ray came back. "Your hand's fine, nothing broken, just bruised. You should be more careful about what you do with it."

"Yes, thank you, I'll find something better to do with it next time," picking up the hint of humour in her voice.

I was called as a witness to the Magistrates' Court for the preliminary hearing.

It was referred to the High Court. The charge was attempted murder. In Rhodesia it counted as murder only if the intent was proved. It did not need to be premeditated, just intended in the heat of the moment. In the eyes of the law the only reason to throttle someone was to kill them.

By the time it got to the High Court I had moved and was living in Johannesburg, but I was told that he was convicted and sentenced to four years. I was also told that he had a very long record and only been out of jail for a few weeks before we caught him.

---

[4] Blacks were catered for by a much larger and more modern hospital.

Chapter 29

Unemployed? Head South!

Britain's dismantling of the Federation of Rhodesia and Nyasaland was ultimately devastating for many Africans. In particular the Malawians, who were unable to return to their families in Malawi and were discriminated against by the local Shona tribe, but for me it was a favour. My employer, the GPO, was a Federal Department; come October 1963, it no longer existed.

The Mech Shop Engineer, my former boss Percy Hulley, virtually railroaded his staff into signing over to the new Rhodesian arrangement. Fortunately for me I had already requested a transfer which had been granted. Apparently the actual words I used; "I would welcome a move to any other department," was the key to getting transferred to "Tyrant" Tony Rawson's section. Rawson had a draconian reputation. I think his fearsome reputation was the deciding factor in the transfer.

As it turned out there was no problem for me in his department. I got on fine with him. He took the time to explain the new situation. He made sure that every member of his team knew exactly what they could expect if they signed over to the new Rhodesian terms compared to the position if they rejected the transfer.

In short, we could sign over and nothing would change, or we could refuse to sign and we would be entitled to all leave pay and not only our pension contributions (normally lost on resignation), but also pound for pound of those contributions. When I brought this up with my ex-boss, Hulley, he dismissed it as wishful thinking.

"Tyrant" Rawson, on the other hand, even worked out what each of his men would receive. In my case it was over £1,700, a little more than twice what I would earn the following year.

Anyone made redundant would be paid an additional one third of the total. Apparently only a very few were unnecessary employees and were *made* redundant, one being the Chief Engineer. Everyone in the lower grades were, of course, essential employees, so couldn't be made redundant.

But no job and no benefits? It was a bad time to be unemployed. Jobs were scarce and half the young men from the GPO would be looking for work. I was planning to marry in February '64.

I took the money; the wedding would have to wait. It was October1963, now I had a healthy bank balance but no income and little prospect of employment within the country. South Africa was booming.

My stay in my flat at Banbury Court hadn't turned out quite as well as I had anticipated; now without a job, I needed the cheapest accommodation available, so I moved back to the Club; this time to that very warm room above the kitchen. I also decided that I needed a car.

Most of the fellows who took the money, as I did, bought a brand new vehicle (new *Ford Cortinas* were £600.). I gave Norman Whelan £150 for his 66,000 mile *VW Beetle.*

***

As a result of a '62 holiday romance in Durban, Jimmy was engaged to Ann from Brakpan, a gold mining town on the outskirts of Johannesburg. After their marriage in November, Jimmy completed his apprenticeship and they moved to a flat in Brakpan. Jimmy had offered to accommodate me should I move south. After trying unsuccessfully for three months to get a job in Rhodesia, I took up Jimmy's offer.

In early December '63, I made the first job-seeking trip to Johannesburg. To help with the petrol expenses I replied to an advertisement from an elderly woman requesting a lift: a mistake. Needing breakfast as well as other stops, she added more than three hours to the journey. She also did her unwitting best to set the car ablaze. Being a smoker, she had flicked a butt out of the window and into the wind. It whipped back unseen into the luggage-well behind the back seat.

"Something's burning," the old girl accused.

"You're right!" I pulled over and stopped.

The cigarette had landed on a folded towel, which was now happily mouldering, just about to burst into flame.

"I'll buy you a new towel."

"Towel? Bugger the towel! Don't smoke in the car!."

She was visiting her married daughter in Johannesburg, something that didn't seem to please her son-in-law. We arrived well after dark so her daughter was kind enough to invite me to stay the night. That was something else that seemed to make the man of the house unhappy. Never mind him, I was hungry, tired and didn't relish looking for Jimmy's Brakpan flat in the dark. However, I think the husband must have selected my pillow. It felt as if I was resting my head on a bag of coals.

***

Jimmy's flat was a two bed-roomed apartment above a busy fish-and-chip shop, opposite an equally busy bus stop. Behind the block was the car-park and entrance to the flats. With accommodation at a premium I was very appreciative of Jimmy and Ann's offer to put me up.

The mines in the area were said to be almost totally worked out but there was plenty of industry. Jimmy worked in the test department of a British company called *Reyrolle*, which specialised in high voltage switchgear. In the South African and Rhodesian mines and industry *Reyrolle* products were known as the, *"Rolls Royce"* of switchgear.

I tried unsuccessfully for several jobs before I landed the one at *Reyrolle,* where I would be assembling and wiring high-voltage switchgear panels.

When I was interviewed for the *Reyrolle* job the personnel officer made a point of telling me that the company only employed blacks and whites, no-one of mixed-race worked there. I wondered why he had said that to me, and I still don't know.

Later, when I was watching a soccer game between the blacks and whites, there was such an overlap of skin colours that I couldn't always differentiate between players. South Africa was a strange place.

Reyrolle was due to close over the Christmas break so I arranged to start in the New Year.

Back in Salisbury, I used that time to pack my few possessions into the *Beetle* and co-operate with our wedding plans for the coming Easter.

On the return to Brakpan the *Beetle* developed a bearing knock, which meant an engine overhaul. This was a time-consuming but not difficult job. However, very careful use of a torque-wrench on the cylinder-head bolts was essential. I never realised how essential.

I didn't have access to a torque-wrench; until then my experience on *Fords* was "damn tight is right." But that, I would learn, was too damn tight on the *VW* head nuts.

The other thing I was soon to learn, was that the torque required on the very big, single nut securing the flywheel on a *VW* was more than could possibly be exerted with a mere two foot spanner. In practice four-foot of leverage would have worked.

The problems associated with a lack of a torque wrench wouldn't be immediately apparent but would wait for the most inconvenient time to manifest themselves.

Chapter 30

Brakpan and Gold Mines

Accommodation in 1964's South Africa was in short supply, particularly so in the Johannesburg area. Jimmy had moved from the flat to a three-bed-roomed bungalow overlooking Brakpan Lake with its well-kept surrounds. It was a big improvement over the flat above the fish-and-chip shop. I found the area very pleasant, regrettably our work-load didn't leave much time to enjoy the area.

The lake was man-made, not only the earthworks which formed the reservoir, but most of the water itself came from the enormous quantity which had to be extracted in order to work more than a mile underground.

Gold wasn't the original reason for Brakpan's existence but had grown to eclipse the old as well as nurture new enterprises, particularly in heavy engineering. All the gold-mining towns had similar dams and associated industry.

The mine was said to have become uneconomical so was on a care and maintenance basis as was its better-known neighbour, Boksburg's *ERPM* mine, which at over two and a quarter miles deep, was the deepest in the world at that time.

I found it amazing that a mere fraction of an ounce, a few grams, of gold in a tonne of rock had already justified mining to such depths. Ironically, most of the metal extracted would be shipped to the USA, where it would effectively be reburied in the depths of Fort Knox. It's a strange world in which I live.

The process of hard-rock-mining is basically excavation by explosives, hot, hard and dangerous work. All the various separation processes required the rock to be crushed to powder before the next stage, which, in the Rand mines, usually involved cyanide rather than mercury.

The area, the *Witwatersrand* (White-Water's-Ridge) was dominated by enormous man-made hills of powdered rock, slowly solidifying. The earth below was a honeycomb of tunnels. It was said that it was possible to walk underground from 25 miles east of Johannesburg to emerge 25 miles west of Johannesburg.

Various schemes were being tried to utilise or beautify these great dirty yellow dumps, from attempts to persuade grass to grow on them to the large and profitable *Nitestar Drive-In* cinema on the summit of one. The *Nitestar* was still in use in 1989.

Earth tremors were common. Local building regulations required all premises to be sufficiently reinforced to cope with this man-made earth movement.

A sudden shocking jar or series of shudders and a workmate, an old ex-mine-worker, might say, "pressure-burst."

Then the old man would reminisce, "We used to feed the rats. When they ran, we ran… in the same direction." Pressure-bursts, as suggested, were the result of the high pressure existing in the rock at those extreme depths. During a burst the "walls"[5] of the tunnel close inwards.

---

[5] mining terminology hanging/left/right/foot/wall

Sometimes it happens gradually, with creaking, cracking warning noises; the rock behaves like a lumpy liquid, shuddering and splintering, almost oozing into the man-made void. At other times the action would be violent, explosive and deadly.

The following photos were taken approximately two miles underground, in the early 1990s, by our mining engineer son, Allan. He worked in the *St. Helena* mine in Welkom, more than 100 miles south of Johannesburg. It's said to be "bad ground." I quote him:

"On the occasion that I took those photos no-one was around, but a year or so earlier a guy was working on a ladder close by the bump and got thrown off and killed by the force of the burst. A year or so later I was developing a tunnel through this same dyke when it bumped and collapsed the last 10m or so of the tunnel, much to my dismay; (fortunately it happened overnight; if it had happened during the shift I'd have lost anyone in the face and I usually had a least 2 guys on the face during the shift)".

"That tall rock mechanics officer (Wayne), shown on the supports in the one photo, was in a face when this same dyke triggered a burst. The face had burst a week earlier and one guy was killed. Wayne was investigating the scene when it popped again and he got completely buried alive. Luckily for him his hard hat ended up on top of the rubble and the crew were able to follow the lamp cable down to uncover his face and chest so he could breathe. It took them another half an hour to dig him out and he spent 3 weeks in hospital recovering. He was one lucky man."

"A few years earlier he'd been in a cage just about to go down when he got a phone call. He told the onsetter (cage attendant) to wait as he wouldn't be long but the onsetter said, "fuck you" and rang the cage away. Shortly after, while Wayne was on the phone, there was a massive explosion and he saw the end of the rope flying out the shaft. 65 men died in that cage along with another 2 workers who were trapped at the shaft bottom by all the rubble".

"They were untouched by the accident but couldn't be rescued in time".

I found it hard to imagine granite and quartz would behave like a liquid regardless of the pressure involved. But it does.

I never went underground on the Rand, my occasional visit to very small mines in Rhodesia had satisfied my curiosity.

Serious footwall failure in cross cut Footwall has punched up into the X cut that was originally 3m high x 3m wide

Footwall failure (uplift)

Rock mechanics officer standing on top of newly installed main haulage support. He is 6' 3" and standing in the cavity left by the collapse

Wayne standing in cavity left by collapse
Photos and italic script by my son Allan Boniface

Our son Allan standing in an undamaged section of haulage
***

It wasn't just the environment that was different in Johannesburg, the people, their outlook, attitudes; everything seemed foreign. It was a flat-out rat-race of a city. The fast buck was king.

In South Africa's Roman-Dutch law a verbal agreement was binding, but I never knew of a modern Johannesburger who would rely on another's word.

In Rhodesia, you could speak to a stranger and get a courteous reply, in Johannesburg you would most likely be verbally ignored, a hard suspicious stare the only response.

The ruffians we had in Rhodesia were tough enough but they were gentlemen by comparison to their Johannesburg equivalent. Crimes of headline magnitude in Rhodesia would go almost unnoticed in this city. However, as in every society, the wage-earners are not the criminals. I was accepted by my workmates, we had a common enemy in the form of the factory manager. He was a small ginger-haired despot from the north of England.

Our UK workmates assured us that he would never get away with his harsh management style in England.

When we got news of his car being blown off the road by high winds during his holiday, someone said, "I hope it wasn't trivial", we all agreed.
***

I found the South African take on firearm ownership strange. I had brought two rifles with me from Rhodesia, an ex-army .303 and a light sporting .22. To register these I had to apply to the local magistrate.

The .303 was no problem but the little .22 was the stumbling block.

"Man you sees, when Christmas comes, these okes takes the .22 and shoots sheep b'coz it don't make no noise," the magistrate explained.

"I assure you I'm not going to shoot any sheep." I replied

"Ag alright, I will give you a license, but you must promise to sell it."

I promised and I did try to sell it. It was late November when young Visser approached me. I liked the guy, a pleasantly friendly Afrikaaner, uncorrupted by the religious bigotry of many of his folk.

"Man, maar dit word 'n lekker geweer! (this is a lovely gun), maar ek moet dit eerst probeer (but I must first try it out)."

"OK." I agreed. I knew it would pass any test and whether he bought it or not it would be proof that I had tried to sell it. He returned it mid-December having decided not to buy. I didn't mind, I liked the rifle and I had done as I had promised. The magistrate should be happy and family Visser? I'm sure they had a magnificent Christmas feast of lamb and mutton. Win, win, win.

***

Reyrolle's assembly shop wasn't my dream job but it paid well enough with more than enough overtime and it had its lighter moments. One was a very unhappy draughtsman who came begging us to secretly rewire a set of panels to save him from a mistake of his.

It was tight and we had to work together but the management never found out. I must admit I always liked to work where the management weren't over knowledgeable; it's a right pain when the boss really knows everything. Quite a different situation to most cases where the bosses think they know it all.

Another time we had a slack period and being bored, someone suggested a fire drill. We had all volunteered as in-house fire-fighters. Only a couple of men had ever had any fire-fighting training and even they needed hands-on experience. What we needed was a fire to fight.

Behind the factory there was about half an acre of clear ground cluttered with scraps of wood and all sorts of debris. We soon had it piled up into a heap about the size of a domestic garage. It wouldn't take a lot of paint thinners to get it going. We used about two gallons. Within minutes there was a great cloud of black smoke rising from behind the factory. From the offices it must have looked as if the factory had a major fire.

I had coupled the flat canvas fire hose to the hydrant and was rolling it down the factory driveway when a white-faced Managing-Director came charging out of the office block, "What the hell has happened?"

"Sorry Mr. Kirschner, can't stop now," as I coupled it up to the rest of the hose which disappeared between the buildings to the fire site where Craig Wilson had a firm grip of the nozzle.

At the signal I turned the hydrant on. The flat, limp canvas pipe was suddenly alive transforming it into a four inch thick rod of fabric-covered-water; solid, sensuous and surging with masculine life.

Craig Wilson, another Rhodesian, had a firm grip of the nozzle giving instruction to everyone on how to control the nozzle against the high pressure rush of water about to arrive. He followed up by instructing us as we each took a turn on the nozzle. I was surprised by the effort required.

The relieved but still white-faced main-man was asking questions. We just carried on having fun. Might as well, we were probably in for a rollicking anyway.

We were wrong, Nat Kirschner was most impressed with our initiative and organisation, nice kind words but that was all, no bonus.

We hadn't told our foreman when we planned the fire drill, he would have stopped us, but I bet he took all the credit he could once he knew that the top man approved.

***

As expected I was missing Eunice. Once the car was on the road again, it was time for another trip to Salisbury. I took a day's unpaid leave and left on the Thursday after work. After sleeping in the car at Beit Bridge, I crossed the border as soon as it opened.

Just beyond Enkeldoorn I picked up two hitch-hikers. One was convincingly female, the other wore a dress but I wasn't sure it was female. I'll never know, I didn't ask, neither could be described as attractive.

I suppose I was a little tired, I wasn't concentrating. As I sped down and over a narrow bridge, I suddenly realised that the right-hand bend in the strips ahead was too sharp for my foot-flat speed. There was no alternative but to plough through the roadside bush. Fortunately the chest-high grass concealed nothing more than small scrub and bumpy ground.

"That was a mistake," I informed my white-faced passengers after I steered back onto the road.

They didn't reply, they probably agreed. They said absolutely nothing until I dropped them off. That was lunchtime in Salisbury. I phoned Eunice at work. Her boss overheard the call and gave her the afternoon off. The wide streets, tree-lined avenues and laid-back atmosphere of Salisbury were all very welcome after the industry, concrete and bustle of Johannesburg.

***

On the return trip the customs man queried, "Anything to declare?"

"No," I lied.

"Cigarettes?"

"I don't smoke." It felt good to tell the truth.

Under the seats in the car were as many copies of *Playboy* and similar (all banned in South Africa) as I could get hold of. The remaining voids were crammed full of cartons of cigarettes. The profit on this cargo would pay for my petrol, a better arrangement than giving lifts to old women.

The car had behaved impeccably for that trip and the following 1000 miles of city driving. The deficiencies in my engine overhaul would wait for a more inconvenient time to develop.

Meanwhile the wedding preparations were well under way. The date was fixed for 28th March, which was Easter Saturday in 1964.

I had always wanted to go to the Victoria Falls for our honeymoon, but not now. I would be driving 750 miles before the wedding, I didn't want to add another round trip of 1200 miles for the honeymoon. I was undecided on the destination; a handy motel 25 miles out of town would do.

I persuaded the company to give me unpaid leave from Thursday before Easter to Friday the following week. Leaving after work on Wednesday, I was once again sleeping at Beit Bridge; so far, so good. The problems started about 180 miles over the border, just past Fort Victoria. A slight vibration had developed into an insistent shaking, the engine began to miss and the no-charge light came on.

"Shit," what else could I say?

I limped into the sleepy little Afrikaaner enclave of Enkeldoorn and stopped to check the engine. The pulley on the crankshaft driving both the generator and fan had broken away from its centre boss.

I nursed the car to a garage. When a young mechanic came out to meet me, I showed him the immediate problem. "Have you got a spare?"

"Gott man, this is Enkeldoorn. We doesn't do mirricles."

"Can you weld it?"

"Kak man, I can never line it up. It won't be worth a shit."

"Just do the best you can. I've got to get to Salisbury. I'll worry about it there."

He refused to take payment, "It's a *cr-r-rap* job, I doesn't want no money. Good luck!"

It was after three in the afternoon when I eased the *VW* into Salisbury. I went directly to *University Motors* for a new pulley.

"We've only got an oversized one, but if you put it on you'll be able to work it in by running the engine. Just keep tightening the bolt."

I had little option. I could try the main dealers, but it was getting late, if they were out of stock I might not get one at all. Tomorrow was Good Friday, almost total shutdown in Rhodesia and the wedding was Saturday morning.

Of course the pulley only solved one problem, the flywheel was obviously still loose and the engine was misfiring badly. So early next morning, at Neville's house, the best man (Jimmy Smith) and I had the engine out. I needed a 50 mm socket spanner for that giant nut on the flywheel. I tried Wavell's brother Len, no chance, but he said, "Hickey will hire you one".

Hickey was a coloured fellow I had heard of but never met. He was still in bed when I knocked on his door that Good Friday morning. He obliged without charge, but insisted on a £5 deposit. He wanted the spanner back. I was a stranger to him.

The engine misfire was due to either a burnt valve or a cracked head, not repairable before the wedding. A three-foot pipe extension to Hickey's spanner generated enough leverage to get the flywheel nut tight enough. Thus a useable, vibration-free *Beetle* was available for the big day, but it was still too ill to use for the honeymoon.

Chapter 31

The Wedding

In the garden of the Park Lane Hotel
Photo Bernard J. McNamara

I was not at all religious. I had no preference as to which Church was involved as long as it wasn't Catholic. Neville had been married in a Catholic Cathedral. The ceremony was long, drawn-out and largely in Latin, a language which no-one there understood. I regarded it as a brainwashing process.

Everything I have since learned about the Catholic Church has reinforced that opinion, from the fact that top jobs within the Rhodesian Police were once Catholic-only[6] to Stephen Fry's statement on the BBC (QI) alleging that the age of consent to sexual activity in the Vatican is 12. Going by recent press reports it would seem this practice extended well beyond the Vatican.

Front row: Jimmy Smith, Margaret Smith, Darrell Dunwell, Diana Dunwell
Second row: Me and Eunice. Behind and between us; Ron and Sybil Cooper
Photo Bernard J. McNamara

Eunice's choice of the little Presbyterian Church in Jameson Avenue was based on looks: cute, neat and with character. That was just fine by me, as would have been the Registry Office, had she wanted that. Of course the Banns had to be read out, but as I was living 750 miles away, I managed to avoid all but one service.

I wasn't anti-religion, I simply didn't believe. As a young child I quite enjoyed the Old Testament stories read to us in kindergarten. Many years later, a Muslim from Pakistan related the same stories in order to explain his faith to me. From that I concluded that the Koran was in essence a version of the Old Testament which, in turn, was often quoted by religious bigots in Apartheid South Africa to justify their actions. Like the Israelis, and possibly the Muslims, they believed that they were the "Chosen People" and had a God-given right to "The Promised Land".

Eunice said we shouldn't see each other the day before the wedding, however there was a honeymoon to organise. Tradition would have to give.

---

[6] Chap 1 p.8 SERVING SECRETLY by Special Branch chief Ken Flower

We decided on the *Falls* after all. Eunice had never seen them and they were my favourite bit of natural beauty. It had to be *The Victoria Falls Hotel* no less. It was possibly the only viable one at the time; certainly the casinos had yet to disfigure the landscape. With hindsight the engine failure was an unforeseen bonus.

As you can imagine I was involved in a flurry of last-minute phone calls. Thankfully luck was on my side.

The Hotel had a room, which they would put on hold while I phoned *CAA*, the airline. Again we were fortunate, the demand for Easter excursions to the *Falls* had been so popular they had put on an extra flight.

Eunice at her home in Hatfield
Photo Bernard J McNamara

The wedding service was reasonably short. The minister wasn't Kennedy-Grant, Tomás's father, who had originally interviewed us. He had all but turned me down. Perhaps my attitude upset him and he didn't like Eunice's reasons for choosing his church. At least we were honest, and as the wedding party would be an assortment of religions, from casual Catholics to hard-headed Calvinists, he might have gained a few converts.

Following the service we were driven in Eunice's Mum's *Morris Oxford* to *The Park Lane Hotel* for the reception. My *Beetle* was tucked away somewhere, supposedly safe from the attentions of the likes of Jimmy Smith: a vain hope!

Thankfully the explicit impact of his artwork is not apparent in the official photos, due to the photographer's skill in placing a bright star of censoring sunlight in a strategic position.

In spite of having a very large extended family, I had lost contact with most of them so apart from Neville and Annette, there were only two cousins with their spouses present. They were Yvonne and Burmie Burmester and Evelyn and Shorty Rosser. I got on particularly well with Shorty, he always had time and showed interest in whatever was happening regardless of the recipient's age or status.

Having only basic formal schooling, Shorty's opportunity in life came with WW 2. Educational requirements were secondary when aircrew were little more than airborne cannon-fodder. Like all the South African servicemen, he was a volunteer. He became a bomber pilot; now, in 1964, he was a Captain with *CAA* (Central African Airways).

***

We drove off from *The Park Lane* in the lipstick-graffitied *VW Beetle* towing the usual train of tin cans the whole five miles to Eunice's house.

Before we left on honeymoon I asked Eunice's brother-in-law, Jim Dunwell, to take the *VW* to *University Motors* for repair while we were away. It was still covered in graffiti. I figured no-one bar me would drive it like that. Someone would clean it. We drove off in her Mum's *Morris Oxford*.

***

In the event, it was Eunice's Mum who cleaned the car. It was her lipstick they had used. Shame, she felt bad, she hadn't realised the extent of Jimmy's artistic enthusiasm. I didn't really mind; for me it was a light-hearted contribution to an otherwise rather staid occasion. Anyway the car was old. I could've driven it all the way to Johannesburg like that.

Maybe it was the subject matter of the graffiti that upset her. After all, her generation was not used to seeing a graphic full-on, life-sized sketch of a bent-over female backside-up in all its naked glory emblazoned in bright red lipstick over the front of a car. Of course the rounded slope of the *Beetle's* bonnet with raised central strip was imminently suitable for such artwork.

The plane left Sunday morning so we had booked in at the nearby *Kentucky Hotel* for our first night. The twin beds were fashionable in the '60s, but the bedside furniture was fixed to the wall. A major furniture reshuffle was necessary to improvise a double bed. We had to abandon the use of the fixed-in-position mosquito nets.

"We never needed them before, why do we need them now?" was Eunice's logic.

Eunice was right; we had only used them under exceptional circumstances in the past. The malaria-carrying mosquito, deadly scourge of the early settlers, had been all but eliminated in the populated areas. This was accomplished mostly by a system which seems to have been abandoned in modern Africa; we knew it as good housekeeping.

Water trapped in household rubbish would otherwise make ideal mosquito breeding pockets. The white-settlers' introduction of reticulated drinkable water and hygienic sewer systems helped to control malaria as well as many other diseases.

The *Kentucky Hotel* was an exception, whatever they did do, they missed a trick when it came to mosquito control. We found that out when we eventually decided on sleep, hordes of buzzing insects engulfed us. Every so often one would go quiet, as she found a feeding spot, it was unpleasant, but malaria wasn't a threat. We were too tired to care.

Reception at Park Lane Hotel
Photos Bernard J McNamara

Chapter 32

The Honeymoon

The plane was packed with holidaymakers. In the seat across the aisle someone said, "Hello."

"Oh! Hello Dennis." It was Spiro Woodhouse's younger brother. I hadn't seen any of the Woodhouses for years. I'm sure Dennis hadn't seen me since I was a child; it was a surprise that he recognised me.

A little while later the Captain spoke on the intercom, "This is Captain Rosser..."

"How about that for a coincidence, Eunice? Shorty's flying us!"

As we approached the upper reaches of Kariba, Shorty came through from the cabin.

"Come and have a look." He invited us through to the front of the *Viscount*.

After a quick description of the controls he said, "Look at the lake."

As far as we could see was a massive thick green matt of *Kariba* weed *(salvinia molesta)*.

"Hell! I didn't know it was this bad." We had all been told, but actually seeing it and knowing that it was expanding faster than it could be physically removed was thought-provoking.

"Yes, about 600 square miles; nearly a quarter of the lake's surface." Shorty informed us.

Once we were back in our seats, Shorty asked all the kids to come through to the cabin in twos and threes, lastly he invited the other adults.

As we approached the Falls, again Shorty's clear, rich, South African Cape accent came over the speakers, "We don't usually do this, but this is a special occasion."

The wing on our side dipped and the four-engined airliner made two figure-of-eight circuits over the Falls to give all the passengers a bird's-eye-view of their destination at exactly the right height for photography.

I sometimes wonder if Shorty had arranged his work schedule to suit us. Perhaps he had. It was the sort of thing he would do.

***

Transport from Livingstone Airport was by *CAA* bus. We travelled the seven miles to the Hotel in Victoria Falls Village without stops. Although the Federation was being dismantled and a custom post had been built, organisation and staffing seemed to be on a more-or-less basis. There seemed to be no objection to anyone simply walking across the border behind the building. The custom post was on the Rhodesian side.

The last-minute room wasn't the best. The best would, of course, look towards the *Falls*, with a good view of the "smoke" (spray) emerging from the surrounding woodland, but every room was within earshot of the rumbling waterfall.

Our ground floor accommodation had a fine view of a mango orchard, but it did have a better arrangement of twin beds than had been the case at the first night at the *Kentucky Hotel*. We quickly rearranged them to make a double. The mosquito nets could still be used, not that they were necessary.

It was ironic really, in the past malaria had made Victoria Falls one of the most unhealthy places in the country, but by then (1964), strictly disciplined and robust control measures had almost eliminated the mosquito population.

My photo of the Falls, Bridge and Gorge from the Viscount
Thanks to Pilot, Captain "Shorty" Rosser.

The orchard had a part-time troop of baboons. We were never bothered by these animals, they seemed afraid of getting too close to buildings, probably for good reason. Vandals of any kind wouldn't be tolerated. As baboons were classed as vermin, there were no limits as to the methods of control. They had probably learnt where trespassing would be tolerated and where it would be lethal.

That grand old Hotel had been built long before air-conditioning and although March was the tail-end of summer and the daytime temperature was still in the upper nineties (36°C+), the interior was quite comfortably cool. Obviously the architect had been skilled in designing for hot climates.

After we had settled in we walked down to the gorge. It was Eunice's first visit. For me, on this trip, I had the time and company to fully appreciate the grandeur of the place. The rain-forest wasn't as wet as it would be when the river was in flood. There was just enough misty drizzle to take the scorch out of the Zambesi Valley's heat.

That tiny rain-forest, together with a larger one on the eastern border with Mozambique, was, apparently, all that was left of the tropical rain-forest which, it was said, covered the entire country hundreds of years ago.

It was certainly busy with bird life, some I had never seen before. A giant shiny black hornbill with an enormous yellow beak was engrossed in some activity. It was obviously much too serious for him to be concerned with either us, or an excited German tourist bearing down on him with a cine camera.

Through the forest we emerged onto the knife-edge, a path along the ridge of land forming the point of the first "V" of the 8-mile downstream, zig-zag chasm. This narrow path begins just under the airliner's wingtip in the photo.

On our left was the main mile-wide 300-foot waterfall, complete with a pair of magnificent concentric full-spectrum iridescent rainbows. On our right the waters of the Zambesi swirled through rapids over 300 feet below towards that superb Victorian iron bridge.

The narrow pathway broadened out into a wider flat area to form an excellent viewing platform overlooking the boiling-pot, the deep pool of angry bubbling water at the north end of the cataract. Across the gorge in front of us was Zambia. We retraced our steps until we could cut across behind the newly-built custom post to the road.

Crossing the bridge to the Zambian side, we made our way down the steep cliff-side path to the stewing water.

I was planning to photograph Eunice with a background of the torrent tumbling into the boiling-pot. As I was getting everything organised in the viewfinder, I became aware of a very big baboon behind her, less than four feet away.

"Come towards me, slowly." I spoke quietly. There must have been something in my tone of voice, because she didn't argue, she actually did as instructed.

When she reached me she turned to look at what had my attention. We moved slowly back to give the animal space. Then we realised that he wasn't interested in us, he was engrossed with the limp body of a second baboon.

The large male was hugging and caressing the head and shoulders of the smaller, lifeless one. This wasn't the grooming or sexual behaviour so common with these creatures, this was compassion. Something I had never even heard anyone suggest amongst wild animals.

As the light faded and the day's heat cooled down to a pleasant warmth, we walked back through the shadows. Once again we by-passed the customs post.

That evening we sat on the extensive veranda to relax and take in the view.

Sunday morning we decided to go on a Falls-come-game-viewing flight. In spite of the greater agility of a small plane, the views were no better than that superb bit of viewing from the *Viscount*. Somehow we just wanted more. We simply hadn't had enough.

The game-viewing highlight was a single, big, boisterous and apparently rather happy bull elephant rollicking along; his head and all appendages swinging from side to side.

Stories of animals, particularly baboons and elephants, getting drunk on fermenting *marula* fruit were common, but this was the first time I had seen any animal behaving as if intoxicated.

Tribal Africans allow *marula* berries to ferment thus providing the base for their very potent distillate, *k'chasu;* a clear, pretty green liquid, indistinguishable by taste from brake fluid, but good for prolonged partying. The taste I know, having tasted *k'chasu* deliberately and brake fluid accidentally.

Nowadays South African shops sell delicious Irish-cream spin-off based on the *marula* distillate, it lacks even a hint of brake fluid unlike the tribesman's version.

This liquor is not to be confused with the city African's evil equivalent *skokiaan,* normally distilled from fermented maize (corn) but with extras added to the mash. Such extras could include rodents, reptiles and the favourites, carbide salts and/or *dagga* (cannabis).

Skokiaan gave rise to a local penny-whistle hit tune by the same name. It would be struck up in the township *shebeens* to warn of an imminent police raid. The Rhodesian (BSAP)[7] Police band brought it to the wider public with their recorded version. In recent years I've heard it used both in a TV ice-dancing programme and as a jingle for *ING Savings Bank*, shortly before a major banking disaster. A warning to investors perhaps?

That afternoon we were back exploring the nooks and crannies of the area. I was surprised that we found the energy to clamber up and down the gorge and walk so extensively in that heat. Somehow we didn't seem to notice and even went swimming in the evening. However we were soon in bed.

The next day, Monday, we took the train to Livingstone just to view the Falls from the rail bridge. Of course we expected it to be much the same as that from the road. The line of sight would be different and the angle of the sun was changing all the time and so the formation of rainbows in the mist was constantly, if slowly, altering. Anyway it was something we wanted. The rail trip was a to-do thing.

The railway was the original crossing, preceding the roadway by some 25 years. The bridge originally carried two rail tracks. It was designed and built when the car was nothing more than a rich man's toy in Europe and non-existent in Rhodesia. In 1930 one set of rails was removed and the bridge modified by the addition of the roadway.

By then the settlers were developing an infrastructure of all-weather roads and low-level bridges which, although submerged in the worst floods, would survive, still being serviceable as soon as the water level dropped to expose the railings at calf height.

Rhodes had wanted the trains to be within reach of the spray of the Falls and I suppose that with the river in flood it might just happen, but for us the bridge would need to be a lot closer to the cataract. As it was, I'm sure the engineers had challenge enough to build it where they did.

----

[7] *British South Africa Police.*

From the coach the picturesque view was unobstructed. It exceeded my expectations. We looked down into the swirling waters of the gorge, along the chasm to a glimpse of cascading water through a brilliantly rainbowed veil of mist. It was the shortest and most spectacular rail journey of my life.

Livingstone Station was not spectacular, and being well acquainted with the legend of David Livingstone, the tired little town offered me nothing. We started to walk back.

We had only walked a few hundred yards when a *Peugeot 404* stopped and offered us a lift. The driver was either the Station Master or the Post Master. I can't remember which.

At the smart new custom's barrier we had to stop and this time we did as required and proceeded through the approved route via the border-post's main-man's desk.

The said official was most put out that we had crossed into Zambia and only now, on the way back, were we going through the correct channels. I wondered if he ever looked outside behind the building, where tourists nonchalantly crossed the border every day, oblivious to the importance of that particular gentleman. I also wondered exactly how I was supposed to pass through his little dominion without leaving the train.

It didn't seem wise to query these points with him. I was well aware of how easy it was to confuse minor officials who have to work to a book of rules. Should one actually use his initiative, his colleagues and superiors would rather highlight his bending of the rules than accept a sensible solution. I could think of a number of suggestions for him but I felt that they might not be welcome.

I apologised for our misdemeanour and promised to obey the rules now that I was aware of their importance.

That afternoon we spent exploring more of the gorge and forest, being careful to avoid the customs man.

Early to bed.

Tuesday morning and I don't have the vocabulary to go on about the Falls, but that doesn't mean that we were satiated. It was the 31st March and Eunice's birthday, her 21st no less. We didn't do more than we had been doing. The honeymoon and the place were special enough.

Of course, as well as exploring every available path, byway, pool and set of rapids we found time to be honeymooners. This we did with great enthusiasm, delight and frequency.

***

Come Wednesday it was time to fly back. We took the CAA bus back to pick up our flight.

Livingstone's little Airport was clean, tidy and not very busy. In fact the floor was clean enough for a long-legged German blonde to spread her brown skirt on the floor, step into the centre, hitch it up around her waist, and step aside to pick up the white shorts she had dropped to the floor; so quick, amazing.

"Did you see that Eunice?"

"What?"

"Never mind."

"Never mind what?"

"It doesn't matter."

"It does now. What?"

"That woman in the brown skirt, she was wearing shorts a minute ago, she got changed right there in the middle of the floor."

"And you watched her?"

"Yes: and I saw nothing. It was amazing."

"Bad luck. Serves you right for watching."

The return trip was on the scheduled service via Kariba Village and not in the luxury of a *Viscount* but in the world's most beloved old airborne workhorse, a *Douglas DC3*, a *Dakota.*

I am also an admirer of those aircraft, but as a spectator, not as a passenger.

After a laboured take-off we flew over the lower reaches of Lake Kariba. Flying at that relatively low level was good for sightseeing, in spite of the bumpy journey reminiscent of some of Africa's worst roads. It was reassuring to see that the area of lake near the wall was free of weed.

At Kariba there was a short but uncomfortably hot wait to exchange passengers and refuel. Slowly we lumbered up to altitude, a long steady predictable climb.

The Country was peaceful, being 14 years before it became necessary for aircraft to take off with acrobatic clowning antics as an avoidance tactic from the SAM 7 (surface to air missiles) of the "freedom fighters."

In 1964, it was beyond anyone's imagination for survivors, including children, of a shot-down aircraft to be executed, not even in the name of "freedom," as would happen in 1978. Equally unbelievable would have been the triumphal crowing, in a BBC telephone interview, of Joshua N'komo, the man responsible[8].

More strange, to Rhodesians, was the gutless silence of the Callaghan Government; not even offering condolences to the families of the British nationals murdered…

We rocked and jarred our way into Salisbury shortly after dark. Sunset from the air was truly spectacular.

Early Thursday morning, I was in *University Motors'* workshop looking at the *VW's* cylinder heads. Both had cracks. I really should have used a torque wrench.

"We have a reconditioned engine you can have for seventy pounds. It's the best option."

"I don't doubt that, but when I register the car down south they'll think it's a stolen engine, you can't believe the hassle. They expect everyone to be crooked. It's normal."

"OK ,we'll grind that number off and stamp the casting with your old number."

"Fair enough, when can I have the car?"

"This afternoon."

---

[8] *Google "Viscount Down" for more information and passenger lists.*

"Thanks."

I forgot to check that the engine number had been "rectified".

***

In Johannesburg I had managed to beat the wait for accommodation by paying the past month's rent on an empty flat in the suburb of Kempton Park. Either the previous tenant had been evicted or had simply abandoned it without paying the rent. So we began our married life with an address to give to the removal company.

There was no point in dashing back too soon and it was an opportunity to see a bit more of Rhodesia. That Friday about noon we turned off at the Lundi River to visit a series of pools which were well-known for their resident hippo.

After watching the hippo wallowing about, we spent the night at the nearby Motel. Typical of white-owned businesses in tribal-trust land, everything was done on the cheap, as white proprietors could never own the land or buildings. It was basic, but clean and comfortable.

An easy stage took us across the border through the little town of Louis Trichardt into a mountainous area where we decided to spend the night at the next available accommodation, imaginatively named *The Valhalla Motel*.

The rooms were round (known locally as *rondavels*) and built in pairs; each pair linked by a common bathroom. Not only affordable, but again it was basic, clean and comfortable; fit for purpose.

We arrived at the flat shortly before the *Stuttafords* removal van delivered our few bits of furniture.

Chapter 33

'64 *Sasol*, Snow and a Horrible Death

Our married life began in Johannesburg's satellite village of Kempton Park on the ground floor of Oakleigh Heights, Oak Avenue number three. It wasn't a bad flat; one-bed-roomed and spacious. The kitchen came with a cooker, a South African requirement at the time. The lounge and bedroom were both square with an entrance hall-come-dining room. It also had an established population of cockroaches, fish-moths and related species.

Hot in summer, cold in winter, the bedroom and lounge windows were directly opposite the row of resident carports, all concrete and tarmac. I hated the place.

The car-space, which lined up with our bedroom, was used by someone dedicated to *Sasol*, South Africa's petrol-from-coal. I didn't care if it was the only viable coal-extracted-fuel in the world, I loathed *the* stinking exhaust fumes when that fellow warmed up his car at five every morning. We got a daily dose.

Eunice cured the insect problem by applying *Johnson's* Pest Wax to the parquet floors. We bought a three-piece suite, double bed and *Formica* kitchen table and chairs from the furniture shop owned by our Jewish landlord.

1964 turned out to be an eventful year in that city, but I can't say any other year would have been different. I had no intention of finding out. I soon decided that South Africa was not for me. Perhaps the work-place stress was to blame, but I think not. It could just have been the culture of violence, a way-of-life, which may have resulted from cosmopolitan inhabitants having to survive in a suspicious and hostile city.

Maybe violence was traditional, after all in the 1880s Johannesburg was mostly a camp of miners, rogues, card-sharps, crooks and whores. It was regarded by the supposedly pious people of Pretoria as a latter-day Sodom and Gomorrah.

It was also the coldest year since the Boer War, complete with snow. The year of serious sinkholes; the year of the Johannesburg Station bomb; the year I saw three work colleagues arrested for separate assaults involving weapons, and the year I realised that I had lived a very sheltered life.

The first time I saw snow was towards the end of June, Eunice couldn't remember her early years in the UK so it was also new for her.

"Isn't the snow lovely?" was her take. I could only agree for a few hours, after that I got quite surly about it.

We were up early and went driving before work just to marvel at everything covered in white. Never had Johannesburg looked so clean.

The roads were clear, still warm enough to melt the snow, driving was a pleasure.

That old car was built before VW fitted petrol gauges, instead it had a reserve tank you just switched over when the main tank petered out. I had forgotten that the car was already on reserve. Once again I was a hitch-hiker, but for the first time in snow.

Of course we were both late for work. Eunice normally walked the few hundred yards to the Standard Bank where she was a clerk.

Running out of petrol was no excuse for being late.

At *Reyrolle* it was different, the whole company played in the snow until we got too cold.

In the assembly shop we cut insoles out of thick felt and stuffed them into our shoes, then spent the rest of the day sitting around makeshift heaters.

That ginger-haired tyrant of a works manager did manage to slide the hanger-style doors open a crack and look at us, only to have his hostile stare returned with a chorus of "Shut the fucking door!"

He did as he was told, but you could sense his bad attitude. He knew he was powerless just then, we knew his turn would come, but no-one cared.

After work I tried all the shops in Kempton Park's little shopping centre looking for some sort of heating device. Eventually a pokey little place came up with a choice of two, one a very heavy and clumsy looking 2Kw model at 3 Rand and a very delicate state-of-the-art infra-red job at 11 Rand. I paid the 3 Rand for the ugly one. Two SA rand were equal to one pound sterling.

Snow in Johannesburg 1964
My photo

Just about a month later, on 24th July, I walked into the flat to be told by Eunice that a bomb had gone off in Johannesburg's main station with more than twenty casualties.

Apparently someone had left a suitcase packed with dynamite and petrol (erroneously reported as phosphorus) on the main concourse of one of Africa's biggest and busiest stations. The bomber did phone in a warning, fifteen minutes before the bomb was set to explode.

A practised, well-organised, competent police force could possibly have prevented death and injury but it would have been extremely difficult to evacuate a station that size without panic. Nobody could expect that from the South African Railway Police.

There was nothing in their instruction book about bombs in public places. The instinct in South Africa was to expect booby-traps to be aimed at the Police. They would be very careful approaching the place.

Mrs. Ethel Rhys, a 77 year-old grandmother, died later from her injuries, her pre-teen granddaughter was close to death but did survive after multiple skin grafts, and is said to have moved to London.

Although insignificant compared to the Twin-Towers' atrocity, the public anger was on a par with that horror. In my opinion the people who condone or apologise for either of these acts are as guilty as the perpetrators.

The bomber, John Frederick Harris, was hanged on April 1st 1965. He had been arrested within hours of the blast and was persuaded to confess the same day. His interrogator was said to be tough and on that day would have shared the anger of the general public.

Harris's comrade-in-crime was John Lloyd. They were already under suspicion for blowing up power line pylons as a protest against apartheid.

Lloyd was in custody when the bomb exploded and had been intensively interrogated. There can be little doubt that the intensity increased after the explosion.

He is vilified by his former friends because they believe his evidence guaranteed the hanging of Harris. Perhaps he simply told the truth. Maybe he really did feel remorse.

Going by internet pages, his former friends seem to feel that Harris was wrongly hanged.

According to their reasoning the terrible pain of the horribly burnt and broken casualties *were not really his fault* but down to the incompetence of the police.

Likewise, the traumatic, drawn-out suffering death of Mrs. Rhys was, by their reckoning, all due to the incompetence of the authorities rather than a deliberate explosion of a combination of petrol and dynamite in a very busy public place.

Some people can excuse anything.

Chapter 34

Sinkholes, Storemen and All

I was glad that the very gold-rich danger area, Carletonville, known for the sudden collapses of apparently firm ground, was to the west of Johannesburg, well away from us. Our area suffered nothing more than the occasional minor earth tremor.

Apparently, in South Africa, the sinkholes occur in dolomite areas when water-filled underground caverns are drained by mining activity. The caverns in the limestone are formed over millennia by the action of CO_2 in rainwater. When the groundwater is removed the rock becomes unstable and can collapse at any time

1964 wasn't the year of the big one, just the one which got the most publicity. The big one was in '62, when a three-storey crusher plant was swallowed up by the earth, killing 29 workers and leaving a crater 150 metres in diameter; bigger than a football field. Subsidence in South Africa can be serious.

But the headline sinkhole occurred on the night of 3rd August 1964 when three and a half houses disappeared into the earth. The sleeping Oosthuizen family of five and their servant within one dwelling awoke too late. They were heard screaming. Occupants of the other houses managed to evacuate in time.

Tragically the family, who all died, had returned early from holiday that day and it was reported that their young daughter had not wanted to sleep in the house that night. Mrs. Oosthuizen also voiced her concerns as the house had obvious signs of earth movement, but was assured by mine management that there was no danger.

No rescue attempt was made, and no bodies were recovered. The authorities decided that the danger to rescuers was too great. I found it very disturbing that part of a house's roof was visible, but volunteers were prevented from even trying a rescue.

The Macmasters had to escape through windows; their doors already blocked or jammed. The Kriels did likewise, their normal exits having dropped into the hole and the Brits family left as their house was cracking up on the edge of the collapse. One family watched their car follow the houses to obscurity.

As the estate was specifically for mine workers, the remaining inhabitants were moved by the mining company to another site into caravans, most of their servants, now jobless, had to return to their tribal homes.

***

I can't remember which employee was first to end up in trouble with the police that year. I think it was Gerry G. He used a kettle lead to put his former buddy, "Spider" Pike, into hospital; something to do with the degree of friendship between Spider and Gerry's wife.

He wasn't fired, but was so filled with remorse and shame he couldn't face his workmates. It was a pity I liked Gerry, I was really sorry to see him leave.

The next wayward one was Swanee, the assembly shop storeman. He had asked me to sharpen his knife a few days before the incident. Naturally I obliged. Why not? I had grown up with knives and other sharp tools; to me a blunt tool of any description is useless.

Anyway, Swanee had not planned on lashing out at anyone; he was with friends. They had been gambling and Swanee was in a good mood, he was on a winning streak. Eddie L. had been losing but he was cheerful; until Swanee decided to take his winnings and leave.

"I'm buggering off, you ouens can carry on."

"You can't piss off now!" Eddie protested.

"No! I'm off right now."

"Fuck you man, you've got all the cash. Give us a chance. Just one more hand."

"Fuck you too! No! "

Then came the violence. Quite suddenly Eddie had blood running down the side of his neck; the newly sharpened blade having narrowly missed his jugular.

Swanee was back at work after court on the day of the hearing. The case had been abandoned because Eddie hadn't shown up to give evidence "I'll get him my own way," was his ominous comment when he returned with his stitched-up neck.

Swanee didn't stay with us for much longer, I think Eddie's attitude got to him.

The third man to leave suddenly with a two-man escort was Fred G. Fred was the machine shop storeman, apparently he was accused of stabbing his girlfriend's husband *in the bum*.[9]

His case never got to court; it seems that when the police went to interview the victim both he and his wife were too drunk to give a statement. As in Swanee's case, the law lost interest.

These were all white employees, the blacks had more complicated lives. The black "Boss-Boy" in the machine shop used to collect a percentage off each man under him: "insurance" to keep the job.

It seems that with one operative there was a disagreement over the premium. This worker bounced the "Boss-Boy's" face against a lathe chuck. The damage was extensive because the chuck was revolving at the time.

Once the injuries were sewn up they were both reprimanded. The company didn't pay them to fight. That they could do in their own time.

I didn't know the exact situation with the "Boss-Boy's" equivalent in our shop, but I did notice that he always left late and varied the time. I think it was a very sensible precaution having heard various promises concerning his future health.

***

Swanee's place was taken by a pleasant little Afrikaaner, Wolmerans, I don't remember his first name, but his problem I will never forget. This unfortunate fellow couldn't resist the simple Afrikaans command "Gooi weg!" ("throw away!")

Regardless of who had shouted, his immediate response was to discard whatever he was holding. It was wise not to stand too close when he was drinking.

Of course, almost everyone had to have a go just to prove the story. I'm ashamed to say that I did too, but only once.

---

[9] The policeman's words

The poor man might have his arms full of small items when someone would bellow "Gooi weg" and the stores would mushroom into the air leaving a frustrated little man reluctant to pick them up in case his tormentor shouted again. Jimmy was a particular offender.

When he had to carry something the unfortunate fellow was reduced to trying to sneak past anyone who might worry him. We were told that it was shellshock. When I asked him about it he said it was the result of a car accident.

Chapter 35

A New Car and Sunburn

On Durban Beach, Eunice nearly five months pregnant (1964)
Photo by Beach Photographer "Scotty"

They only did two things when a privately imported car was registered in South Africa: check the engine number and the weight.

When University Motors in Rhodesia replaced the *VW* engine, I had anticipated a problem with registering the car in South Africa. Any variation in the engine numbers would be bound to result in aggravation.

I could visualise a messy tangle of red tape, which would have me traipsing from office to office of stony-faced and confused little apprentice Hitlers.

The garage owner, a well-spoken Englishman, laughed off my concerns.

"We'll just erase that number and replace it according to the book."

Unfortunately he hadn't followed through on that promise and I had forgotten to check. My car now contained an unofficial engine, a variation I hadn't mentioned to customs at the border. I could be working some sort of scam. At least that's what the South African authorities would expect.

However, I knew the attitude of the type of man likely to be employed in the physical checking process. Their ambitions were limited to an easy life with the occasional backhander.

I had to consider the alternatives. In the case of an expensive car, anything a bit dodgy could involve a major problem or a hefty bribe. However, with a near worthless old *VW*, any investigation would be more effort than any possible reward.

Reyrolle had the gear for the quick solution; an angle-grinder and a set of number stamps.

Within 20 minutes the engine was in full agreement with the paperwork. My attempt to give it a bit of age with a rub of a dirty thumb did nothing to make it look original, the shiny new grinding shone brightly through the dirt. If it was queried I would have to act aghast and think fast.

I need not have worried; at the checking facility the man recording engine numbers was, as I expected, paid to write down what he read. He had no difficulty in reading my nice new number, he had no interest in its history or how it got there.

Likewise the fellow on the weighbridge didn't even look at the reading. He had weighed thousands of *VW*s, they were the most popular car in the country. He knew the weight of every variation in the models. He also knew the run-around he would have if the weight was wrong. It wasn't going to happen.

Now that everything was correct I went to Kempton Park Town House to make everything absolutely legal.

So far I had resisted the temptation to spend too much of my redundancy money on a new car, but now I weakened.

In Rhodesia where the *Mark 1 Ford Cortina* at £600 was the same price as the *VW Beetle*, I would have chosen the *Ford*. In South Africa, the *Beetle* was as cheap as the *Ford Anglia*; for me, no contest; I bought a new white *VW*.

***

We soon made a weekend trip to Salisbury in our new car. I had the journey well organised. We left at midnight on Friday, to arrive at the border just as it was opening at six. Stopping at Pietersburg, Beit Bridge and Fort Victoria for petrol, we arrived in Salisbury just after noon.

What a pleasure it was, the laid-back relaxed atmosphere, the clean well-kept streets, the flowering tree-lined avenues and the quiet, tidy, spacious suburbs. I loved my hometown.

After a nap we visited friends and enjoyed the ambience of the place.

We left in the early hours of Sunday morning. After we had travelled about six miles, a fellow flagged us down. He had run out of petrol. I obligingly backtracked four miles or so to Togo's Service Station, where he very rudely and abusively knocked up the attendants.

"Very sorry baas, it is a'lockit. We hev not the key."

I'm quite sure they did have the key, but with this man's attitude there was no way they were going to serve him. In their shoes I would have done the same.

He climbed back in the car cursing every black man alive or dead. Now he was insisting on going another mile back to Macey's petrol pumps.

"They'll be closed." I knew there was no point in anything being open so early on a Sunday.

"They'd better not be. I'll wake the bastards up. They'll serve me."

As he approached the attendants' sleeping quarters, it was obvious to me that there was going to be a repeat performance of bad temper and profanity against men who would have been pleased to help him, had he simply been polite.

"Close the door Eunice."

"Are you leaving him here?"

"Yes, I've had enough of that idiot."

"He's got a long walk!"

"Good. He needs to learn to be civil, and especially when you need a favour you have to be pleasant. If we had time he would've had a much longer walk."

As the car drove off, he ran after us waving his arms. I expect he had something to say, but we couldn't hear him. I could imagine his anger. The thought pleased me.

Having got rid of that nuisance we had a good trip back.

***

Weekends in the flat could be boring so we did a lot of driving about, simply sightseeing. On one occasion, following a violent hailstorm, we drove into the densely populated flatland of Johannesburg's Hillbrow.

On the windward side of the high-rise buildings the hail had broken so many windows it was difficult to find unbroken panes. Hailstorms on the Witwatersrand are ferocious and feared, quite capable of causing serious damage to a car's bodywork. This could be directly from hailstones bigger than golf-balls or indirectly by the aggressive panic of drivers trying to get their cars under cover.

I was quite unsettled by the confinement I felt in the flat. One November Friday, at eight in the evening, I felt particularly restless.

"Are you tired Eunice?"

"No."

"Let's go to Durban."

"Alright," Eunice was always prepared to do anything new or different.

"How far is it?"

"Maybe three hundred and fifty miles."

"OK."

By the time we got to the town of Harrismith, about halfway, we were too tired to drive any further. It was well after midnight. We booked into a local hotel for a most welcome rest.

Before eleven on Saturday morning we booked into the upmarket Beach Hotel. Comfortable and luxurious it overlooked the most popular stretch of sandy beach just north of the array of seaside merchants hoping to fleece the few out-of-season heat-resistant holidaymakers. November was hot. Durban's hectic days were in the pleasant winter warmth of June and July when the central inland high plateaus could be bitterly cold.

Within half an hour we were swimming in the Indian Ocean after having our photo taken by the ever-present lens-man, Scotty.

"Pull your tummy in!" came the order.

"The man said, pull your tummy in." I smirked at my five-month-pregnant wife.

"I was talking to you, not her." Scotty put me right.

Of course he got the laughs he wanted and his shutter clicked on genuine smiles.

It was time to catch up with a bit of rest, deck chairs would do nicely, so we hired a couple and settled down in the hot but comfortable sun. We had realised that our tender un-tanned skin would be vulnerable in that sunlight. It was something you learnt early on in Africa, so we wore our tops, our legs we never considered; in Rhodesia they had had enough daily exposure to cope. In Johannesburg we had hardly been outdoors. Sunscreen was yet to be available.

That Durban sun was warm and relaxing, so easy to drift into a lovely deep sleep.

As soon as we were awake we knew that we should have covered our legs. I should have known better, as a child I'd been severely sunburnt. I guess either my memory was lacking or I must be a slow learner. True it was only the tops of our legs... But it was memorable.

Chapter 36

Back to Rhodesia

I am aware that I was biased, but I could find nothing to like about Johannesburg; had we moved further south to the Cape, it might have been different. I have always found the Eastern Cape relaxed and friendly. I craved the uncluttered space and laid-back atmosphere of Rhodesia.

We wanted to buy our own house as soon as possible, having realised that in the long run it was the cheapest thing to do, and we had looked at houses in the Kempton Park area. However, prices were escalating daily and we could get far better value in Rhodesia, which gave me another excuse to return.

So when we went up to Salisbury over the *Reyrolle* Christmas shutdown I went job hunting.

The personnel officer at the GPO was a bit pompous at first. He scanned through my work record and got quite unpleasant about a complaint involving me. The grouse concerned a female upset by a wolf-whistle, and there was me thinking that I could emit a particularly flattering whistle: lusty, long and loud.

I had to stifle my laughter and admit to a few black marks.

"You'll have to repay the redundancy payment, which you can do over time because I suppose you've spent the cash. Are you prepared to do so?"

"Well, I can pay it back in cash, but I'm not going to pay it back at all."

Apparently he wasn't listening. "If you repay the money we can offer you fifty-five pounds a month."

This time I didn't resist laughing, I'd been on eighty-five per month in 1963 when I left the Federal GPO and I had been offered two other jobs. The best was with *Reyrolle,* but in Zambia, the other, which I accepted, was with the Salisbury Electricity Department, at twenty-five pounds a week.

"Sir, you are wasting my time and your time."

Now he became far friendlier. "Well, if you reconsider, do come back."

"OK. Good bye."

The next day I was in the "mech shop" where I used to work, just talking to the fellows, when Tom Hayes approached me. Tom ran a section parallel to Percy Hulley's group in the same workshop doing the same sort of work. He probably knew more about me than Hulley did. I had noticed him checking over my work when I worked under Hulley.

"Looking for a job? Come work for me, never mind the redundancy, I'll start you as an Established Skilled Technician on a hundred-and-ten pounds a month."

It was amazing how a government department could have so many conflicting but bendable rules.

"Thanks Tom, but I've accepted a job as an electrical fitter with the council, same kind of money."

"OK, but think about it and if you change your mind come back."

Now we just had to go back to Johannesburg to pack and tidy-up. We would stay with Eunice's parents at first until we got our own accommodation.

It didn't take us much time to pack. As the removal van left the flats we pulled out and drove around to our landlord to drop off the keys.

"These are the keys to flat 3 Oakleigh Heights, we're moving out."

"When?"

"Now."

"You have to pay a month's rent in lieu of notice!"

"I paid for the month before I moved in, remember?"

"That's immaterial, you still owe us a month's rent. It's the law."

"If you don't rent the flat immediately, or get someone to pay ahead as I did, let me know and I'll pay up."

"Where's your furniture?"

"In Rhodesia."

"What's your address there?"

"I don't have one yet. Good-bye."

"Bugger you! Go! Voetsek!"

His use of the South African word, understood by all the country's dogs to mean that they weren't welcome, was most impolite.

We understood each other. I left.

Back in Salisbury I started work in the Council's Electrical Sub-Station Workshop overhauling switchgear and transformers.

The Workshop was exceptionally well-kept, the change-room toilets and showers were the cleanest I have found anywhere, absolutely spotless, a pleasure to use. Later when I worked for the ESC (Electricity Supply Commission) I discovered how bad that type of workplace could get.

It was not mentally challenging. On arrival the equipment was often caked in oily dirt. The internals could be clogged-up with acidic sludge but that was unusual. The Council's preventative maintenance was of a high standard unlike that of its country-wide cousin, the ESC.

The oil filtration plant was plumbed-in, housed in a room with an epoxy-coated floor and polished copper pipe-work, the whole kept spotless. Our boss, Steve Skelton, had a right to be proud of his little empire. He was backed up by Alfie Wright, a born Rhodesian, who remembered my dad from before World War 2.

"Was your dad in charge of the Park?"

"Yes."

"I remember him, I was with my pal, we were on our bikes having great fun riding through the flower beds and your dad caught us. He gave us such a hiding I never broke another flower in my life."

There was nothing for me to say, I had heard about the incident but I never thought I would be working directly under a man who, as a child, had taken a thrashing from my dad. I need not have been concerned, both Alfie and Steve turned out to be first class bosses.

One of the stories told by old-timers concerned two little boys playing in the original storm-water tunnel under Kingsway (now Julius Neyrere Way). Bill Nelson was one of the pair, Alfie Wright may have been the other.

Rectangular in section, the drain was big enough to cycle in, which of course kids would do. I don't know if they were on their bikes, but they were having fun.

They didn't hear the thunder; they were oblivious to the sudden storm. Within minutes they were well out of their depths and being swept along in the surge.

They only managed to clamber out after they had been washed into the flooded Makabusi River about half a mile or so downstream.

Bill laughed about it when he told me the story, but that was more than thirty years after it happened. I don't think he thought it was funny at the time.

Chapter 37

Allan and 44 Logan Road

We had never intended to stay long with Eunice's parents and accommodation in Rhodesia at the time was freely available, so we soon moved into a one-bedroomed flat.

The Roman Gardens flat was on the first floor of a seven-storey block in Second Street, between Baines and Montague Avenues. We settled in quickly. The baby was almost due so there was no point in Eunice looking for a job and she was looking forward to being a full-time mother.

Being about as anxious as any expectant father could be I wasted no time getting her to the nearby Lady Chancellor Maternity Home as soon as the labour started, about mid-night Sunday 14th March 1965.

A pain-killing injection brought the labour to a standstill. Allan wasn't born until the early hours of Tuesday 16th March 1965.

Fathers weren't allowed anywhere near the delivery ward and I couldn't simply sit and wait, so I kept going for little drives in the car. When Allan finally arrived they displayed him at arm's length and said "What a lovely little man," which was fair comment but to me he looked just like all the other babies. I wasn't allowed to touch.

I phoned Eunice's mother as requested, it was 3 am! "It's a boy, six pounds five ounces. No, we haven't decided on a name yet and Eunice is fine."

I wasn't at all worried about fatherhood. At twenty-three I was still young enough to think I knew it all. Of course I was wrong; I was only just beginning to learn about parenting. By the time I knew enough I no longer needed the knowledge.

In Rhodesia it was customary to wet the baby's head, so I took the *Sub-Station* workforce (all male) to the early-evening *sunset-strip* show at *The La Boheme* nightclub. I'm sure this was a new experience for some of the fellows and I don't think Steve Skelton was too enthusiastic. However, he was gracious and perhaps curious enough to come along.

Between leaving work at five and the show starting at six there was just enough time to achieve that happy mellow mood. Our table was on the edge of the dance-floor; ringside. Steve made the mistake of sitting next to the floor, a naïve innocent.

The stripper had three things in her favour: she was a passable dancer, she obviously had had years of experience and we were getting merrier by the minute. The highlight for us was when she insisted on sitting on Steve's lap, causing him great embarrassment.

This set the pattern for the next few celebratory drinking sessions.

***

We were still looking for the best affordable house to buy. It was a buyer's market, but mortgage repayments were pegged at a quarter of the man's earnings and just as well because more would have been very difficult to keep up.

Someone suggested I try the Land and Agricultural Bank. It was set up to finance farmers and civil servants, however it had some repossessed houses which it would sell to the general public on deed-of-sale mortgages.

With a deed-of-sale it was agreed that if the purchaser failed to pay a single month's instalment, the seller could demand that the whole debt be settled within 30 days or the buyer could be evicted.

Wise heads advised against this sort of deal, but there was no deposit to pay and the first instalment was only due at the end of the month. I liked the arrangement; since when had I listened to wise heads?

We settled on a three-bedroomed bungalow on an acre and a third in Hatfield, about halfway between the city-centre and the airport. It was just two miles from Eunice's parents, near enough, but not too near.

The soil was sandveld, lacking in plant nutrients, but clean. Something Eunice valued. In her opinion children and mud were inseparable. She had no desire to challenge the sticky, staining tenacity of the rich, red, northern-suburbs' clay.

***

It was June 1965 when 44 Logan Road became available, it had been empty for a month or two. We went round to check it over before actually moving in. Wearing flip-flops and shorts I strode in and immediately jumped out again, nearly knocking Eunice over in the process.

"What's wrong?" she demanded.

"Shit! Look at me! Bloody fleas!" Little black dots peppered my feet and legs.

"Oh damn, more Johnson's Pest Wax!"

"Not this time," I replied, "here we can use *Gamatox*." The house was empty and well away from the neighbours so there should be no complaints about fumes.

"Gamatox?"

"Don't you remember; those tablets you light?"

"Oh yes, but we won't be able to go inside!" Eunice's disappointment was obvious. "Isn't there something else?"

"Not anything as easy and nothing as good. That stuff kills everything."

"Right! and just who's going to light the *Gamatox*. The way you came out of there I don't suppose it'll be you?" There was an edge to her voice.

"Don't worry. You panic for nothing; it's easy."

"Don't worry, it's easy? Is that because you think I'm going to do it?" The edge sharpened.

"It's OK, everything will be fine. You'll survive." I didn't deny her assumption.

"You can forget that idea right now!" She was in absolute rebellion.

"You'll be fine. Trust me. I wouldn't ask you to do anything I wouldn't do myself. Remember, I've already had my turn." I had no intention of asking Eunice to do the job, but I didn't tell her.

"Yes, but you didn't stay long; I've never seen you move so fast before."

We went down to the local chemist where I bought the *Gamatox* and a tub of *Vaseline*.

"What's the *Vaseline* for?" Her tone wasn't very friendly.

"You'll see. You put it on your legs, it traps the fleas." I could feel the tension all the way back. Eunice's silence said it all.

At the house I covered my legs with a thick layer of *Vaseline.*

Having lit the *Gamatox* and locked up I checked my legs expecting to find them covered with immobilised fleas. I was most disappointed, only four.

We came back the next day to air the place.

Once we were settled in, Eunice's Dad loaned me a drawing board and squares and I drew up plans for a garage-come-workshop. I decided to make it twenty-five feet by fifteen thinking that would be as big as I would ever need; afterwards I always wished it was bigger.

Having had no building experience I relied on Eunice's Father, a plumber by trade, for guidance. He had spent a lifetime in the building industry. In Durban he branched out into house building and in Rhodesia he had built their house in his own time.

I laid out the foundations and Clement, our garden employee, made a smashing job of the trenches in the compliant Hatfield sand. The building inspector said they were the neatest trenches he had seen.

A cement mixer was too expensive, so the foundation mix of cement, sand and crushed granite (ballast didn't exist in landlocked Rhodesia) would have to be mixed by shovel; heavy work. I recruited three Malawian Africans from work to help Clement and me. It was done at the end of a long hard day.

Now the challenge of bricklaying; not so easy, but Eunice's Dad came around and got me started. After six months of weekend work it was ready to be rendered. Again I decided to learn and I did; I learned that it was a tough, difficult job, made worse by hot weather and bone dry brickwork. The bricks would suck the water from the mix, making the render too stiff, almost impossible to work. I did try spraying the walls with a hose, but the water simply disappeared. However, the job did get done.

Building the Garage
My photo
***

Once the garage was built, I used some of my remaining redundancy spoils to buy woodworking equipment and tools as I needed them. I tackled jobs as they came up as opposed to planned projects.

We had always said we would have a family of two children; planning on a two-year wait before we started a family. I'm glad to say Allan beat our plans, so we decided he needed a companion and Charlene arrived on the 22nd September 1966, followed by Allison on the 5th May 1968.

Plainly my birth control expertise was flawed so I approached our Catholic family doctor to arrange a vasectomy. Not surprisingly he was against the operation and tried to persuade me to use a timing method but, luckily, even the combination of the Catholic Church and London Rubber Co. are no match for Mother Nature; Brian arrived on the 20th March 1971.

By then I was working at Lion Match and I arranged a vasectomy through the Company doctor. Fortunately I was too late and Brian was already on the way. Having those four children was the outstanding highlight of my life.

Charlene, Brian, Allison, Allan (1971).
Photo by Stella Nova Studio

The photographer has captured each child's character especially Brian's. He never stopped having fun

Chapter 38

Granny and the Slide

Using a forked tree to bend the tubes for the slide. My photo

At that time, every slide I had ever seen was a simple straight chute, but once, in an American magazine, (National Geographic I think) there was a picture of a hump-back slide. I had to make my own version.

The slide was supported by the "A" frame of the swing, which meant that the kids would have to run around or through the arc of the swing when using the slide.

Some said my concept was dangerous, but we only had one accident requiring stitches and one broken arm; in the process the kids did learn.

I think the cause of visitor Suzanne's stitches was down to an excited child's poor judgement when he tried to run past the swing while she was in mid-swing. Allison's arm broke when she decided to jump off the swing at the maximum height. Allison was a swing enthusiast; she had to explore every possibility.

Eunice's Mum was enthralled when she saw the slide, "Oh I do like a slide." That, of course would have been as a child, well before WW 2; there wasn't much left in the London of 1948 when she emigrated.

"Well, have a go." I encouraged her, "The kids won't mind, in fact I'm sure they'll be thrilled to see Granny on the slide."

The slide ended almost at ground level, but you came down with enough momentum to simply stand up as your feet hit the soil. It wasn't so much of a knack, more a natural reaction; and for the kids it was automatic.

Allan Airborne
My Photo

The children had it down to a fine art, as could be expected. They also had their own ideas as to how to improve on my work. It involved using *Cobra* furniture wax to speed things up. That made it super slippery, fast enough for them to take off as they flew over the bump.

Granny, as always, was smartly dressed wearing a knee-length skirt, and an equally elegant top. She was the secretary in a local firm of attorneys.

Eunice was concerned that the slide might soil her Mum's outfit. "Here Mum, sit on this. It'll keep your dress clean." She handed her Mum a towel.

I don't know if being fourteen feet off the ground worried Granny. I think her difficulty was more a matter of trying to preserve her modesty at the same time as seating herself on the towel.

She didn't manage either, neither did she finish the descent standing up, but she was remarkably fast. The kids said she broke the speed record.

"Have another go Granny." I suggested.

There was no need to hear her reply; her look was definite enough. She seemed to have lost her enthusiasm for slides.

Hatfield may have been down-market but it was magic for our children.

My photo

Chapter 39

An Oil Problem

"What are you looking for?" Eunice was, and still is, very interested if I go scratching about in her kitchen; in fact even more so after that memorable night. And memorable it was; now more than forty years later, she still has a negative reaction to the two words "linseed" and "oil".

"I want to boil up some linseed oil"

"Why?"

"I'm refinishing that gunstock and the raw stuff takes too long."

"Well, use whatever you like as long as you clean it properly".

Which was very generous of her but I knew linseed oil better than she did and I knew better than to use any of her cooking utensils. I knew my wife. But I didn't know what else she might have which might be suitable.

"Don't you have anything that can be thrown away afterwards?" I asked.

"Will this do?" Eunice was holding up an empty coffee can.

I took the can. It looked OK. There was a tiny soldered-over spot on the bottom where the vacuum had been drawn. But that wouldn't be a problem, after all, any school-child, who was awake in the physics lessons, could tell you that a boiling liquid doesn't exceed the boiling-point temperature. The melting-point of solder is well above the boiling-point of any kind of oil, everyone knows that.

"Thanks, that'll be fine." I poured a cupful or so of oil into the can, placed it on the solid plate of our cooker, switched it on to high and left it to boil a bit. Eunice was elsewhere in the house.

After a while, when I went back to check the oil, there was a ring of fire around the bottom of the can. I had been wrong about the solder, it had melted. Now what to do? Clearly I needed to get that oil out of the kitchen. If I simply carried the can outside I would leave a trail of burning oil. I didn't want that.

More thought was required.

No problem. I knew what to do. The can had a tight fitting lid. I would slam the lid in to place, turn the can upside-down, the steaming vapour would escape through the little solder-hole and I would whip the whole lot just five paces outside to safety.

As it turned out there was a little problem, the little hole was too little and the tight-fitting lid wasn't tight enough.

I made the first two paces before the pressure in the can overcame the fit of the lid and the kitchen floor became a six foot circle of orange flame.

Eunice reacted immediately by knocking off the main switch and plunging the whole house into darkness, except for the kitchen. In the kitchen everything was clearly visible in the oscillating orange light, even the thick black sooty cloud which now covered the ceiling.

I needed to do something and I needed to get it right this time. In the UK you'd simply phone the Fire Brigade but this was the third world. The Municipal Fire Brigade would not respond in the area.

The part-time local Hatfield team would probably arrive while the embers were still glowing and with great enthusiasm and even more water, proceed to destroy anything that may have escaped the blaze.

I've since learnt that the black cloud of oil fumes was the perfect component for a flashover which would result in the instant ignition of the house. I didn't know that at the time.

I dashed to the bedroom and gathered an armful of bedclothes and dumped them over the burning oil. Problem solved. I was quite proud of myself. I had saved our house, surely that was good enough for a few brownie points. I looked towards Eunice, anticipating a hero's reception. I could see she wanted to say something but didn't seem to be able to find the words. From the look on her face, hero wasn't going to be one of them. I could tell.

Now that the electricity was restored I looked around the room and up at the ceiling. The black cloud had dispersed. Oily black stalactites of carbon hung from the ceiling, light fitting and pelmet. Everything had its own messy decoration of black spreadable soot.

I looked at the still wordless Eunice and concluded that I needed some fresh air. I used the car to find the air. I returned about three hours later, the kind of fresh air I needed had been some distance away.

Eunice was now standing on the serving table just finishing off the clean-up. She had also found those words. Words I never knew she was aware of. And so many!

Chapter 40

Matches, Motors and Male Pain

It didn't take long to decide that the ESC (Electricity Supply Commission) was a mistake. Moving from the Council's organisation to the ESC was like moving from a five star-hotel to the local doss-house.

Nine months after I joined I left for a much more promising job with the *Lion Match Company* as a potential manager. The plan was to learn how to make matches and simultaneously pass the South African Certificate of Competency in Engineering. Making one match is simple; making 160 million every day is not so easy.

Lion Match was a South African Company and SA law required every company using more than 1000 horsepower to have a certificated engineer on every shift. The match Company figured that as they had to have a manager, he should also be that engineer.

The certificate was basically a safety requirement. Not particularly high academically, it was extremely broad-based covering civil, mechanical and electrical engineering. Designed to establish whether the candidate actually knew what he was doing and whether he could work safely. It was notoriously difficult to pass.

I was given an office and five white heavy-cotton jackets, styled along the lines of a sports coat. I had to wear a clean jacket every day. Laundry was done in-house by full-time employees using a truly massive machine, which had probably been made by the company.

My training started in the log-yard where the eight-foot logs were stacked and kept wet by sprinklers. It was only possible to peel veneer from wet wood and both matches and, in our case the boxes, were made from veneer.

We used two types of timber: Rhodesian-grown pine for boxes and poplar imported from South Africa for the splints (matchsticks). Attempts to grow suitable poplar in Rhodesia had failed. The local climate produced a hard brittle and wasteful wood. Not that the pine wasn't wasteful, it was awful to process; our management were the only ones bloody-minded enough to use it.

The logs were fed into the billet-saw via a motorised conveyor, all at coffee-table height. The counter-balanced, five-foot diameter blade would rise throbbing through the log as the operator wound a little handle, first up then down. As the blade sank beneath the table the worker, standing in a pit waste-level to the saw-table, would reach over and push the billet over to the debarking machine.

If you were going to be a manager in *Lion Match* you had to have hands-on experience of every production process. From the company's viewpoint this approach worked very well. As a worker I always found a knowledgeable boss a hindrance if not a downright nuisance.

The billet-saw was the first machine I was going to work.

The squat, short-legged, long-armed and pleasantly ugly operator tested me with his greeting; "Mungwanani baas."(I see you)

"Mangwanani, m'rara heri."(I see you, how did you sleep?), I replied, passing his test.

"M'rara t'rara." (I slept well, and you?). His broad round Malawian face broke into a Cherie Blair grin of perfect *pre-Coco Cola* teeth. As he grinned he exhaled less than perfect breath, breath you could taste.

I jumped down into the pit, pressed the button to feed the log into position on the saw and with novice enthusiasm wound the giant blade through the log. With a feeling of satisfaction I spun that little wheel in the opposite direction. The blade dropped below the table and I was about to reach over to push the billet to the debarking machine.

"Cherie Blair's" arms were locked around me as I watched that fearsome great blade bounce back, pulsating its way through the air where my armpit would have been.

I could have kissed that beautiful, sweet-smelling, black man.

Clearly the ancient machinery was built when workers had to think for themselves.

***

November 1972, having worked my way through all the machinery and processes of match manufacture, I was now suitable to run a factory; specifically the Malawian factory.

I wouldn't be the Manager; I would be the Technical Assistant to the "Manager." The "Manager" would be a Malawian sitting behind an impressive desk. All I would have to do was make everything, plant and personnel work effectively. It would have been an interesting challenge. However, I would have been on bachelor status and our fourth child, Brian, was just eight months old. I thought about it, decided that the family came first and resigned. Apparently a rash decision but in the light of subsequent events, I believe it was a wise one.

Two months passed before I secured another job. It was with a hire-and-fire outfit which specialised in electrical machinery repair, mostly motors, generators and transformers. They didn't think my family came first; in their opinion the firm was supreme. After a year they fired me, partly because of my headstrong attitude, but mostly because they wanted to employ a former more amenable employee. Once again we had no income.

One incident which may have influenced the boss occurred when an excited and irate customer arrived with a large motor which I had recently tested and signed out.

"A hundred and twenty miles round trip and the bloody thing's up to shit!"

"You sent this out and it's out of balance. Didn't you test it? Run it up." My Irish boss was as annoyed as the customer. It took four men to manhandle the motor. I said nothing, there was no point in protesting that it was fine when it left my test department.

As they placed it on the floor, I noticed that the coupling flange had been left on the motor shaft and only three of the four bolt studs had been removed. That stray stud would cause major imbalance.

Oh yes! This thing was going to vibrate with a vengeance, but the coupling was the customer's responsibility; nothing to do with me or our firm. I would give them a little more rope.

Not mentioning the stud, I connected up and switched on. The 600 lb. motor immediately went into a slide, dragging the leads with it across the floor. The vibration was even more than I had expected.

"Switch off! For Christ sake!" Paddy McGloghlan (my boss) screamed, he was now fuming. The customer was smug-faced with a sort of told-you-so expression.

The motor was still spinning too fast to see the stud. I said quite innocently, "Are you sure there wasn't a bolt left in the coupling?"

"Of course not! Who would be that stupid?" Paddy ranted, giving me a black look.

I managed to resist telling him exactly who had, in fact, been that stupid. He would soon find out. All eyes were on the coupling as it slowed down and the stud became visible. The customer was suddenly less sure of himself but I would still have to run the motor to check it without the stud. It performed perfectly as I expected. Dynamic balancing of a machine wasn't an extra, just part of the repair service.

The client had no one to blame but himself. There were no apologies.

It was my turn to be smug but I didn't say anything; I didn't have to, my attitude said it all. Diplomacy has never been one of my faults. However, that didn't help my job prospects, especially just then.

After I was fired, the jobless situation got worse, Eunice went down with badly swollen glands in her throat; mumps. Not surprisingly I also developed a sore throat, but it didn't stop there.

I had applied for a vaguely advertised post which promised remuneration beyond anything I'd previously earned. I phoned in reply to their letter and explained the situation. They were still vague about the exact nature of the job. The manager came to our house and interviewed me in our bedroom.

There was a reason why he interviewed me in my bedroom. Everybody thinks it's a big joke when a grown man gets mumps. I assure you it isn't, but men aren't allowed to cry. Any movement, any contact below the waist, was extremely painful; not just for a few days; the swelling and discomfort lasted weeks; four of them.

I'm sure I must be the only man in the world to be offered a door-to-door insurance job while lying flat on his back with goollies the size of grapefruit. I turned the offer down. How could I sell something which I considered insincere if not an outright con.

I cannot put the degree of discomfort into words, but obviously I needed to stay as still as possible. However, the remarkably gentle but firm stabilizing effect of a pair of Eunice's (super stretch) panties, was very welcome, if limited, for my very tender grapefruit. Sod the jokes.

Chapter 41

Second Cars and the Beira Shoot

With Allan approaching his sixth birthday and due to start school, we needed a second car and it had to be cheap. I found a *Borgward Isabella* for £80. The engine was newly reconditioned to a very high standard; the drive system was good and the bodywork was sound and easily tidied up with a quick respray. Eunice stitched up a new roof-lining from balloon cloth. Unfortunately *Borgward* never designed their suspension for Africa.

It was on the school-run that the left front wheel became fully independent. Fortunately Eunice managed to use the momentum to guide the car off the tarmac onto the gravel verge, leaving a semi-circular gouge in the road.

She phoned me at Lion Match,

"The front's collapsed. Should I wait for you?"

"No! Look in the Yellow Pages for a breakdown firm. Get them to tow it home and dump it next to the garage. Do it as soon as possible. If the cops find it, it'll end up in the VID and then we've got big problems".

The Vehicle Inspection Depot (VID) was Rhodesia's answer to vehicle safety concerns and was a remarkably thorough organisation. I had visions of a prolonged and expensive experience.

That was in 1971 just after I had sold our plot at Christon Bank. Having fixed the suspension, I decided to use some of the money from the sale of the plot to trade the *Borgward* for a *VW Kombi*. Not a factory *Kombi* but a van with windows and, unusually for the time, it had sliding doors on both sides. We bought a second-hand tent for our first camping trip; most new stuff was scarce and expensive in sanction-bound Rhodesia. For our beds we simply took our mattresses.

The try-out excursion was to Gatooma, about 90 miles south-west on the Bulawayo Road; we had entered their shooting club's annual competition. They said the town had a campsite.

I can't remember if they charged us. They should have paid us; it was all but derelict. However, we found a clear patch of gravel where we pitched the tent, made a fire and had a meal.

We were feeling tired and so, early to bed.

***

"Daddy, something's biting me."

"Shut up Charlene. Go to sleep you'll wake the others."

"Ow! Me too, something's biting me."

"And me." came a chorus.

"Bloody hell! You're right." I lit a gas lantern and unzipped my sleeping bag. It was crawling with little dark red, almost black dots.

"Shit! Bloody ants!"

The next half hour was spent with wet flannels wiping ants off ourselves as well as everything else before we bundled the mattresses and children into the *Kombi*.

Finally we joined them and settled down to sleep; a jumble of mattresses and humanity.

After that, the Gatooma shoot was a day trip; and old Fred Maughan enlightened me on ant control. "Talcum powder; just cover the site with talcum powder. It gets into their joints and they can't move."

It worked very well but only if everything was dry.

Of course we got a lot better organised the next time when we went down to Beira on the Mozambique coast. Camping on the beach, we combined a seaside break with the Beira Shoot. It was the first time the three youngest had seen the sea and the first time Allan was old enough to appreciate it. Brian was only just crawling but he enjoyed everything; it was in his nature to enjoy whatever life could offer.

Although the competition was serious the highlight was the prize-giving and party. The innate hospitality of our Portuguese hosts was almost embarrassing. The wine barrels were in full flow.

They didn't believe in annual floating trophies; so there was an abundance of superb handmade trophies; all to keep. The alcohol level caused the prize allocation to flounder a bit but some Rhodesians stepped in to help and eventually the prizes were dished out to much applause.

By the time we got to the food, no-one really cared who won what. The menu was a magnificent feast of barbequed seafood, poultry and beef with all sorts of savouries and delicacies. The *vino* was so good in the balmy African evening.

Driving back to our camp the *Kombi* was producing a strange rumbling noise from the front wheels. Fearing bearing trouble I took it into a local garage where the mechanic happened to notice a box of .22 ammunition on the shelf under the dashboard. *"In Mozambique non; no can get."*

"You want? You take; no problem. Take." I gave him the 50 rounds of British target ammo. It really seemed a bit strange; with intense international sanctions imposed by Britain we had no difficulty buying British ammunition. Our shortages were more a matter of exchange control; imports had to be paid for in advance and exports went through highly devious channels. Russia is reputed to have made a fortune selling Rhodesian chrome to the USA, (this at the height of the "cold war"). At the same time Russia was arming and training terrorists to fight us.

"Obrigado, obrigado!" The mechanic was obviously pleased by my generosity; he stripped and thoroughly cleaned both front wheel bearings and brake mechanisms; checked the alignment and presented me with a remarkably small bill.

The *Kombi* was fun but even after I fitted it out as a camper it left a lot to be desired for a family of six. When some Hippo Valley Sugar shares I had bought escalated in value I sold half and decided to buy a new car.

The choice was limited to a *Citroen, Peugeot or a BMW-engined Cheetah*; all were locally built in the ex *Austin, Ford and Mercedes* plants. I didn't want to consider their stable-mates, the *Datsuns* and horrid but durable little *Renaults*. Unfortunately there was a two or three-year waiting list for any of them.

I tried a wanted advert for a *Citroen;* and a nine-month-old *DS20* came up. The asking price was as much as the owner had paid for it brand new; but I gladly paid up. We both knew that with the waiting list in his favour he could have got more.

It was by far the best and most prestigious car I would ever own; but it was no camper.

I needed a camping trailer. Next project.

The *Citroen DS 20*
My photo 1972

Chapter 42

Sanction Busting

In the past I had never been successful in getting a job through an employment agency but I had to knock on every door. This time it worked. The agency couldn't give details of the job except that it involved sanction busting and that I would be forbidden to speak about it off-site. They gave me an address of an office.

There I had to fill in a long and comprehensive application form in the presence of a personnel officer. "We'll let you know in the next few days", were his parting words.

***

"Yes, you have a job. Catch the bus outside the Jameson Hotel at six tomorrow morning. Report to the electrical assembly shop," a phone call informed me. The bus's destination was not mentioned but it would return everyone to the same place in the evening at about seven.

I didn't read the terms of employment; I had a job; I knew the pay; that was enough. The waiting group of passengers varied from the reasonably neat and clean, wearing shirts, shorts or jeans to a group of dirty vests and jeans containing similarly unwashed humanity. They were back-packers; mostly Germans, Aussies and Scotsmen. Some wore those everlasting products of African township industry, impossible-to-wear-out car-tyre sandals.

Later, on-site, I met other, more civilised Germans, seconded from *Mann* and *Siemens,* who were, respectively, the diesel engine and electrical equipment suppliers.

The bus was a 56-seater and nearly full. Surveying my fellow workers through the haze of tobacco smoke, I thought, 'Hell I won't be long in this job.'

It was only when we disembarked at Norton 26 miles out on the Bulawayo Road that I discovered that the factory built diesel-electric locomotives. These were state-of-the-art, with electronic engine management control; totally mind-boggling for the old-guard senior Rhodesian Railways personnel, both in maintenance and administration.

The operators and technicians would need specialized knowledge. Rhodesian Railways made no training provision for either. Not surprising that none of the 36 DE 5 locos were fully utilized and therefore branded a failure just because stubborn old men didn't want to finance training or strain their brains.

With the rest of the country busting a gut to beat sanctions the Railways seemed to think that they were some kind of sacred cow. At the time I joined *PDC* nobody foresaw the ignorant obduracy of the Railways' technical management as a serious problem.

PDC, (Penhalonga Development Corporation) was a name invented as a sanctions-busting cover. *Rio Tinto Zinc* would have been a bit of a give-away.

Our factory employees, who went to the German manufacturer of the prototype model, DE 1500, had their film and photographs confiscated by that factory's management.

That was because it was feared there might be something in the background to indicate that the plant was actually manufacturing NATO tanks. It was the early 1970s and Germany was forbidden to make armaments.

Today, with the exception of sniper rifles, Britain's small arms are made in Germany; the superbly accurate sniper weapons are made in Portsmouth by *Accuracy International.*

Initially I was employed assembling and wiring components. Fortunately a vacancy occurred in the test section and I was offered the job which I gladly accepted. In the assembly shop we built and wired the various modules which we then fitted onto the frames. The frames and bogies were built on site; the cabs partly on site and partly by a local company, *Morewear Industries.*

In the Test Section the circuitry was checked and tested before we connected up to a load tank and made sure the unit delivered its specified 2000 BHP. All the procedures and data were laid out precisely; in German. Likewise the drawing symbols and codes were foreign to us.

When I started in Test, the four Rhodesians in the section worked under German *Siemens* engineers who were supposed to get the project up and running. They preferred to talk in German and give orders but not explanations. Of course they slagged us off. In truth there was a notable lack of co-operation from these men.

Factory's Mechanical Engineer having fun
Photo supplied by factory (PDC) in 1975

Richard Walton, Prime Minister Ian Smith and Ben Adelsky
Locomotive Factory Norton, Rhodesia (Paint Shed in background)

Prime Minister Ian Smith Exiting Loco
Factory supplied photos (1975)

One rumour claimed that, should Rhodesia be unable to fulfil the contract, *Rio Tinto* would build a facility in South Africa to enable *Siemens* to complete the order. This may or may not have been true, but there was little doubt that when it came to final testing and commissioning the Germans dominated the process.

Personally I think their attitude was a mixture of egotism and job-preservation, after all, for these men, Rhodesia was a holiday-in-the-sun.

Our General Manager was Peter Sacchi. Peter's father, Gino, had been a draughtsman for Bleriot, the first man to fly the Channel. In 1917 Gino settled in Rhodesia. In 1921 he designed and built a man-powered aircraft with the intention of using it on his farm. The extract at the end of this chapter is from a *Shell Oil* publication and is more informative.

Peter was smart enough to cope with that kind of Germanic arrogance.

His response was to employ Richard Walton. Analytical, practical, academically well qualified and experienced in both electronics and heavy current engineering, Richard was the ideal man for the job. I knew Richard from school; I didn't know he was going to turn out to be so clever.

Richard joined the team, watched the Germans, asked questions and mostly got fobbed off with vague answers. Eng. Winkenbok (the top German) and Albert Emerling were exceptions, keen to respond to intelligent questions.

Without knowledge of German, Richard never-the-less worked late into the night at home over the next few weeks to produce English translations. He then informed those Germans that they were no longer required. Their Rhodesian holiday was over. Winkenbok, Albert Emerling and Albert's alcoholic colleague remained.

The time to test a completed DE 5 was worked down from five or six weeks to ten days. It's true that production faults were reduced dramatically, largely because all departments could now communicate easily in English.

While I was working there I applied to the Institute of Electrical Engineers for technician membership on the strength of a C & G pass at Full Technician level (at the time equivalent to the HNC.) I was interviewed by the controlling board. I recognised one member from past experience. I had been unimpressed then. Now he seemed to want to make his mark.

This Glaswegian (by his accent) hadn't read the same conditions of membership as I had. He was insisting that I would have to write a detailed thesis based on the work I was doing.

I had come across this character when I was in my final term at school. He was standing in for our normal woodwork master who was on long leave.[10]

Anyway, during our final practical exam, this character, as one of the invigilators, made his way round to the working drawings of everyone's exam paper and surreptitiously marked an obscure detail with a cross. That detail was designed to be missed by the less capable. It was a small hump on a tenon; a joint made without it would lose marks.

---

[10] In Rhodesia it was normal for teachers to accumulate enough leave and then take an entire term off.

Naturally no one was caught out by that detail, but when the results (marked in the UK) came out, the whole class had obviously been marked down a grade. I had already picked up on the trap and didn't need that idiot's help; instead of a first class distinction I only managed a second. It was the only distinction in our class. I wondered how his place on a board of engineers could be justified.

A week later a letter arrived informing me that my membership was approved and the thesis was not necessary. I never met the Glaswegian again.

The country was experiencing a year-and-a-half of drought. In the hot, dry weather, the inside of a loco on test (our workspace) would reach 60° C.

Between tests we cleaned out and refilled the load-test water tanks. They were just deep enough to have a little swim. To cool down we would jump into the cool clean water before the next load test. Fortunately, our test section was away from the workshop and obscured from the offices by the paint shed.

Regrettably, the next test would heat the water, sometimes to near boiling point, so our recreation was rather restricted; amazingly, once cool, pond skater beetles and other water creatures would appear. This was baffling because the surrounding area was totally dry for miles.

***

The following describes Sacchi's flying machine.

PRIZE of thousands of dollars awaits the first person to fly a man-powered machine over a half-mile, figure-of-eight course. Many have tried, few have even got off the ground. A Rhodesian almost accomplished the feat way back in 1921, but there was no prize then, nor was he after money. He simply wanted to survey his farm from the air.

Gino Sacchi came to the country in 1917 and settled at Makwiro, 80 kilometres from Salisbury. No ordinary immigrant, he had lived with fame at his fingertips as draughtsman for Bleriot, first man to fly the English Channel.

In 1921 Sacchi designed and built a 'sky-bike', in which he planned to fly around the farm. It was made from bamboo, canvas, steel wire and aluminium at a cost of under $30,00. The pilot sat facing the rear, providing power by pedal, chain and aluminium shaft.

At the very first attempt Sacchi actually got the craft aloft and kept it there for several moments. Exhausted, he next asked his faithful servant Masumo to make an attempt. Frantically though he pedalled Masumo only succeeded in crashing headlong into the bush.

There is no record of any further attempt, but Sacchi must still rank almost certainly as the first airman to get off the ground in a man-powered machine. Unfortunately the record cannot be officially claimed because there were no official witnesses!

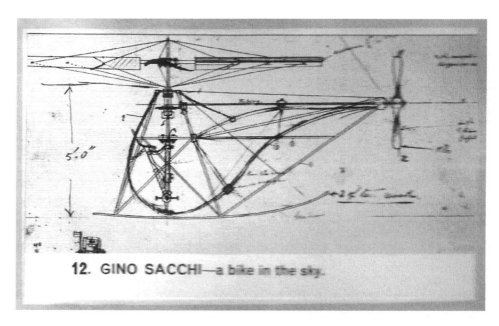

12. GINO SACCHI—a bike in the sky.

The Gino Sacchi man-powered flying Machine
(extract from a Shell Oil Publication)

Chapter 43

Camping: Army Sponsored

Politically the country was changing. Mikhail Kalashnikov's little designer-gem-of-death was being filtered into Rhodesia. The AK 47 had already established M'butu in the Congo and Idi Amin in Uganda as wealthy tyrants and now it was wreaking havoc in Angola and Mozambique.

In Rhodesia some remote farms, being soft targets, had been attacked and the occupants murdered. However, after the farmers armed themselves and returned fire, the preferred weapon of the "freedom-fighter" became what is now called an IED. In Rhodesia they usually took the form of a Russian anti-tank mine, powerful enough to instantly dismantle the family car or whichever vehicle happened to trigger it.

In a country twice the size of Britain and with a population less than that of Scotland, it was easy to secretly bury something in a dirt road. Sometimes, boosted by placing a 50kg bag of ammonium nitrate fertilizer under the mine, they were devastating. The fertilizer bag would be sliced open and a cup or two of diesel fuel poured over the contents; this combination was more powerful than its equivalent weight of dynamite.

Later, effective mine detection vehicles were developed. In the meantime some army personnel used their initiative. I heard stories of enemy captives being tied to the front of vehicles to indicate where mines were buried. Other defensive measures included booby trapping the weaponry in arms caches. The men placing the mine would get a "surprise" when the fuse was inserted.

Sometimes the rifles were sabotaged to self-destruct when fired and there was a little trick with the hand grenades. Let me explain. The Russians supplied two types of these. One was a normal type with a time delay which allowed it to be thrown clear, the other was instantaneous, for use in booby traps. These were identical apart from the lever-retaining-pin-rings.

The instantaneous grenade-pin had a bumpy ring. By swapping the rings in an arms cache anyone disturbing an enemy booby trap would have a chance to survive. Of course a "freedom fighter" throwing a doctored grenade would have an immediate problem, usually described in Rhodesian army slang as a "headache."

In 1973 more manpower was required, so older generation reservists were called up. I found myself spending four weeks in a platoon guarding a witchdoctor, officially known as a spirit medium. It was feared that he was likely to be kidnapped and used to influence his followers against the Rhodesian Government. It would be difficult to find a job further removed from my Air Force reserve job of armourer or the various skills of my companions.

Our refresher training had been, at best, scant. A day on the range with the SLR (7.62mm self-loading rifle) and the LMG (light machine gun), both new to us having been introduced after we thought our soldier-playing days were over.

The powers-that-be thought it more important to teach us their way to drive than to develop firearm skills. They spent a week trying.

We could already drive… our way. The main difference was in the amount of paperwork involved, the red tape.

We didn't give a damn about their office procedures, besides it was said that the cab of a vehicle was the most dangerous place to be in an ambush. Not many wanted to be a driver. I certainly didn't.

Having been given the order that we *would* pass, the instructor gritted his teeth as he handed out the official permits to drive military vehicles. We had never taken him seriously and he didn't like us.

At the village we relieved a platoon of coloured[11] national servicemen. The tribesmen were obviously pleased to see that whites had replaced that group. Apart from general mistrust and lack of confidence in their ability, there had been a couple of incidents. The Africans regarded these as serious and highly offensive crimes rather than simple, unthinking misdemeanours or mistakes.

The first involved the store of thatch, laboriously gathered from the drought-stricken land to repair the huts before the hoped-for rainy season. One night the coloureds had found it necessary to use a flare. It landed fairly and squarely in the thatch. Eighteen months without rain meant it was impossible to replenish the contents.

The second incident was the work of a night picket who challenged a white "shirt" walking towards him.

"Hima! Hima!" The "shirt," ignored the order to halt and kept coming. The guard fired and a white-breasted donkey died.

"At least his aim was good," was a remark I heard. "For the thatch as well," someone added.

Another thing the locals found deeply upsetting was the open funnel-shaped urinal these characters had installed in the middle of the village clearing. Apparently they were afraid to leave the village confines alone, day or night. It was the first thing we tore out. All traces of the offending device were obliterated.

From our point of view we couldn't complain, the coloureds had excavated a new latrine for us. We could only improve their shower by replacing their twenty litre oil drum and tap with a "proper" shower drum equipped with a spray-head. The mechanics remained the same, a long bough supported on a forked branch allowed it to pivot to ground level for filling. A large boulder was used to counterweight the drum to keep it overhead. The arrangement was in the open, totally without any attempt at privacy. No one seemed to mind.

We had a small water-tanker, our water supply, which we trailed behind the *Landrover* twenty-six miles to the operations centre at Sipolilo for filling. We also filled two 44 gallon oil-drums for the villagers' water supply. Their usual water supply, a nearby stream, was now a bone-dry rocky gully.

---

[11] In Rhodesia and South Africa this was the acceptable term for people of mixed-race. A coloured would be offended if you referred to him as "African".

The rains broke with great enthusiasm while we were there. Our tents were better protection than the unprepared huts. The rocky stream-bed separating us from civilization became a thigh-deep torrent. To cross it in a *Landrover* would require the removal of both the fanbelt (to stop water splashing onto the coil and plugs) and the doors. However, in this case, the doors had long since been disposed of. Most operational military vehicles were doorless; simply to enable the driver to escape if the vehicle was immobilised in an ambush. No passengers were allowed in the cab.

Our camp was at the verge of the escarpment where the 4000 ft. highveld plateau began to descend to the 2000 ft. lowveld valley. The deluge of rainwater drained away within an hour or so. It left the surface of the sandy soil glistening with specks of mica or vermiculite, as if sprinkled with Christmas glitter.

Chapter 44

The Camper and a Handsome Old Gun

Back in civilization, what a pleasure to soak in a hot bath and ease the grit, mica particles and debris from newly discovered body cracks and crevices.

At the Norton loco factory we were well on top of the job, although down to three in the section. Time dragged a bit between tests. I showed Dave D'Eath how to peel prickly pears picked from a nearby plant and discovered a common interest in firearms with Albert Emerling.

Albert wanted a pistol; sanctions and fear of attack had created a shortage. People totally ignorant of weapons were carrying them. I often caused offence when I suggested that they were a danger unless they were prepared to put in the time to become proficient. Albert was a German and knowledgeable about guns.

As it happened I knew of an old, but superb, revolver. In the obsolete *.455 Webley* calibre and almost certainly made by *Webley*, but engraved with the supplier's name "*Coggeswell and Harrison*," as well as tasteful decoration, it was a handsome piece. Brought into the country in the late 1800s and handed down in Denis Beatty's family, it had never been registered. A dismissive wave of his hand told me what Albert thought of paperwork.

Ammunition was more of a problem, unobtainable new and likely to be unreliable second hand. Albert decided to make his own. I offered to make the powder.

"Flowers of sulphur and potassium nitrate?" the chemist raised his eyebrows.

"Ja, I've got some mildew on the roses. Sulphur will sort that."

"And the nitrate?"

"Oh! That's for my biltong. I always put a bit in with the salt. That way it never goes off; even in damp weather."

"That'll be a dollar twenty-five."

"Thanks."

The charcoal I ground to a fine powder through wire gauze and sieved the three constituents through an old nylon stocking before mixing them into the dark grey powder. Of course I couldn't match factory-made black powder, but I knew it would work.

Albert used a lathe to turn the cases out of solid brass bar. Drilling the primer hole off-centre allowed him to use little starter pistol blanks as primers and filled the first one with my home-made powder. Yes it worked, but so much smoke and even more mess. The old revolver might have been made for black powder, but Albert realised it would need intensive cleaning to protect his pride and joy unless modern non-corrosive powders were used.

Mike Hooke, one of the fitters, came up with an idea. He had some bolt gun cartridges, designed to shoot bolts into concrete, why not take the powder from them?

I now know that the contents of one would have been too much, I used two; much too much.

The target was a 4x4 inch plank of pine. The bullet from the home-made powder was only embedded flush with the surface: not a lot of power there. I was watching the target, expecting the new load to bury the bullet well into the wood, but no, still just the depth of the bullet.

"Oh shit Albert, that's not much good."

"*Look at the gun!*" A highly agitated Albert screamed.

"Shit! Bloody Hell! I'm sorry," was all I could say as I looked at the bedraggled tatters of what had been such a fine example of an English gunsmith's art. The bridge was missing and two chambers had been blown completely away.

Once the excitement had died down Albert stopped muttering and started thinking; he reckoned it could be repaired. It took some quality steel, careful machining, high-tech welding and hand-fitting for Albert to manage a first-class refurbishment. Unfortunately it had lost all its collectable value, but it should have worked. I never found out; I had nothing more to do with it.

***

Having disposed of the *Kombi,* I had started to build a camping-trailer. My specification was simple: big enough for me to stand and stretch, a waterproof covering and a dry floor.

Someone gave me springs, Bob Flood, a Scouser from work, donated stub-axles and wheels and the loco factory supplied various small but useful items; regrettably I had to buy the rest. Fortunately, steel sections and whatever else I needed were Rhodesian-made and available in spite of sanctions.

When opened out, the result had a 12x15 foot off-ground footprint with a 6x15 foot extension canopy over the ground. The only external guy ropes were on the canopy. The walls and roof I braced with internal diagonal ropes to form a self-supporting structure. A local canvas goods manufacturer tailored a fine, neatly fitting tent. Of course, the trailer interior needed final tidying up, but it was serviceable; now we could camp in comfort.

The photo was taken at Kyle Dam on the Mtilikwe River in the southern lowveld. We had been to the Triangle Sugar Estate's annual small-bore shooting competition and extended the break to a tour of the region. This included the Zimbabwe Ruins and would have covered Gona-Re-Zu game reserve; one of the best in Africa.

Unfortunately, the authorities restricted entry to four-wheel-drive vehicles. We were only allowed as far as a viewpoint on the north bank of the Lundi River.

"Are those hippo Dad?" On the far bank across three or four hundred yards of water were some large dark grey rounded shapes.

"No! Too bloody big. They're boulders, just rocks."

"I think they're hippo." Eunice likes to argue.

"Right, I'll get the scope. You'll see." I went to set up the target spotting telescope.

"Dad; your rocks are moving!" That would be Charlene, she has a way with words.

I managed to set the scope up just in time to focus on the biggest hippo I've ever seen disappear into the water.

The Camper in Use
My photo

***

Driving through the neighbouring Hippo Valley Sugar and Citrus Estate, the molasses paved roads were calf-deep in oranges and grapefruit. It seemed to go on for miles, like squelching orange snow. Tractors were grubbing up citrus trees.

Was there something wrong with the fruit? Absolutely not, those sweet ripe oranges and superb juicy grapefruit were perfect. An undercover reporter by the name of Nicholson had got a job with the company and exposed their sanction-busting arrangements. Without their markets, citrus was uneconomical to produce so the plantations were uprooted; another nail in Rhodesia's coffin.

Thanks Nicholson.

We toured the sugar mill; the children and Eunice always speak of an enormous pile of sugar being piled even higher by a bulldozer. I have to smile when I recall the boast on the sugar-packets; *untouched by hand*.

At Great Zimbabwe, (the ruins), we wondered about who and why. Certainly there was plenty of evidence of gold trading, but why walls sixteen feet thick? Just who did "they" want to keep out? Alternatively, who needed to be kept in? What was apparent was that the original builders were not the final occupiers. The build quality showed variation over time from a very high standard to shoddy.

No mortar at all was used in the build. Years later when Charlene mentioned that at school in the UK the teacher derided her but did manage an apology the next day. The teacher would learn; Charlene doesn't get things wrong.

Not that Charlene's a know-all, she simply keeps quiet when she isn't certain and of course she has accidents. On that trip she managed to get a thorn embedded in her eyeball just on the edge of the pupil at about 5 o'clock. The nearest medical help was at the *Hippo Valley Sugar Estate's* clinic.

It was a public holiday but a young doctor was available.

"I'll have to take you over to the African clinic, we don't have the right gear here."

We followed him over to a spotless, superbly equipped mini-hospital.

The doctor was most impressed with this little six-year-old who accepted the next hour of discomfort without a murmur.

"I've managed to get it out, she should be fine, but when you get back to Salisbury, take her to an eye specialist to make sure. I'll give you a letter for him."

"Thank you so much, what do we owe you?"

"My pleasure; there's no charge; compliments of the company; we're part of *Anglo-American*."

Chapter 45

Very Sad News

There was very bad news waiting for us when we got home. In response to pains in his chest, Eunice's dad had been referred to a cardiac specialist. It seems he was given some sort of stress test. Perhaps it was because Ron Cooper was a man who wouldn't give in easily, perhaps it was just bad luck, but that great, cheerful, healthy, Londoner who had waltzed in for a heart check-up, didn't make it out. He was 71.

Eunice's sister, Diana, had driven her Dad in to hospital on account of the likelihood of his battered old truck being stopped in a random roadworthy test, which it may or may not have passed. She waited patiently for two hours for her Dad to emerge. Eventually she went looking for him only to be told that the test hadn't gone to plan and he had passed away.

The funeral was quiet and dignified, attended by a stunned gathering of family and friends.

As with every death there was a lot to go through and tidy-up. He had made the mistake of appointing the bank as executor. This meant that the family, in particular Eunice's brother John, did all the work required, for which the bank charged the estate as well as their usual percentage.

My contribution was to fix the gearbox on his *Vauxhall Velox,* the second gear was missing; Eunice volunteered me to find it. I was glad when her brother John came round to give me a hand under the car. Once out of the car I worked out a cheap fix with a couple of spacers. Not guaranteed, but sound enough for the time being.

"Will it last?" her Mum asked of me.

"Cross your fingers and sell it," was my advice.

***

As the security situation intensified the call-ups of the civilian population became more frequent and, for school leavers, longer. At one stage the initial period had grown from four and a-half- months to three years. As an older reservist, my once-a-year four-week spell had multiplied to twice-a-year four or five weeks of compulsory camping.

My early winter call-up in March 1974 was in Mukumvura, the point where the borders of Zambia, Mozambique and Rhodesia meet. Just across the border in Mozambique was Tete, the oldest European colonial town in Africa, established by the Portuguese more than 400 years ago.

I say European colonials because incoming Africans were also technically colonials, having displaced the native stone-age San and Koi (Bushmen) during the same time-frame as the Europeans had arrived.

Because the San had no conception of animal ownership or plant cultivation they gathered the crops and hunted the domestic stock. Both black and white farmers took a dim view of this, regarding the Bushmen as vermin to be hunted down and killed.

They were driven into the Kalahari Desert of Namibia and Botswana where their few descendants live to-day; very definitely as second-class citizens.

Mukumvura camp was large and well-established; having been originally built and occupied by a sizeable contingent of South African Police who had subsequently decided to abandon us and withdraw to their own country.

Even though they were always busy, the ablutions were more than adequate. There was never a queue for the bubbling pit of the twenty-metre communal latrine block or the pack of forty or fifty open-air showers. The showers' waist-high hessian barrier had sagged a bit, but would be an adequate screen from any roving eye below knee-level.

Most of the ground had been churned into a fine dusty sand-pit by hundreds of feet and the odd vehicle. The previous occupants had thoughtfully laid the tent floors with polystyrene packing. It was a by-product of the anti-personnel-minefield and did contribute to our comfort. The local frog population also approved of the hollows in the packing. Of course, where frogs are plentiful you can expect snakes. I suppose they must have kept their presence below the surface where the frogs were.

For the first time in my life it was on that camp that I saw a snake eating a frog but it wasn't in a tent. I wandered over to a group engrossed in something under one of the water trailers. There, a frog was head-first, half-way into the grossly distended mouth of some kind of snake. If anyone got too close the little act would freeze; even the frog stopped kicking.

Strangely, the next time I witnessed a re-enactment of such an engrossing bit of nature was some thirty-five years later in my back garden in Bassett, Southampton.

Our task at Mukumvura was to guard the engineers while they laid the mines, however, there was a slight glitch; there were no mines. The supply had run out. Initially we did little bar ride alongside the minefield in trucks while the army thought of what to do with us. It wasn't comfortable but it wasn't bad.

The floors of the lorries were covered with two layers of sandbags topped off with thick conveyer-belting, (improvised anti-IED protection). We could only hope that if required it would work. That, I believe, was possible provided the anti-tank mine wasn't boosted with a 50 kg bag of fertilizer.

There was a bird, an eagle, so graceful and elegant in the air he would glide silently above, following us with no more than an occasional slight twitch of his wings to keep track of our route. His easy effortless flight was in refined contrast to the ugly festoon of vultures on the dead trees at the end of the minefield. They waited there for the next unfortunate animal to wander in to die. A headless carcass of a hyena lay untouched for three days before the vultures started to feed on it. We could only guess that they were so well satisfied that they were getting fussy.

It was said that they could land on the anti-personnel mines softly enough to be safe, but after feeding their clumsy hopping take-off attempts could prove fatal.

The dehydrated remains of eight or nine cows occupied one patch in the danger zone. The fence on the Mozambique side had been cut and the cattle had been driven into the minefield in an attempted crossing one night. The next morning's patrol had the unpleasant task of shooting the distressed and suffering animals.

After a few days, it was decided that we could be occupied guarding the engineers while they repaired the fence on the far side. It was in that situation that I realised what a difficult decision it would be to pull a trigger on another man. It was the closest I've ever been to shooting anyone.

About ten of us had dispersed into the bush alongside the minefield while the engineers cleared an access path to the other side and were busy repairing that fence. I had found a tiny bit of shade under the gaunt remains of an *agent-orange-*devastated mopani tree and settled down to wait for another day to pass me by.

The bush bordering the mines had been sprayed with America's favourite herbicide forming a corridor of dead and half-dead vegetation. How successful it was in hindering illegal border-crossings is debatable but it must have confused the hell out of the wildlife.

Those superb craftsmen, the weaver-birds, would have had a torrid time trying to satisfy their finicky mates with hedgehog-like nests of stiff, prickly grass-sticks; a major down-grade from their usual fluid masterpieces. It was said that even with pliable green grass, the female would tear the first efforts apart until the nest was to her liking. I felt sorry for them in their present predicament.

Of the trees, the baobabs were the most spectacular losers. These massive age-old grey sentinels of the bush turned pink and could be blown over by the wind. One was lying on its side hundreds of yards from the sprayed area.

Most of us had not had recent modern army training, but we knew how to wait. It was remarkably quiet; even the fence repair was being done in silence. In an almost uninhabited, no-go area, the few locals wouldn't wander off into the bush without contacting the army beforehand. Anyone else was enemy. We were told that a Cuban "advisor" had taught them how to clear a path through the mines. We were expected to shoot on sight: *but he had better be carrying an AK*, was the *Catch 22*.

"Hima hima," I recognised the voice of our amateur sergeant; a geologist in civilian life and a photographer in the Air Force, now conscripted to play soldiers with real bullets.

I was jerked from the anaesthesia of my day-dreams by the shouting. The geologist was on my left, running diagonally away from me but towards my line-of-fire. About eighty yards away a pair of olive-green shorts and off-white shirt was about to disappear into the far bush. My sights were on him, suddenly I didn't want to shoot, but I was going to and I would have hit him, my shooting at the time was too good to miss.

"Don't shoot, don't shoot for Christ's sake," the scream came from a fellow who thought I was going to shoot the running sergeant. True he was about to come into my sight-line, but I had seen him and my shot would have cleared him by a good two feet. I hesitated.

It was too late, my target was gone. As I lowered the rifle two more figures popped into sight for a moment, too quick for a shot.

Back at camp I was told to report to the commanding officer; "Muk" Micklesfield. "Why didn't you fire."

Apparently from the neat clean clothing I described and the fact that he was obviously an adult they believed he was the Cuban causing so much trouble. I had let the side down. Had I shot him I would have been a hero. Of course if he had turned out to be a civilian I would have been in deep trouble; "*Catch 22.*" I didn't see an AK. Mistakes were too easy. In one incident a group of farmers took out "insurgents" who were in truth undercover operatives.

Describing this man as an adult was relevant because many "freedom-fighters" had been abducted as school children, causing schools to close. They would return from Tanzania as young teenage killers. Their leaders, the older hard-core survivors, had been trained in Russia, China or East Germany. The range of weaponry available to them was whatever they could use from the Soviet non-nuclear arsenal.

Sometimes I'm glad that I didn't pull the trigger and I hope I am never responsible for anyone's death. At other times, when I think of the needless killings, especially the indiscriminate IED explosions, I wish I'd ignored the *don't shoot* call.

In the minefield adjacent to the camp was a small, bleached-white human skull. I was surprised when one fellow said he wanted it. Amazingly an ex-regular army alcoholic volunteered to retrieve it. I am sometimes baffled and disturbed by human desires and behaviour. Who would want such a trophy or ornament and why would someone risk so much to get it?

When I first saw a picture of Edvard Munch's "masterpiece" *Scream,* it reminded me of that little skull and the man who wanted it; a darker facet of humanity perhaps? I am in awe of the art-dealer who got $40 million for the painting. I have no understanding of the buyer.

The next 1974 call-up was still in winter. This time we had a bit of training beforehand. About 150 of us reported to KG VI (King George VI) Barracks as instructed, where they made us abandon our tin trunks. Mine, fitted-out to stand on end as a portable wardrobe, combined with a folding stool and six feet of two-inch fold-up foam mattress, was my version of camp-life luxury.

The military reasoning was that the trunks caused injury in the event of an IED blast. Of course they were probably right, but we felt that there could be more serious implications to being instantly airborne in a partly dismantled lorry filled with military paraphernalia.

Having left my kitbag at home as unnecessary, I was reduced to a couple of large plastic fertilizer bags for my gear. I was well pissed-off.

Now we were going to Inkomo Barracks for training. We were going to cover the four-month programme in seven days. It was up before six in the morning; very poor food, bed at ten or later, an ice-cold shower the first night, stuff showering after that.

Map-reading was restful until the five or six mile find-your-own-way-back exercise started an hour before dusk.

Only one team made it back without help. They picked the obvious route across the river bridge. Our conscientious leader had to go roughshod overland and find a river crossing to avoid imaginary ambushes. River crossings can be fun in daylight but in pitch dark, stupid is the right word.

In the end the instructors came looking for us. We were ferried back to camp in the back of a five-ton *Bedford*, clinging to each other; a swaying mass of standing humanity, too crowded to sit down.

The range work I enjoyed, especially the night shoot. I had an old hunter's technique for low-light-aiming; it worked well. The skirmishing exercises, where every second person runs three steps forward as their neighbours give covering fire, was more interesting. Doing it from a moving vehicle into the bush was particularly hairy as we always used live ammunition. You had to trust in your neighbours not to hit you. To encourage us to keep our heads down the instructor was firing over us. The fact that we had seen him down three or four beers increased the desire to be close to the soil.

My group were about half-way through the exercise, "Freeze! Freeze, don't move!" It was the instructor's voice.

I was already on the ground in the firing position, but I tried to get lower. What the Hell had happened? Then two shots, not over our heads, just a few feet behind me. Oh shit!

"OK relax, it's all over."

I looked behind to see the instructor walking away with four foot of headless snake dangling from his hand. It was probably a cobra, they were the most common reptile of that size in the area. Apparently our activities had disturbed the creature and it was just trying to escape, en route it had slid under the chest of one fellow who was prone at the time. Fortunately he didn't move. The bullets flying around were certainly a greater danger than the snake. I was far more scared by the trigger-fingers than any snake. When it was all over the sense of well-being was almost euphoric.

These sessions were inherently dangerous as a subsequent incident proved. It involved Dennis Beatty, the former owner of Albert's blown-up revolver. That camp was the last time I saw him.

On a subsequent call-up he was with a group which included members of the mixed-race community. Dennis died on that call-up from gunshot wounds received during training.

Although enthusiastic about firearms, members of that community were said to lack appreciation of consequences. Rumour has it that one death was the result of the person investigating a weapon malfunction by looking down the barrel and working the mechanism without first removing the bullets.

Training over, we were split into three groups. One for Hippo Valley/Triangle Sugar area, now a very active hotspot, another for the spectacular Honde Valley tea growing estates, where it was said, "There are so many anti-tank mines they are like mushrooms." My group was sent to a location about thirty miles west of Mukumvura, known as Katanga.

The accommodation varied from tents to three-sided thatched "rooms." The walls were thin upright logs; the traditional African building construction but without the mud infill. The thatch on the open side extended to make a veranda. A couple of layers of sandbags surrounded the base.

Five others were in with me. Pete the Dream is the only one I can remember. Pete the Muscle and Pete the Drunk were in other groups. The nicknames? Well, we had three Petes. The Drunk is obvious, the Muscle was a diminutive bodybuilder. At maybe five foot he weighed 180 pounds (12 stone 12 pounds). He really was all hard, sharply defined muscle, even between the ears. And the Dream? A really nice guy, a probation officer in civilian life, but he made the mistake on the first morning of telling us that he had had a wet dream.

On patrol it was normal to take turns carrying the Bren gun, but the Muscle insisted on having it. I think it made him feel safer. I was careful not to point out that, in an ambush, the machine gunner would be the prime target. Neither did I mention that the modification to 7.62 ammunition seemed to have destroyed its reliability. Anyway, it was heavier than anything I wanted to lump around the bush. I liked my rifle and I liked to have The Muscle on the same patrol as me.

Chapter 46

Some Weaponry

The Katanga camp's purpose was to provide a presence as well as watching over the local protected village. How we were occupied was up to our Commanding Officer. The group we relieved had, by all accounts, been in several exchanges of fire with the enemy. However, all the incidents had occurred at night and there had been no injuries on either side.

Apparently their CO was gung-ho and seemed to think he was on a hunting expedition. He would lead patrols out at night on optimistic but hopeless search-and-destroy missions. They were lucky to survive. Obviously their CO believed the Rhodesian morale-boosting propaganda which claimed that the enemy would only attack soft unarmed targets.

Fortunately our CO had no illusions about the enemy or their weaponry. In civilian life he was a supermarket proprietor, but formerly he had been a big-game hunter in Zambia. He knew that an AK bullet would shred your innards as it turned over and fragmented in your flesh; effectively an explosion. It was immaterial whether a hard-core Russian-trained gook or an abducted school kid pulled the trigger. He had no intention of proving what he already knew. We removed the lorry's headlights and rigged them up at key points like the com-(communications) tent and, of course, our make-shift bar. We stayed in at night.

During the day we patrolled through the bush for four to six hours. The start and finish points were varied each day. There was no pattern to the routes. The winter nights were cold but the days would be in the upper ninety degrees F. It was the Zambesi Valley.

A few yards from our three-sided hut was a stack of ammonium nitrate fertiliser, a five metre cube of high explosive; supplied by the government for the villagers' use as fertiliser. If a resourceful "Freedom Fighter" had thought to use one of their anti-tank mines to detonate that stack, both our camp and the African village would've been obliterated.

"You know that if the gooks put a bag of that stuff under one of their twenty-five kg anti-tank mines it'll blow any vehicle into little pieces," I pointed out to our OC.

"Yes, I'll send in a report."

From the JOC[12] the message came back, "There has been no incident of the fertiliser going missing. We have no concerns about that possibility."

Within three months back in civvy street I was told that some IEDs had, in fact, been boosted by ammonium nitrate originating from some of these stockpiles.

By now we had produced mine detectors *(pookies)* which could detect metallic mines while travelling at up to 70 kph (47 mph); possible because the *pookie* could pass over the mine without triggering it.

---

[12] Joint Operations Centre.

This was achieved in service by making them light and fitting them with extra wide tyres (*fat tackies*)[13] salvaged as scrap from the South African car racing scene.

The mine detector's name came about when one of the manufacturers' wives saw it. She immediately said "Oh that's a pookie." *Pookie* being the colloquial term for a cute little monkey otherwise called a night-ape. The name stuck because anyone knowing the animal would immediately make the connection.

Interestingly, during one call-up, Eunice's brother, John, was pulled off patrol duty due to his deafness and required to drive one.

Fortunately someone in authority realised in time that a p*ookie* driver needed acute hearing and John was transferred elsewhere.

Of course any vehicle was vulnerable to command-wire-detonated devices and within six months the Russians had supplied non-metallic mines to the "Freedom Fighters." This and more sensitive IEDs meant that detection had to be based on ground disturbance which slowed down the process. The pookie was adopted and adapted by the South Africans in 1982 as the Veldspringkaan Mine Detection Vehicle. Some features were further developed in Britain by ERA Technology in the 1980s as 'surface penetrating radar'.

In service (1976 to early 1980s) twelve were destroyed by explosions. All but one of the drivers survived. The death was not from a mine blast but from a direct hit by an RPG missile. I have no knowledge of the injuries the drivers almost certainly suffered.

When it came to equipment our opponents were only limited by their lack of ability to operate it. The photos show some of their equipment; most seized in cross-border raids by Rhodesian troops against "unarmed refugee camps". In truth the Rhodesians had to destroy a large amount of armaments because it was logistically impossible to transport the enormous quantity back to Rhodesia.

A number of Rhodesian weapons were making their appearance; from backyard machine guns, Government-made, round anti-personal bouncing bombs (slightly smaller than a football) and at least three combat shotguns. One, the Striker, was adopted by an American manufacturer in the 1980s, used in movies and banned from private buyers in the USA in 1994.

All these photos were taken at the Morris Police Depot, Harare by Mike Jesson in 1980.

Yes, Mike is the same man, the *VW* rollover-learner-driver in 1958 when I was the required licensed passenger supervisor and we were racing Jimmy and Wavell.

Even now most Rhodesians have no idea of the enormous scale of the armament which was being assembled against us in neighbouring countries. There is no doubt that our shoestring weapon industry turned out some remarkably effective killing devices, but against the combined Soviet and Chinese input it was miniscule. In the real world we had no hope.

---

[13] Fat = wide, tackie = slang for plimsoll = tyre.

Katanga was my last camp with the Army. Apparently the Air Force found themselves doing work beyond their usual remit; unpleasant stuff, much more suitable for the talents of National Servicemen. The following call-up was my introduction to the little anti-personnel bouncing bombs.

Rhodesian Mine-Protected Vehicles (Leopards)
Photo courtesy Mike Jesson

I joined the other recruits at the New Sarum air base where we boarded an ancient DC 3 transport plane and left for Thornhill base, 200 miles to the south-west. Any of us could have elected to go by our own transport and some did. On board, a few were discussing the pros and cons of doing just that, so I joined in with my contribution:

"I thought about going by car, but my *Citroen's* thirty years old now (by then I had changed the *DS20* for a *Big 15 Citroen*) and anything that old can fail at any time, regardless of the condition. I wonder when this plane was built?"

No one replied; that old Dakota was almost certainly pre WW 2, way older than my car. We travelled the rest of the way in silence.

At Thornhill I found myself part of a four-man team having a pre-six a.m. high-protein breakfast. One fellow spoke my thoughts, "I love steak and I can enjoy a full pint of milk but at six in the morning it's not quite the same."

Soviet Tanks
Photo courtesy Mike Jesson

Soviet Amphibious Personnel Craft
Photo courtesy Mike Jesson

I wondered what we were about to do.

"You're on bomb filling," was the reply when we asked.

I doubted it would be those practice bombs of my early service when Ian Jackson had that interesting experience with flash powder. Hopefully it would be something new to me; maybe frantan (napalm) or more likely high explosive.

Our transport to the site was one of those durable, ugly and claustrophobic little *Renault R4s*. The facility was a single storey rectangular red-brick building the size of a small bungalow.

We entered a hallway with doors to a changing room complete with showers and toilet on the left. The doors, directly ahead, led to the main working area, of about 100 square metres. At the far end was a work surface under a large steam-heated metal hopper. The hopper contents could only be drained inside the workroom; filling it was done from a room behind a dividing wall. It was filled with flakes of what looked very much like cornflakes but with a lingering smell you could and would taste for days later; TNT.

Steam was used to melt the TNT. Our job was to pour this stuff into the cricket-ball-sized inner cores of bouncing anti-personnel bombs. This inner was surrounded by marble-sized high-bouncing rubber balls and encased in a sheet steel outer. They were designed to bounce once and explode at head height.

There was no provision to jettison these devices in a safe condition which is normal with bombs, in other words they had to be dropped live before the pilot landed. A *Canberra* bomber carried 300 and dropped them in lots of 50.

Of course they had to be loaded in the live condition but were said to be safe to drop four feet onto concrete. The *Canberra* bomb bay is four feet from ground level.

It was another job usually delegated to National Servicemen and always carried out with great care.

Overalls, wellington boots, respirators, gloves and full-frontal liquid-proof aprons were waiting for us in the change-room. At the end of the shift we scrubbed down everything including the floor and showered enthusiastically, but you couldn't get rid of the feel, smell and taste of TNT.

I mentioned previously that our forces would sometimes booby-trap an arms cache by arranging for the anti-tank mines used for IEDs to explode as they were armed. In addition, the rifles could explode on firing or be fitted with a tracking device. The Soviet hand grenades came in two basic variations; one with a time fuse, the other would explode the instant the lever was released.

The intention with the instantaneous grenade was to be used as a booby-trap. The lever would be restrained somehow with the pin removed in readiness to kill the next person to disturb it. These instantaneous grenades could be left anywhere such as inside an empty upturned tin can, drinking mug or under the body of a dead or unconscious comrade. I was told of cases where a wounded and booby-trapped terrorist had moved and blown himself up; a sort of own goal.

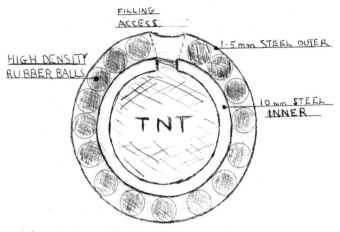

FILLING ACCESS

1·5 mm STEEL OUTER

HIGH DENSITY RUBBER BALLS

TNT

10 mm STEEL INNER

BOUNCING A-P BOMB : PISTOL (DETONATOR) NOT SHOWN

Basic construction from my memory of 40 years ago (dimensions approximate)
Rhodesia's anti-personnel bouncing bomb
The granddaddy of cluster bombs (now banned).

The official procedure for dealing with possibly booby-trapped enemy bodies was to attach a rope to one wrist, retire to a safe distance and pull the body clear of any possible explosive. An unofficial but quicker alternative was a burst of rifle fire to jerk the body about to set off the explosive, if it existed.

***

Between 1976 and 1978 something occurred which I am convinced involved one of the modified mines. Late one night there was a single, very powerful explosion. The sort you feel as well as hear, but it was also, obviously, quite far away.

Every weekend I travelled the old, little-used section of Twentydales Road south of Salisbury Drive, en route to our rifle club. I usually had the family with me, the range on Gus Luginbuhl's farm was a great place for kids to explore.

The Sunday following that explosion that route was blocked off. No problem, I went the long way round, but I decided that I would make time to find out just why a perfectly serviceable bit of old strip road was now out of bounds.

There was only one house off that road, Mrs Norton's school-run would be a few miles longer now.

It was more than a week before I was able to investigate the closure from the opposite end which would give access to the Norton home. That route was blocked immediately past their turn-off. I parked up and walked about two hundred yards. towards the small stream. I knew the area well, everything looked normal, no sign of road works.

As the road curved downhill towards the bridge the strips weren't there any more, instead there was a giant crater big enough to fit a *small car*.

I know that rainstorms can cause extreme damage, but there had been no rain or any kind of storm. In my experience the only other possible cause, and the damage was typical, would have been a boosted anti-tank mine. As no deaths had been reported the logical conclusion was that one of the booby-trapped mines had taken out the perpetrators.

I found that was a much more pleasing thought than Mrs Norton and her children or possibly my family and me becoming casualties. I hoped my assumption was correct.

Of course this was only a guess but strict press censures and propaganda cut off accurate information. Any threat near the Capital would be glossed over if possible.[14]

---

[14] Many things simply weren't reported. Sometime the newspaper would have large sections of print obliterated. I've only recently seen the passenger lists of the two Viscounts which were shot down. I know they are genuine because two casualties and one survivor were known to me personally

Chapter 47

Callous Callaghan

At the factory things were going smoothly and my turn came to go on a *tractive effort* run. These were required by the Railways before they accepted a loco; final proof that the engine had enough power. Richard Walton always went on the test, but he might need one of us as a second pair of hands.

The running sheds were in Bulawayo so we flew down, booked into a hotel and got up at 3 am to start the test. At the station we were joined by the driver and our company's resident technician in Bulawayo, Tom Billington.

The test involved pulling the maximum load up the steepest slopes and recording the current, voltage, speed, various temperatures and pressures. To load our train, everything they could muster was coupled up; in this case one hundred-and-forty axles. That's when I learnt that trains are measured in axles; at least they were in Rhodesia. A wagon could have two, four or six axles.

The two hundred miles to Gatooma was mostly uphill, that took care of the testing. At Gatooma we had lunch and waited for a green light to start back.

Tom had a problem; it was an important day, a birthday or anniversary, I'm not sure which but he was due to take his wife out and didn't want to be late.

"OK, I'll see what can be done," Richard said, and phoned the control room in Bulawayo.

"Fixed-up, we'll have green lights all the way back," he smiled.

"Yes, but what about the tacho'?" from the driver, "I'll be done for speeding."

"No problem I'll sort that," and Richard proceeded to remove the paper recording roll from the tachograph. "I'll say it jammed."

I'm glad to say that Tom made it back comfortably. It was the only time I met Tom and his wife Annette. Tragically she would die in February 1979.

The Billington family had been for a break to Kariba. Tom and his young son travelled by car, but because of possible ambush attacks on road vehicles (our GP had a bullet pass through his trouser leg in one incident) Tom's wife went by air. It was the second Viscount airliner shot down by Nkomo's "freedom fighters." There were no survivors.

Of the fifty-four passengers at least four[15]; were United Kingdom citizens. Regina Chigwada was *Air Rhodesia's* first black air hostess.

Once again Britain's premier, Jim Callaghan, was completely silent. The "freedom fighters" were armed by Russia, with *Strella (SAM 7)* missiles and it is believed that they were specifically trained to target civilian airliners.

Both Callaghan and Wilson had close contact with the Kremlin. They refused to comment. Were they complicit? By their silence they certainly seemed to condone these murders. To this day I have yet to hear a British premier offer condolences to the relatives.

---

[15] Miss Margaret Davies (35), Mr. Peter Gray (67), Mr.Michael Harraghy (37) and Mr. Ronald Isitt (55)

Local Africans were defenceless against these gangs and had suffered beatings, rape and murder in order to recruit them to the "freedom" cause. Realising their predicament the Rhodesians set about "turning" them.

Once they were trained and armed they proved invaluable in seeking out and destroying Nkomo's "freedom fighter" SAM 7 gang. But only the foot-soldiers were eliminated; the instigators lived on to grow rich and pompous at the expense of their impoverished people.

Chapter 48

Coming to Terms with Reality

Being aware of the downhill slide into corruption, violence and economic failure affecting the countries to the north, east and west of Rhodesia, it was easy to conclude that Rhodesia would be the next sufferer of this African sickness. Clearly it was likely that our children would not reach adulthood in Rhodesia.

"Before we leave we must take the kids to show them as much of the country as we can." Eunice insisted. Naturally I went along with that.

Bridal Veil Falls Inyanga 1969
My photo

We had already spent holidays in the Inyanga area, a place of spectacular waterfalls and mountain scenery including the 2,450 foot (750 metre). Matarazi Falls, the sixth highest in the world. Viewed from the top you look down onto the vast expanse of the Honde Valley. With an annual rainfall of three metres (over 120 inches) it was the tea growing area of Rhodesia.

Trout were bred and released into the cool mountain streams of Inyanga and rods were available for hire to the casual angler. My problem has always been actually catching the fish. On the last visit we had our two canoes which were fun but didn't please the fishermen.

We had also twice visited the Vumba mountains. The first was unplanned; we had been on the way to Beira in Mozambique for a shooting competition. However, we arrived at the border a day before the Portuguese officials received our weapons clearance so when they turned us back we decided on a little detour.

Although our old *Kombi* had to struggle its way up the steep slopes, my initial anger was transformed into pleasure once we entered the lush, relaxing, mountain forests of the Vumba.

There we camped at one of the excellent Tourist-board-sponsored sites.

That was before both the Vumba and Inyanga became "red areas"[16] and the possibility of being blown up was still in the future. When that happened the roads were implanted with, probably, the highest density of IEDs in the country; the greatest concentration being in the Honde Valley. Perhaps that was because of the easy access to the enormous weapon stores in Mozambique.

***

Early in 1975 we camped at Kariba, on the lakeside. There we lost money in the Casino, visited a croc farm and simply relaxed. The fashion industry's demand for crocodile belly-skin had endangered the wild population so farming was seen as a profitable control measure much preferred to simple hunting.

Where crocodiles had been wiped out most fish species disappeared as well, leaving that particular waterway dominated by catfish and *platannas,* those pregnancy test frogs.

Crocs weren't bred on the farms; the farms being stocked by collecting eggs from the wild and hatching them on the farm. The farmer was only allowed to take ten percent, leaving ninety percent to hatch naturally. Now in 2014 it would seem that Kariba's croc population has multiplied extensively and includes some very large specimens.

The wonderment on Brian's face was his reaction to seeing a baby croc emerge from a cup-sized, squeaking egg as the farmer cracked it open. The squeak indicated to the farmer that the egg was ready to hatch.

Brian wasn't the only one filled with wonder.

We were also told that they would be slaughtered when they reached two metres which would be in two or three years if fed on pork. Apparently, using the equivalent weight of catfish as croc food had little effect on growth. Going by the enormous size of some of the crocs in Lake Kariba they must have had a pig-rich diet or something similar. Of course humans remain a food source for them and are said to resemble pork.

---

[16] Attack likely.

One afternoon, when Brian walked into the camper dripping wet, I bawled him out. He replied with a crestfallen look, "You said we could play in that boat, and I got a bit wet, and Allison said I looked silly only being half wet, so I got all wet."

"You mean you went swimming?"

"Yes."

"You've seen crocs. To them you look so very yummy. They can have you if you're just near the water. Don't go near that boat or the water again, ever!" Of course after that we kept a closer watch over the antics of Brian and Allison.

The other danger near the shoreline of any water in that part of Africa is bilharzia; a disease caused by a parasitic worm which enters the bloodstream through the skin causing irreparable internal injury. Usually infecting the bladder and kidneys, sometimes the brain; it is curable but you have to live with the damage done. It can be fatal.

At the end of December 1975 we went to the Victoria Falls and Wankie Game Reserve (now spelt Hwange). There had been attacks on farms and there may have been car ambushes but news was very closely censored. We were not yet travelling in convoys although we did carry weapons.

At the Falls we toured another croc farm, not as tidy as the Kariba one, more of a tourist attraction than a farm. It included a large captive beast with most of his tail missing.

Allison and Brian watching baby crocs emerge from eggs

One bedtime Brian complained of a festering lump underfoot. He always seemed to wait a day or two before he worried about little things. The cause was a thorn which had broken off under the skin. Too deep to extract with a needle or penknife, I resorted to an old home remedy; a hot poultice of sugar and soap. The next morning the thorn was out, stuck to the poultice; a neat, clean little hole where it had been.

Two days later we were ducking through some undergrowth when Brian yelped and muttered that something had stung him. Within a few minutes his face had swollen up closing his eyes down to mere slits.

The local clinic didn't even try to guess what had stung him but gave us some anti-histamine tablets and cream. It was a few days before the swelling went down. Brian didn't complain he simply did what he was always so good at; he got on with enjoying life.

Two years later, on 2nd November 1977, the *Elephant Hills Casino Hotel* at the Falls was destroyed by fire. A SAM 7 heat-seeking missile missed its passenger aircraft target and homed-in on the Hotel's kitchen or air-conditioning system. Again this was hushed-up; the tourist trade was too important to frighten.

I have since discovered that the rocket was launched from the outskirts of Livingstone in Zambia and was actually one of the seven fired at civilian aircraft. The two planes brought down by Strella missiles were only hit after the gang relocated to Kariba. (see Viscount Down by Keith Nell).

The incident was reported as an attack on the Hotel. Aircraft were yet to be hit.

Chapter 49

Redundancy by Journalist

At the locomotive factory we had finished the 35th Rhodesian built, high-tech German mainline loco and had been marking time building a batch of ugly little diesel-hydraulic shunters. The next order was for a fleet of French-designed DE 8s. Rough, tough, simple and almost idiot-proof mainliners, they were favourites with the laid-back Rhodesia Railways.

Bad news came in the form of a devious little British journalist by the name of Kenneth McIntosh[17].

McIntosh had already written an article exposing the sanction-busting help Rhodesia was getting from all over Europe. Most of this help was motivated by financial gain but there was also a feeling of goodwill towards us from a section of the British population; in particular from those who had served with Rhodesians in the British forces and were aware of Rhodesia's contribution to every British war since the 1896 Jameson Raid.

A young man by the name of Harris left Rhodesia to volunteer for the Flying Corps during WW 1 and simply stayed on in the RAF, in the process gaining the nickname of "Bomber" when he was in charge of Bomber Command[18].

At the outbreak of WW 2, the tiny white tax-paying population built eleven training airfields for pilots as well as supplying volunteer pilots. One of these men would become the Rhodesian Prime Minister, Ian Smith, who had broken off his university studies to volunteer and become a fighter pilot.

Most of Rhodesia's politicians had been on active service in the war and had a lot of friends in Britain, but not all the pilots trained in the country were on our side; Tony Benn, who also trained in Rhodesia, often spoke against us. He should have known that he was siding with the Russians, and he must have known that they were Africa's prime suppliers of free-of-charge war-weaponry, most notably the AK 47. If not, what was he doing in politics?

Of course there was nothing of high moral value with McIntosh, he was just doing a grubby little job. By the time our Special Branch arrested him he had already deposited a large amount of material with his sister in Scotland with the instruction that if anything happened to him she should pass it on to a newspaper. He seems to have failed to tell her that it could have been used to bargain with the Rhodesians.

Rhodesian SB officers visited her in Scotland and requested that his writing be surrendered to them with the promise that her brother would avoid prison if she complied.

---

[17] My information is based on Rhodesian News reports and our management statements, (wikileaks mentions McIntosh ref... Cable: 1974STATE082339_b, apparently a communique from Kissinger)

[18] RAF 44 Squadron was known as Rhodesia Squadron until Harold Wilson got his knickers in a knot over UDI (The Unilateral Declaration of Independence).

She refused, instead doing as instructed by McIntosh; as a result 50 whites and approximately 250 blacks were jobless when the loco factory wound down. But McIntosh went to jail; some consolation for the factory workers. It was an especially bad situation for the African workers and worst for the Malawians whose only route home would involve a circuitous air journey via Johannesburg; far too expensive for their limited means; all because of the stupidity of sanctions.

It wasn't long before McIntosh's escape was manipulated by the British; easily done because a nasty piece of work, Chief of the Rhodesian Security Branch, Ken Flower, was a double agent[19].

However, McIntosh's freedom didn't last for long, at the airport his nerve broke and he left by road for newly-independent Mozambique. Once over the border he handed himself in at the nearest police station. Unfortunately for him the man in charge decided that the best person to handle this situation would be his Rhodesian friend. One phone call and McIntosh was a convict again. Of course this was a major story for *The Rhodesian Herald*, the country's newspaper.

The factory kept going building the little shunting locomotives for a few months. It only closed while I was on call-up in February 1976. However, I was kept on until the end of the month after I returned from the Army.

***

That call-up was to the Umtali area on the Mozambique border where relations with our politically re-aligned neighbours had deteriorated considerably since McIntosh's escapade.

First impressions were anything but promising. Our Sergeant-Major appeared to be on his first active service call-up and totally out-of-touch with reality, shouting out orders as if he was in a TV comedy. We knew that the young soldiers called us "Dad's Army," but this pillock didn't have to live up to it.

At one stage he was pacing about when he bent forward for some reason and his glasses fell to the ground unbroken and unnoticed by him. The decent thing to do would have been to tell him but as he obviously didn't think we were decent human beings, no need to disillusion him.

Eventually he did find them after he had investigated a satisfying scrunching sound underfoot. His puzzled expression changed to something near tears when he discovered exactly what he had trodden on so fairly and squarely; a little light relief for us.

That night I was put on guard duty within rifle range of the border; with that in mind I was careful to stay in the shadows. I could see very well but didn't want to be seen.

Unsurprisingly, our blustering, bumptious Fuhrer decided that a tour of inspection was in order.

"Where the hell's the guard here? There's no one here!"

"I'm here staff."

---

[19] I recently heard Flower confirmed as a double agent by David Owen during a BBC Radio interview.

"What the hell are you hiding for?"

"Because I'm not planning to get shot; the border is just over there and if you can see me so can a sniper. This is the real world, not toy soldiers."

"Huh!" as he stalked off.

I thought he might put me on a charge, but I heard no more.

The next day I was put with three other fellows to guard a remote bush airstrip. There was the shell of an old bus we used for accommodation and an oil-drum barbeque for cooking.

On the third day it was my turn to cook. I had just started when a smart little civilian craft landed and disgorged a poncey white business suite, a politician.

Apparently it was a visit meant to boost our morale. I wondered just what the powers-that-be thought this particular fly-boy could do for our morale.

Another aircraft appeared, painted in camouflage, it was obviously military. The pilot must have seen the politician's plane on the runway and unsure as to what it was about to do, he had to abort his landing. As he climbed away and turned left his wing made contact with the branches of a tree sending the aircraft spinning into the distance; too far for us to even try to find the crash scene. Clearly survival was very unlikely. No one could face having a meal..

Soon a *Land Rover* arrived.

"You're going to the crash site."

As the vehicle stopped another one pulled up behind it and suddenly the occupant was addressing us.

"Who's Boniface?"

"I am."

"You're an electrician?"

"Yes."

"Come with me, we've got a job for you."

It seemed strange that the army would go looking for an electrician at that time of night, but a lot of unusual things were happening in those days. Of course it is possible that the Army knew that one of the plane's occupants, "Rusty" Routledge was a neighbour of mine. I knew Rusty from the GPO college where we had been on one of the courses together. I had no social contact with his family and didn't know he was on the plane.

Apart from my personal feelings the authorities wouldn't want specific details of the incident to be disclosed to relatives in case they contradicted the official version.

I knew that the three occupants of the plane had all been killed, but it was only a few months later that I learned that one of them was "Rusty". He had only recently moved into a neighbouring house.

***

The electrical work turned out to be a remarkable stroke of luck. The Army had requisitioned the old Meikles Hotel as their Area HQ, but with the building due for demolition the wiring had been stripped out for scrap; now the army needed it to be reinstated.

There were two other call-up electricians involved, one a contractor, the other, with the rank of sergeant, was in charge. We would stay in the new hotel until the old one was fit for habitation; all meals would be provided by the hotel in the main dining room. Luxury in the army, unbelievable!

I could tell immediately that this job would keep us occupied for the rest of our call-up. I also knew that during that time only three bedrooms would become habitable and the first area to be fully functional would be the cocktail bar complete with refrigerator.

***

There was a garden courtyard in the centre of the old hotel which was now totally overgrown. Amongst the weeds was a plant unfamiliar to me. It was about three foot wide and four foot tall.

"Dagga," (cannabis) our leader informed us, "I'll have to tell the manager and he'll have to inform the police."

Instead of a rush of officialdom, two African labourers appeared. Within two days the whole area, with the exception of that plant, had been restored to bare earth.

"What about that one?" I asked one of the men.

"Which one?"

"Over there, under the window."

"There's nothing there baas. I can't see anything."

I gave up. This fellow simply wasn't going to admit that he might know anything at all about any cannabis plant. He wasn't going to touch it. He was already in denial or maybe he was planning to return when no one was about.

There was a delay of three days before the police appeared. The delay was said to have been down to the Hotel manager's inertia, but the police could have been watching in the hope of arresting someone. They said that the cannabis was worth about $1,700. With hindsight we could have given the situation more thought.

***

For a call up it was a right skive; we worked army office hours. One weekend I even managed to hitch-hike the 170 miles home. In retrospect, it could have turned out badly for a lone unarmed man in army uniform, but I had done it before from Bindura and I was still young enough to be blasé about the possibilities.

We had to leave the comfort of the new hotel once the health department had exterminated the population of giant cockroaches in the sewers. Going by the pristine state of those drains I thought the insects were doing sterling work. I suppose the inspectors were more concerned about where the cockroaches would have their next meal.

We paced the job well and completed the rewiring just in time to catch a lift home in the back of a *Land Rover.*

In Norton a few of the admin staff were still at the locomotive factory. I had only to tidy up and say goodbye. My wages to the end of the month and any other monies would be paid into the bank. Right now I needed to find another job and being the last to leave I would be last in the queue.

"Peter Sacchi wants to see you," was the message I got over the phone.

"Good morning Mr. Sacchi."

"Good morning. There's a supervisor vacancy coming up in the emerald cutting section. Would you be interested?"

I couldn't remember even having seen an emerald before, but a job was a job. It wasn't the time to have doubts.

"Yes, I'm very interested; thank you."

"I'll put a word in for you. You'll have to have an interview as well as a police security check and report. But I'm sure it'll be fine. You know where to go in *Pearl Assurance House?*"

"No, but I can find it. Thank you Peter, good bye."

"It's on the fourth floor. Good bye and good luck."

To me the cutting laboratory was a workshop not a laboratory, but what's in a name? It occupied the fourth and fifth floors of *Pearl Assurance House.* Three cutting sections; large, standard and reject occupied the fifth floor. The maintenance workshop and offices were on the fourth.

I was responsible for the reject section, where the cutters had to make the best of heavily flawed stones. They did this remarkably well. All the cutters were African, they did first-class work and were highly productive, however, a few years later, after Zimbabwe's independence, Rio Tinto moved the cutting operations to India. Apparently the Indians were paid less. I found that surprising; unless there was a hidden agenda.

The cutting machines were made in-house to the designs of Ken Cole, a highly talented toolmaker with a hobby of violin making.

Of course I had to learn how to cut stones, which I did using odd bits of quartz, agate, aquamarine and BWB[20]. With the *Rio Tinto* equipment it was easy and relatively quick; compliments to Ken Cole.

Cutting emeralds is quite different from cutting diamonds in so far as emeralds are cut for maximum size so that determines the angles of the facets. Diamonds are cut for brilliance. Their high refractive index means that light entering the stone can be bounced around, split into rainbow colours and out again to make it sparkle. The critical angles necessary and the diamond's hardness make it very time consuming to cut.

Colour, clarity and rarity make emeralds valuable. Cutting skill gives the diamond its beauty and marketing skill makes it valuable; they are not rare.

My section cut the rejects, stones of borderline value, the dozen cutters each turning out between fifteen and twenty-five stones a day.

The new position was on an "A" contract which meant that the benefits were even better, but I found the work extremely boring, perhaps I should have developed an interest in jewellery making.

---

[20] Broken wine bottle. Wine bottle glass makes excellent imitation stones.

Basically my job was to issue, check quality and keep track of little green stones. Sometimes if a stone was badly flawed and wasn't worth cutting, I would crush it and just say that it broke. Occasionally I would need to do a bit of basic maintenance on the machines. Of course, I also had control of the cutters but on the whole they were almost perfect employees. They had a job for life with status way above their peers, working for the best employer in industry; certainly the best I have ever had.

However, like workers everywhere, there will always be someone who will try to pull a fast one. In a new job it's important to spot the first attempt, particularly if it's clumsy. My trial came from Kenneth.

A big, bearded, pleasant and personable man, he claimed to be ill and needed to see a doctor. It was the Thursday before the Easter break.

"Sir, I am not very well, I must go to the doctor."

I could see that the nearest cutters were taking note of the proceedings. The outcome was obviously of interest to them.

"OK Kenneth, I'll phone the doctor and arrange transport." *Rio Tinto* met all medical expenses and had arrangements with local GPs for their African staff.

"No…No I must see my own doctor, the pain is too much."

"Where is your doctor?"

"He is in Charter Road sir."

"Charter Road? How will you get there?"

"I will walk there sir."

"And back?"

"Oh yes sir."

"But Kenneth, I can't let you walk. Not when you are in so much pain. I will take you there in my car, at four, after work." I heard a few sniggers from the other cutters.

"Ah, but the doctor, he will be closed at four o'clock."

"That's unusual does he close every day at four?"

"No sir, only on Thursdays. On Thursdays he goes to Harare Hospital for patients there."

"Oh dear, I'll have to take you at lunch-time, then I can wait to bring you back."

"Yes sir." Kenneth nodded and went back to his cutting bench.

At one I called out, "Kenneth, come with me, I'll take you to the doctor."

"Ah!...Now it is much better sir. Now I am well. The pain is gone."

"Are you sure? I can still take you; just in case." More sniggers in the background.

"No, no. now I am quite alright."

"I'm so glad, but if you have any more pain just tell me," now laughter replaced the sniggering in the wings.

***

Rhodesia declared its independence from Britain in 1965 as the USA had nearly 200 years before. With this Unilateral Declaration of Independence it spurned the protection of the UK and put the Country outside the Commonwealth. We could go it alone, or so we thought.

What we had really done was to open a door to Communistic interests (Russian and Chinese). Harold Wilson didn't simply stand aside for them; he actively helped them by instigating the most punishing sanctions he could, regardless of the effect on British industry. The French, Germans and Japanese were delighted. At the UN they all voted for sanctions, while their trade envoys were queuing up to do business with Rhodesia.

As in all wars, the side with the largest industrial backing would win. The "freedom fighters" had the backing of both Russia and China: we could not win.

In a nationwide broadcast in 1976, Prime Minister Ian Smith announced that agreement with Britain had been achieved. We would have a black government.

Initially it would be in coalition with the peaceful black front-runner Bishop Muzorewa. That may have worked but the USA got involved and Jimmy Carter insisted that to fulfil the American[21] definition of democracy Mugabe and Nkomo had to be included.

***

"What are our choices? We have to leave; just look at Mozambique, Zambia, the Congo, any which one. They're all bloody basket cases since independence. You've heard Portuguese refugees talking about the "Re-education" camps. We know about the rape and butchery in the Congo. Alice Lenshina's[22] 700 or so followers in Zambia who sought refuge in a church but were murdered on Kaunda's orders simply because they refused to vote? And that was in the early '60s. What did the rest of the world do? The West; sweet sod all! Britain's Government didn't mind at all, and the East? They supplied the guns".

"Why should Rhodesia be different?" I was having a rant based on a mix of rumour, some personal knowledge and numerous reports.

"Can they really wreck everything? Why should they? Surely even the dumbest must know that hospitals, schools and roads are essential?" Eunice always made allowance for common sense.

"I don't think the average African would argue about that, but the political leaders will grab all they can for themselves, their families and cronies. The law won't count. The ordinary decent man in the street, black or white, but mostly black, will pay the price, and even if we don't what about our kids? We have no option. There's no hope for Africa now, not in our lifetimes."

"Where can we go; Britain, or maybe Switzerland?"

"It'll have to be the UK. Stuff Switzerland!"

"What's wrong with the Swiss?"

"They're fussy buggers: prim and proper: everything must be just right. The neighbours will be telling us when and how to mow the lawn or empty the trash. At least you've got a British passport and I should be able to get one."

---

[21] To follow the American example we would have to commit genocide against the native inhabitants.

[22] I had spoken to John Dicks, who was an eye-witness after the act of the scene of the Lenshina massacre. He said with obvious emotion, *"The Church walls were running with blood"*.

The decision had been made, we would settle in England; there would be no going back. We made our plans and decisions based on hearsay and opinions from whoever.There was no shortage of suggestions. "The winter's not so bad, a good warm jacket will see you right," from Belfast home-townie, Joe Dunn.

"The summers are fine," said a workmate in 1976, just after a three week dinghy sailing holiday. He never mentioned that 1976 was the hottest UK summer on record.

1978 was about the worst time to emigrate. Only three countries in the world would accept Rhodesians; South Africa, Switzerland and the UK. South Africa was bad news in my opinion, I had lived there for a year and I didn't like it.

Eunice said "If we go there we'll only have to move again and we'll be so much older." Of course she was right, we should have left in the early 1960s when we were younger and could have settled in a choice of countries without punitive financial restraints.

Passports were interesting. We had to apply via the British Embassy in Pretoria, where for some reason they refused to put the children on either mine or Eunice's passport. However, twelve-year-old Allan (born before the Unilateral Declaration of Independence) could have one, but only valid for six months and our other three children would be put onto that one. This can't be explained by logic, it had to be political chicanery.

Shortly after I received my passport, the Embassy sent me a letter, I quote;

"As you were not born in Britain and are married to a so-born wife, we require you to return your passport to be amended."

It is true that when Eunice was born in Wallington on the outskirts of Croydon, a London suburb, Hitler was doing his best to destroy London, but to the best of my knowledge he failed; London remained in the UK. I wondered where the Embassy recruited its staff.

After carefully reading everything written on my passport, I decided that it was quite fine, especially the words "Right of Abode".

However Allan's document was different; according to that our children could only stay for six months. Quite obviously that would cause a problem if we decided to stay in Britain. It seemed to me that the UK Embassy in Pretoria was being deliberately obstructive. We would worry about that six months clause in England.

Years later, when Brian applied to join the British Army, he was most welcome. No problems for anyone prepared to fight for Britain.

Having no idea of housing or anything else about Britain I wrote to my half-sister Molly, married to Stan, neither of whom we had ever met, asking for as much information as possible. She wrote back, "You had better come and stay with us until you can get settled."

When we eventually arrived in Southampton we queried our status with immigration. They seemed to be baffled but not surprised. I overheard something like "that B-team in Pretoria," but I think it was simple political manoeuvring, a semi-official by-product of sanctions. Later we had the children naturalised.

***

Leaving Rhodesia was not only hampered by passport problems; there were strict financial controls needed to maintain the value of the Rhodesian dollar.

Unauthorised Rhodesian currency was valueless over the borders. Unauthorised foreign currency within Rhodesia was a criminal offence. A Rhodesian dollar had increased in value in relation to the pound from fifty pence before sanctions in 1965 to between seventy and eighty-five pence in 1979.

Obviously, anyone emigrating needed as much cash as possible. A family was allowed $1000 (about £750) to emigrate. "Holiday allowance" with four children was $1000 each year or $2000 over two years.

Naturally ways to circumvent these rules were always being discussed. Illegal practices like secreting foreign banknotes on your person were a shortcut to a prison sentence followed up by demeaning strip searches every time you crossed a border.

I met one transgressor, a Jewish fellow, who complained with much feeling, "They make me stand on a chair and look between my buttocks every time I go south."

I wasn't surprised, his storage potential was definitely above average.

A legal suggestion from Prof. Richard Harlen sounded good to me. "What about a classic car, they're getting more valuable overseas now? But the condition has to be very good."

Regrettably, I thought age was more valuable than make. What I regarded as a relatively new *Jaguar* was by then a classic in the UK, and the *Citroen DS20* I already owned would be a classic by the time we settled in Southampton.

However I did not know that, so I bought a UK built *Citroen Big 15* from an old man, a Mr. Small, who had bought it new and was still very much in love with it.

I re-sprayed it; Eunice did the re-upholstery.

That old man cried when I took it back to show him. His wife was ecstatic but said that I should have painted it maroon rather than the original black.

Next I bought a *Riley RMA.* "It's been primed, just needs the final colour coat."

True it had been primed, but it needed a bit more than the finishing paint. The existing grey primer had to come off and I filled the dents and various flaws with body-solder before a coat of red lead epoxy primer was applied under the metallic green top-coat. Next a clear lacquer for the final gloss.

The nuts and bolts I had cadmium plated and the shiny bits re-chromed. All this was done before reassembly.

I used beech and imbuia to re-rim the steering wheel. It looked quite good but I lacked the time to finish shaping it to my satisfaction.

The Riley Before and After
Upholstery by Eunice
My photos

The Citroen Big 15
The seats, carpets and door panels are Eunice's superb upholstery work
My photo

Chapter 50

Safety First

"Dad…can I have a razor blade?"

"Pardon?"

"Can I have a razor blade please?"

"And what are you going to do with a razor blade?" Our ten year old daughter, Allison, was a close second to Brian, our fourth child, for the title of *casualty-visit-champion.*

"My homework; I have to make a balsa wood plane."

"OK, but if you cut your finger I will smack you."

She thought for a moment…"Alright! I won't cut my finger." From her hesitation and emphasis on "finger" I knew exactly what she meant. Whatever she cut it wouldn't be her finger. It might be the skin on her finger, but it wouldn't be her finger. I've always believed that she would've made an expert loophole-lawyer.

I broke a double-edged *Gillette-style* blade and gave one edge to her and then I carried on making a bow for Brian. I should have been working on the *Riley RMA.* The bow was a promise I had made in the past to Brian. It was the last opportunity I was likely to have to keep that promise before we left for the UK. I always tried to keep my word.

Right then I was in the process of cutting and planing thin strips of beech to laminate into the traditional shape of a cupid-style bow.

The spinning planer blades were guarded by a spring-loaded cover designed to be pushed aside by the work-piece. The current problem was the thinness of the wood. It was inclined to slip under the guard and stick. My remedy was to flick the guard aside with my thumb, easy when your thumb was on top of the guard; in fact it swung aside just as easy with my thumb in front of the guard… but only once.

When you did that, your thumb also travelled through the path of the spinning blades.

"Shit" I looked down, the end of my left thumb was quite unusual, instead of being neatly rounded, it was spread out like the petals of a meat-red flower. End-on, in the centre, was a little patch of neatly planed bone. Before it even started to bleed I clamped my right palm over the injury. There was absolutely no pain.

It must have looked strange as I shut the planer down and locked up my garage while clasping my hands together.

"Eunice! Take me to hospital."

"What have you done?"

"Never mind what I've bloody well done! Just ask Jill to look after the kids and get me to casualty." Fortunately Jill Vaughan happened to be visiting Eunice at the time.

"Let's see."

"No, just get the car keys and let's go."

At casualty the nurse looked at the tattered end of my thumb. "You've made a mess of that, haven't you? How did you do it?"

"On a wood-planing machine."

"That was silly." As if I didn't know. "Sit here and put your hands palm down on the table," she said calling two more nurses over.

I was already embarrassed by my carelessness, there was no need for her to remind me, but I said nothing. There was no blood, my quick response had completely prevented any bleeding, and still no pain.

The helpers knew exactly what to do. They grabbed a wrist each and pinned me down with all their weight. It was the only time I have ever been pinned down by a couple of pretty young or, come to think of it, any female. Various possibilities crossed my mind, but it wasn't the time or place for fantasy.

The boss-girl reappeared carrying a little bowl of brown liquid.

"Iodine" was her smiling reply to my unspoken query. "This is going to hurt," she said, still smiling as she lifted my thumb and dropped it into the bowl of iodine, "but we have to do it." There was a hint of pleasure in her voice.

Hell… she was so very truthful! Until then I'd felt no pain at all. I don't think she realised just how much the sudden shock of pain hurt. The end of your thumb has a honeycomb of nerves and mine were all severed and nicely spread out; an ideal arrangement to feel the full power of iodine. I clenched my teeth and kept my thumb in the iodine, but I had to react somehow; I found I was suddenly stamping my feet. Once I realised what I was doing I did manage to stop. Now I felt the injury, in fact the pain lasted for weeks; well into the healing process.

After ten minutes or so, that wicked witch-woman with the East-German accent came over to sew me up; the one who seemed to be a permanent fixture in casualty.

I hoped she didn't recognise me. The last time she'd sewn up a cut on me, I had been talkative and made some derogatory remarks about Mugabe. The nurse assisting had caught my eye and shook her head.

Three days later there was a red line growing up towards my armpit. Witch-woman's stitches had gone septic and I had serious blood-poisoning. I had watched her run the thread under her thumb-nail before she stitched me up. I thought, "she thinks she's mending a shirt or something." This time I kept quiet but watched her actions very carefully. No problems this time. However, if my anti-Mugabe remark had caused her to deliberately infect me, I wonder about the fate of our military personnel who were treated by her.

The wound couldn't be closed completely, there wasn't enough skin; my thumb ended in a patch of bare flesh covering the neatly planed bone. "That will heal slowly by granulation. Keep the dressing on. It will take about three months." She was right.

Allison completed her project without injury but even now she does her best to ensure that I don't forget that day.

Chapter 51

Taking the Gap

Having been granted the maximum holiday allowance for two adults and four children, we had to keep up the pretence and buy return tickets. Of course the deception meant that the kids thought they were coming back so never had an opportunity to say their goodbyes. Now I wish I'd told them in time, but before the authorities could react to any information. The minimum response would have been to reduce our allowance to a thousand dollars (the emigration allowance) but no doubt we would have had other difficulties.

As it was a criminal offence to export anything valuable without official approval, we were thoroughly searched as we exited through customs. For that very reason I had mounted castors on an old tin trunk. The rather flimsy metal had to be backed up with two sturdy pieces of wood. Even the keenest eye would have had difficulty seeing the glued joint in these. So our three gold coins and a few emeralds were slipped out, encased in two blocks of apparently solid wood.

***

When I returned to tidy up and emigrate officially I called in at the Rossers to say goodbye, Shorty warned, "Don't even think of smuggling anything out. They will catch you, and it will be prison!"

"Don't worry Shorty, I won't get caught." I assured him. But he did worry and repeated his warning emphatically. I never told him that whatever I wanted to sneak out was already out. I would be leaving absolutely clean.

However, when I did emigrate, every crack and crevice of our two containers of belongings, including the two cars, seemed to have been investigated. I have often wondered why they even thought I was worth all that attention. How would they cope with someone who was affluent and had worthwhile possessions to smuggle out of the country?

***

On the initial trip, the crew of *the South Africa Airways'* plane were superb and paid particular attention to our children; something we both appreciated on that long flight. Politics sent the plane around the bulge of the continent. A 6,000 mile flight, which should have taken eleven or twelve hours, took thirteen or fourteen hours. It also meant a refuelling stop at *Ile de Sol,* a facility built by *SAA* specifically for the purpose.

For the children and me it was our first time north of the equator, not that Eunice could remember her early years in London. In the darkness of the early hours, we could see absolutely nothing of the land mass below.

We didn't exactly see England either, the bright November morning sun displayed an endless vista of rolling white cloud, "It's a mild eleven degrees at Heathrow," came the announcement. Eleven degrees wasn't a daytime temperature I was familiar with, nor would I call it mild.

The plane circled for almost an hour waiting for a slot to land. Under the cloud it was much darker than I expected and although we hadn't seen the outline of England, we did see London; lots of London. I've always felt it was a pity we didn't know enough to identify the areas below.

The first thing we did, I got wrong. Trying to save UK currency, I followed a backpacker's advice to go to Earls Court, "Where someone's always selling a *Kombi* type van. You can buy one cheap and drive to Southampton."

There was a van for sale, and I'm sure a bunch of backpacking youngsters would have made a success of it, but not for me.

Looking at my uncomplaining family, sitting on our piled up possessions, on the Earls Court pavement, in the cold London drizzle, I realised that everyone who really mattered in my life expected me to wave my magic wand and put everything right.

The first taxi refused our custom but the next one piled us in with a smile. When he dropped us off at Waterloo I paid the fare in valuable English pounds and rewarded his good nature with a pack of twenty *Benson and Hedges.* I had bought a carton in the duty-free with Rhodesian dollars specifically to use as tips. They were made in Rhodesia, but after sanctions mainly for export, although also available in the airport's duty-free for the near-useless Rhodesian dollar.

At Waterloo, the guard, a very helpful black man with a strong Cockney accent, loaded our baggage into the guard's van and waved aside the offer of cigarettes. We all remarked on how the train, the station and the surrounds were so remarkably dirty; it was 1978, the *Winter of Discontent* was on the way.

The Southampton taxi driver cheerfully distributed our pile of cases and black tin box between the boot and the roof rack. I think this bunch of strange but friendly folk made his day.

It was on the roadside, outside their house in Harefield, Southampton, that we met our saviours, my half-sister Molly, and her husband, Stan. Stan was a big-hearted man who had served in North Africa in the war; a toolmaker by trade, he was near retiring from his position as a foreman with Ford Southampton. Three of their four sons as well as their foster son Ben Goodman, had married and left home, the fourth, Danny, was newly divorced and living with them.

Born in Rhodesia but twenty years older than me, Molly had been deposited with family in 1923 at the tender age of three following her Mum's death. She never saw our Dad again, circumstances just made it impossible.

We will be forever grateful for the welcome and continuing support of Molly, Stan and their family. They really didn't deserve to have the six of us in their three-bedroom Southampton ex-council house, it was an extremely generous act of kindness, which we can never repay but will always remember.

Deciding that it was time to retrieve the emeralds and gold coins, I borrowed a saw from Stan and cut open the blocks encasing them. I noticed Stan and Adrian exchange glances as I extracted the items. Of course, while I was the legal owner, I wasn't allowed to export them without a permit; I was officially on holiday.

Having concealed them so carefully, it would have caused considerable delay and inconvenience, had I declared them at Heathrow.

Chapter 52

The Tidy-Up

Naturally it was cold, it was November, and we were in the UK, but it was the sun that fooled me. Of course it could be cold in Rhodesia as well, but you could walk into the mid-winter sun and warm up. I soon discovered that England had a different and quite misleading kind of sun. Although I felt cold indoors, it was considerably worse outdoors in spite of the sun. In other ways it was even more confusing.

Throughout my formative years, the sun rose in the east, arched up until it was directly overhead before it eased itself into a glowing red sunset in the west. In the winter it took eleven-and-a-half-hours and twelve-and-a-half in summer. With such total reliability it was easy to know the time within half an hour either way. You could tell with certainty whether it was nine in the morning or close to any other hour, and you instinctively developed a sense of direction related to the sun.

My UK initiation was so different, the sun seemed to hang about at nine all day. My sense of direction was completely confused in Southampton's jumble of streets. I found my way about, but I often walked much further than necessary. Rather than the sun traversing the sky, it seemed as if the streets were re-orientating themselves.

We needed accommodation and a council house would be quite fine but not according to the Southampton council. They informed me that we didn't qualify for a council house as we had voluntarily left our former home. There was a blanket "no" from the banks and building societies as soon as I told them I was working in Rhodesia, and the mobile home site owners lost interest when they realised that we had four children.

Just two weeks after arrival I went back to Rhodesia to work three months notice, to emigrate officially and to arrange the export of as much in the way of goods and chattels as possible. The holiday monies we had already claimed were greater than the emigration sum but I was allowed $20 in cash, travel money which converted to £13. I took that in the form of twelve pounds and two rand; the two rand because the bank didn't have another pound note.

Why such draconian financial laws? Simple answer; sanctions, every import was overpriced and had to be paid for in advance from domestic production and the same applied to the bush war. There was no meaningful external aid. The Canadian educational aid to our University which I saw was nothing more than scrap. No doubt the book value satisfied a hole in the Canadian budget and someone's conscience.

To me, the fourteen years of sanctions against Rhodesia are positive proof that, given good management, integrity and a challenge, Zimbabwe could be profitable and affluent, even under very adverse conditions.

However, now in 2015 the country is reported as being extremely chaotic with corrupt management in every sector of business and government. The resulting poverty and hardships of the majority are adopted by *good-cause* Western charities.

This just gives an easy-out for the political clique and their supporters who either ignore poverty and starvation or side-track as much aid as they can to their personal advantage.

In my opinion it's unlikely that outsiders can ever solve Zimbabwe's problems. Of course the Chinese, who are now reported to control the country's mineral wealth, may not be foreigners in the future.

I left Eunice job and house-seeking. The job she got was as a ledger clerk with, at the time, Southampton's premier but run-down *Polygon Hotel*. She gladly accepted the first available house. It was a housing association unit on the Lordshill Estate.

The houses were recently built and it had a garage as well as a parking lot. This was very handy as I was planning on bringing two classic cars over in place of cash; my costly ruse to overcome the Rhodesian currency controls.

When I boarded the plane for the flight back it was with an almost empty suitcase, all it contained was a few lengths of rubber trim for the *Riley* and a few copies of *Playboy* and similar. *Playboy* could be a handy little beer-money earner. In Rhodesia censorship and foreign currency restrictions had combined to make them unobtainable and therefore valuable. Any importer using his foreign allowance for such frivolous goods would soon lose it.

The flight to the refuelling stop at Ile de Sol in *SAA's Boeing 747* named *Magaliesburg* was fine, well up to their usual high standard, comfortable with good food and service. My wallet was like my suitcase, it contained nothing useful outside of Rhodesia. As the plane was taking off there was a loud bang and the whole aircraft shuddered.

"What was that?" someone demanded.

"Must be lightening!" another replied.

"This is your captain. We have a technical problem and will have to jettison fuel before we can land again. We will keep the delay as short as possible."

For the next three-quarters of an hour we flew around in circles on three engines dumping jet fuel into the Atlantic. Occasionally we would pass by brightly-lit island holiday complexes, only a few hundred feet below.

As we disembarked I asked a hostess, "What happened?"

"An engine blew up. This plane's jinxed! When something goes wrong, it's always with this thing!"

I don't know where we actually landed, but the island's currency was the peseta so I guess it was Spanish. I was acutely aware of having absolutely no useful money. What could have been quite a pleasant break turned out to be a long boring wait.

The airline arranged a meal for everyone while they organised accommodation in various, mostly half-built, hotels. It must have been challenging to suddenly cope with an unexpected jumbo-jet-load of passengers. I ended up sharing a room with a conversationally challenged fellow, which did little to improve the situation.

The man-made beach was very inviting, but I never even had a pair of shorts to use as swimming trunks and my camera was in the UK. However it wasn't all bad, there was only one topless bather, but she had a superb figure, was well tanned, and obviously enjoyed the well-deserved male attention. Who could blame the other females for covering up?

It was after midnight the following day that we left on the replacement plane, the one which had delivered the new engine, bolted under its wing, as though it was pregnant, about to deliver its offspring.

Landing on Salisbury's three-mile-long runway was a comforting feeling even if more than a day late. I was tired enough not to care that I was the last leaving the baggage hall. In fact I was soon quite glad about that because I could see that absolutely every case passing through the "nothing to declare" channel was being opened, and in my suitcase were the banned *Playboy-type* magazines. Men had been locked up for that.

The only alternative was the "something to declare" channel. I was still thinking hard at the counter.

"So! What do you have?" He wasn't unfriendly.

"I've got some English money." I lied.

"And in the case?" he asked, pointing at the case at my feet.

"Just some rubber trim for an old car, otherwise it's empty," a half-truth. "I can show you".

"No, don't bother, it's OK," he waved me through.

I went on my way trying not to show the relief I felt.

Eunice's sister, Diana, had come to meet me. Again I was lucky she had been on the point of leaving thinking that I must have missed the plane. That wasn't surprising, I suppose, as the plane itself was more than a day late and a different one to the one which had left Heathrow.

Our part-Staffordshire bitch, Tippy, was of course overjoyed to see me, but totally at a loss when I took her back to the empty house, searching each room again and again for the rest of the family. A memory I find more unsettling now than I did at the time.

I was fully occupied trying to complete the rebuild of the *Riley* and fulfil the emigration formalities. Fortunately we weren't too busy at the University, mostly because my immediate superior was young enough to have a hefty military commitment and spent most of his time on call-up. A lot of University time went into the rebuild of that *Riley*, but it was hope for the future and the well-being of my family had priority.

Ian Smith's power-sharing agreement with the peaceful black leaders wasn't good enough for America's newly elected Jimmy Carter. With the typically scant knowledge which America's colonial descendants have of Africa, he decided that the "*freedom fighters*" represented the majority and vetoed any agreement reached without them.

Please remember that after the colonials settled in America in the seventeenth century the native population dwindled to near extinction.

This is in stark contrast to the British African Colonies where the native populations multiplied many times over. America is governed by the descendants of the colonial settlers and African slaves; a population closely equivalent to us, the white Rhodesian settlers, but not quite the same. There was never slavery in the history of White rule in Rhodesia.

Considering the enormous backing the "*freedom fighters*" were getting from Russia there can be little doubt that they were anything more than foot-soldiers, and, very often, cannon-fodder for the Soviet cause. Of course we (the Rhodesians) couldn't win, but we didn't want to know and, with a continuous drip-feeding of munitions and recruits to the other side, the war had to escalate.

Many people realised the gravity of the situation and left the country, which made things worse. I had no objection to armed conflict, but it was pointless after you had already conceded defeat. Life in the UK would be a new and challenging experience.

***

In 1979 I was selling up to emigrate to England and Kenneth, who had been the emerald cutter with the mystery disappearing illness, arrived as a potential buyer.

"Mungwanani."

"Mungwanani, Mmurara heri?"

"Murara terara", we exchanged greetings. "Are you still working in the emerald department?"

"Oh yes."

"Tell me, do you have any stones at home?"

"Muningi (plenty)" he grinned, his heavy black beard framing two full rows of perfect teeth, typical of Rhodesian Africans.

We both laughed, I was confident that none of my stones had been pilfered, but I was aware and sometimes in awe, of the ingenuity in deceit of any population living at breadline level.

Mind you, the breadline wasn't necessary for cunning theft. A few months before this conversation, I had been told that a complete month's consignment of emeralds had left the mine and been missing ever since. To visualize a consignment, imagine a large pack of cereal but with little green stones instead of the cornflakes.

Without warning, the police had raided every employee's house. The consignment was never found, but Melvin G, a long term supervisor, had a fair collection tucked away in various places, and those the police did find.

Melvin was generally well-liked, but he had taken an instant dislike to me, perhaps he sensed my own caution when we met; something about Mr. G. made me uncomfortable. Of course he went to prison, where I'm sure he did some useful networking.

I looked at Kenneth and wondered about that consignment, and, for a moment, whether it would be profitable to buy some stones from him…

Absolutely not, I decided that the less I knew the better. The emeralds I had were legal, I had bought them and they were already in the UK.

Admittedly I had evaded the Rhodesian exchange control laws and having smuggled them out of Rhodesia I could hardly declare them to the UK customs, so, I suppose technically, I did smuggle them into the UK.

***

In the mean time I had an enormous amount of work to do on the second car, the *Riley,* which we hoped to sell in the UK.

The bodywork was made up of steel and aluminium panels nailed to a wooden frame, supposedly ash, but really beech, and actually rotten. It was a traditional coach-built vehicle. The wood had to be replaced. I used what I had to hand, beech and some African *mafutu.*

When I bought the car I was told that it had an engine knock, "Sounds like a big-end-bearing, but it can't be, there's almost 100 pounds of oil pressure."

When I finally started the engine there was no doubt about the noise, or the oil pressure. It was obviously serious, but what was it?

Lying under the car with the sump off and the engine running, I held a can of oil up to the oil pump while I watched the crankshaft spinning around. There was plenty of oil getting to the outer bearings and more than enough on me, but the centre-main and big-end bearings were totally dry.

The engine had been incorrectly assembled after a reconditioning job. It had to come out, be completely stripped and reassembled with the centre bearing-housing reinstalled the right way up. There was no alternative.

At least it was interesting, a twin-cam *Riley* original, a multitude of parts, far more than any other engine I had worked on. There was only one possible sequence of dismantling and subsequent reassembly. Very time consuming.

Eunice had sewn up new seat covers and roof lining before she left, I only had to fit them, easy enough, but time was running out, however I got it driveable.

Three days before I was due to leave, the authorities demanded a valuation of everything before they would grant export permission.

Fortunately the auctioneer valuator, Ian Ferreira, had been in my class at Churchill School. He listed everything and together we worked out and sometimes guessed the most suitable valuations which would be acceptable to export control.

I drove the car for the first time the five miles to the exporter's warehouse. The next time would be from the then, very decrepit King George VI docks (now the very posh Canary Wharf), in London to Southampton.

I sold whatever I could, packed what might be useful, and abandoned the rest on the front lawn with a help-yourself-notice.

One scavenger held out a lump of metal, "This is an FN breech-block?" It was half accusation half incredulous question.

"Yes, I know," I answered.

"What the hell's it doing lying on your front lawn?"

"Well, I couldn't get my hands on the rest of the rifle and I sure as hell don't need it where I'm going. If you think you may need it you're welcome to take it".

He threw the piece down in disgust.

My advertisement under *Miscellaneous* in the local paper read:

Kenwood $150, wheelbarrow $125,
50 metre hosepipe $50, red carpet $50
baize carpet $30,
house $12,000.
Phone 52080.

Everything bar the house sold quickly. For the house I only had one reply.
"This house, where is it?"
"Hatfield, I replied."
"Sorry, not interested, but I like your style."
"Thanks."
That seemed disappointing but turned out to be most fortunate, because had it
sold I would have had to leave the money in my frozen bank account which simply
dissolved in the subsequent economic mess of Mugabe's Government. As it turned
out it was twenty years before I could move the money, but the tenants paid it off
and I sold it for real pounds.

Recently, when Zimbabwe adopted a version of the US dollar, all accounts in
Zimbabwe dollars, regardless of value, were reduced to zero. However, mine had
already been wiped out by Zimbabwe's nut-case economy and subsequent
inflation.

I left the house in the hands of the local estate agent, a Mr. Issy Kaplan, an old
Rhodesian who had known my Dad. There was nothing in writing, just a
handshake.

One tenant did a moonlight flit without paying. The next morning, when Issy
heard about it, he went to the property, seized a trailer which he found there and
sold it to pay the rent.

As rents went up he increased the mortgage repayments instead of paying cash
into my bank account, a very wise move.

Strangely, you can now pull up that house on Google, just type in *44 Logan
Road, Harare*.

Chapter 53

A Step Change in Life

Back in Rhodesia I settled down in the unnerving quiet of our three-bedroomed house. How I missed my noisy squabbling family. I still had to work my notice and sort everything out before actually emigrating.

The first night I was back little Shaun came charging around from next door asking for Brian. I've never again seen a child so crestfallen as when I told him that Brian wasn't coming back.

Ten years later in 1989 we heard that Shaun was trying to contact Brian again. It was just after Brian's fatal car accident.

∗∗

I had decided to have an early night and had only just got into bed when the room lit up with a fluctuating orange glow. A few seconds later it was joined by a rumble of what could have been thunder. It was Wednesday, 11th December 1978.

There was enough light in the clear Rhodesian night to see the thick black billows of smoke above the massive red glow of fire in the distance. It had to be the fuel storage depot a few miles to the north-west.

As I was watching a great balloon of flame billowing up into the night, one of the tanks exploded. This time the noise was much louder.

The phone rang. "What do you think that was?" Eunice's mum asked.

"It has to be the *Shell Depot*." I knew the area and I didn't believe that either *Lion Match* or the power station would burn with such intensity. I was right.

The fire was beyond the capacity of the Salisbury Fire-fighting Service, however they did limit the damage and with additional water-cannon flown in from Johannesburg it was out by the end of the week.

Fortunately no lives were lost and to me the unsung heroes were the African tanker drivers who rescued loaded fuel tankers from the flames.

Everyone who works in the petroleum industry would know that going near a fully loaded tanker in that situation would risk being engulfed in a massive fireball at any moment. Those drivers were gutsy men.

No-one doubted that this was sabotage and I believe it was established that Russian limpet mines had been attached to the tanks by members of Mugabe's ZANU group although Nkomo's ZIPRA faction also claimed responsibility.

Amazingly, after 12 years of sanctions and war, Smith's Rhodesia was still viable and able to limp along without foreign aid.

Now, just over two decades after Independence, in spite of enormous injections of outside help, Mugabe's Zimbabwe relies on the begging-bowl for sustenance.

The Africans I knew and worked with were always willing to work hard and better their lot. It seems strange that their political leaders prefer to beg for charity and impoverish their people in the process of lining their own pockets.

One night a series of distant explosions came from the nearby air base to break the silence. Apparently there had been a rather futile mortar attack on it.

The perpetrators had not wanted to be close enough to be caught up in return fire or be captured. I imagine that they believed (with some justification) that they wouldn't be taken alive, in any case, possession of weapons of war was a capital crime in Rhodesia. Paradoxically, if they did survive they could change sides. The Rhodesian Army had discovered that a "turned" terrorist was invaluable.

The fire at the fuel depot had obviously caused problems, but most people managed to get by on their rations; I don't know how many others did what I did and supplemented their petrol ration with a mixture of benzene and benzol; it can't have been many or those would also have been rationed. The fifteen or so percent of benzol was only added to increase the octane level for smooth running. Apart from being very unpleasant to inhale and a powerful carcinogen it was very destructive to rubber. The new trim I had brought over from Southampton and fitted to the *Riley* was all but destroyed by fumes from the benzol content in the fuel. Presumably, being confined in a shipping container during transit back to England concentrated the effect and caused the problem.

Eunice's job quite clearly could not support us. Not wanting to break into our savings, she had done well to buy, really cheap, both a cooker and a fridge from students as well as mattresses from the *Hotel*. We had brought our camping gear with us, so for the first few days I joined in the in-house camp.

Molly and Stan's son, Adrian, passed on a three piece suite, I went in to *Currys* and did my best to get shop-soiled appliances cheaper than their asking prices. Now I needed a job. *Petters* at Hamble were advertising for a panel wireman. It was almost twenty years since I had done that type of work and I never enjoyed it but it was a wage starting Monday. Now I needed a car.

A banger of a *Renault* was advertised for £150 which the female seller was prepared to deliver the following morning.

Early the next day the car arrived and I listened to some fiction about the drive from Winchester. From the steaming exhaust the car obviously hadn't travelled much more than a mile, so either her Winchester was a lot closer than mine or she was lying. However I had to have a car for Monday and I bought the headache; a horrible thing, that *Renault*.

Petters had been making petrol and diesel engines since 1896. In their Hamble factory they produced *Westinghouse's Thermo-King* units for refrigerated vehicles. As an employee I had no complaints, but I needed a more varied and challenging role. Being on night-shift was the wrong kind of challenge. When an electrical fitter's job came up at Marchwood Power Station I applied and got it. I think someone at Marchwood knew the engineers I had worked under in the electrical supply authority of Salisbury (now Harare).

I know, according to *Google,* the power station only opened in 2009, but that is the present one. I worked at the original one in 1979. That was, of course, the oil-fired facility generating 600 megawatts.

The Kariba hydro system on the Zambesi River, powered by a man-made lake of 2,500 square miles, only produced 600 megawatts (since increased to 1200) at the time. That meant flooding land 100,000 times bigger than Marchwood's 16 acres and about 900 square miles bigger than Hampshire.

By all accounts, with today's technology, a solar system could have matched that output on land a fraction of that size, but more than Marchwood's 16 acres; food for thought.

The *Central Electricity Generating Board* was a nationalised industry. I was amazed at the wastage of tools, materials and clothing. Perhaps I was super sensitive; everything I had encountered in Rhodesia was high-mileage.

The *CEGB* was different. In one instance, the employees had a short (3-day) fork-lift driving course. It was outdoors so we were issued with waterproof overalls, which we kept. I was issued with a comprehensive kit of new tools and although I had to hand them back when I left they would not have been re-issued because they were now second-hand. Many had never been used. Officially they were scrapped. One reason given in favour of scrapping the chrome-plated tools was that the plating could lift and cut the user. That was possible, but unlikely and easy to spot, anyway the few I mislaid at the time and therefore couldn't hand back, haven't peeled to this day.

It was a very civilised place to work, the surroundings were lush and green, there was a clean, well-kept canteen and a block of excellent showers. It could only be described as most favourable employment, with reasonable rates of pay; but still we had to tap into our savings.

I think we could have got some sort of state aid but I never knew about it. As a child I had benefited from the goodwill of friends and relatives. It was a debt I could never repay. Once, only once, I had handouts of new but near unwearable shoddy clothing from some do-gooding women's group. Not only was I expected to be enthusiastically grateful for this useless tat, but their attitude made me feel like something quite untouchable. The experience left a lasting bad taste in my mouth; never again. Neither Eunice nor I wanted what we regarded as charity. I had to get a better paying job.

Fortunately, I read *The Telegraph,* fortunate because that's where the giant, obscenely-rich, Saudi Arabian *Aramco Oil Company* advertised for personnel.

Appendix

Family History

My Father's Family

My father, Owen Boniface (1882-1956) in 1902
After seven year apprenticeship with Barnham Nurseries
Before leaving for South Africa in 1903/4

Owen Boniface standing right
with other early Rhodesian Settlers circa 1911
Family photo

Owen, Evelyn and Friend
Curators House Salisbury Park 1920s

Evelyn, Neville and Owen 1938/9 Winson Road Hatfield
After 1930s Great Depression and Alcohol

My father, Owen Boniface (1882-1956), was the youngest of seven children of Eliza nee Smith (1840-1930) and John Boniface (1842-1932). John was a shepherd and worked in the Yapton, Felpham and Westhampnett areas of Sussex.

Born in 1882 in Yapton, Sussex, Dad had been lucky enough to stay at school until 13, before serving a seven-year apprenticeship with Barnham Nurseries in Sussex. I say lucky, because the 1891 census records his two oldest brothers, 13-year-old William and 11-year-old Mark, as farm labourers.

At thirteen, Owen started work with John Marshal Nurseries in Barnham. By the time he had completed his seven year apprenticeship the firm had been renamed Barnham Nurseries. From there he secured a head gardener's job in Ascot. I believe the company was called John Husband Landscape Gardeners.

Owen migrated to the British Cape Colony early in the twentieth century. I have a postcard he sent from Cape Town in 1904. After working for six years for a firm called Charles Ayres he got the job of Head Gardener at the late C.J. Rhodes's Groote Schuur Estate.

Rhodes had bequeathed it to the State. It was yet to become the Teaching Hospital where Christiaan Barnard carried out the World's first heart transplant so many years later.

After The Union of South Africa was formed in 1910 he moved to Southern Rhodesia, where he was Curator of the Public Gardens in Salisbury from 1913 to 1933.

In 1914 he married Henrietta Carter, who had been the housekeeper to the Bishop of Cape town. They had two children, Jack born in 1914 or 1915 and Molly born in 1920 and presently living in her own bungalow on The Isle of Wight.

When he was in his mid-teens Jack became very ill and underwent surgery. I'm told that he had a brain tumour. Whatever the cause, he went from being a very successful student and sportsman to being committed to a mental hospital. He died in 1945 at the age of 31.

By now Dad was suffering some of the worst effects of alcoholism and was also committed to that hospital. There he received electro-shock-therapy. At the time it was administered without anaesthetic, however, he always said that it saved him, presumably from permanent hospitalization. My Mother said he was never the same again.

While he was in the hospital he spent time with Jack and said that Jack had recovered and should be released but it never happened.

The hospital was 300 miles from Salisbury where we lived, I don't think my parents saw Jack again. They couldn't get to his funeral. I was five; I never met Jack.

Neville was born in 1937 after Dad was released from the Mental Hospital and I arrived three years later when Mum was 43.

This Postcard, of Groote Schuur at the time, was sent by Dad to his sister Kitty.
Dated 4/12/1907

When Dad migrated to Cape Town in the British Cape Colony in 1904, every man in the Cape and Natal (both British colonies) who could sign his name or owned property of £75 or more in value, had the vote, *regardless of race, colour, or creed;* effectively the same right to vote as existed in Britain at the time. However, when the Union with the Transvaal and the Orange Free State was formed in 1910 the non-whites living in those two provinces were denied the vote. After the National Party was elected in the late 1940s, voting rights for non-whites in South Africa were completely withdrawn with the introduction of apartheid.

Dad voted in the first Rhodesian election which took place in 1923 and the sparse female population provided the first woman Member of Parliament in the British Commonwealth, Ethel Tawse Jollie.

He survived the common tropical diseases, notably blackwater fever, the usually fatal complication of malaria. Many years later when I was about eleven, at 69, he was very ill with tick-fever. By the time he allowed us to call the doctor he was through the crisis.

"He's made it through the worst," the doctor said, "he'll be OK now". It wasn't surprising that life spans were short.

***

Salisbury's (Harare) First Town House
Destroyed by Fire circa 1930
postcard dated 7 July1924

X marks the Grave of Eliza and John Boniface
In Yapton, Sussex
unsigned postcard

Eliza (nee Smith) 1840-1930 and John Boniface 1842-1932
my Grandparents

My Mother's Family

Jean Prieur du Plessis, a ships' doctor, was born in Poitiers in Poitou, France in 1638. Although it is claimed by the family that he was related to Armand du Plessis, better known as Cardinal Richelieu, no proof has been found. However, it seems that the connection might be applicable to a lesser French robber-baron; not as infamous as the good Cardinal.

In any event Jean was a Huguenot and the Catholics, with considerable help from Richelieu, were doing their utmost to rid France of all challengers to their hierarchy. The Huguenots were particular targets. So after fleeing initially to Holland, Jean joined those recruited to bring skill and education to the Dutch Cape Colony.

Carel Prieur du Plessis was born on board the *Oosterland* in Table Bay on 18th April 1688.

It's obvious from the estimated 70,000 du Plessis descendants living in South Africa today that Carel, his siblings and their offspring were enthusiastic about making babies; apparently not all within wedlock.

It would be nearly impossible to include all my South African relatives in a family tree so I've depicted a direct line of parentage on my mother's side from 1638.

The Huguenot Museum in Franschhoek, South Africa filled in the gaps.

Hester Helena du Plessis (nee Muller)
My Grandmother
1865-1908

Evert du Plessis 1866-1956 my Grandfather
Oupa to the Family
family photo

Jean Prieur du Plessis (*1638-1708) x Madeleine Menanteau
↓
Carel Prieur du Plessis (*1688-1737) x 1712 Cecilia van Marseveen
↓
Jacobus du Plessis (*1734-?) x 1756 Anna Boeiens
↓
Carel Petrus du Plessis x (*1782-?) Anna du Plessis xx 1794 Sara Petronella Celliers
↓
Charl Jacobus du Plessis x 1812 Hermina Catharina Kleynhans
↓
Evert Phillip du Plessis (*1820-1846) x 1840 Martha Jacoba van Rooyen
He died on his farm *Klaassejacht* leaving an estate of 1 wagon, 24 oxen, 40 cattle and 5 horses.
↓
Gert Thomas du Plessis (*1843-?) x 1866 Johanna van Rooyen
↓
Evert Philippus du Plessis (*1866-1956) x1888 Hester Helena Muller (*1865-1908)
↓
Gertrude Evelyn du Plessis (*1897-1959) x Owen Boniface (*1882-1956)
Owen already had 2 children,
Jack (*1914-1945)
and Molly (*1920- to-date)
by his first wife, Henrietta Carter.
↓
Neville Boniface (*1937-2011) and **Eveart Boniface (*1940- to-date)**
↓
Read **MY AFRICA** for the follow-on.

***

In the 1860s, the Boer brothers, Diederick and Nicolaas de Beer, may or may not have cared whether they were citizens of The Orange Free State or the Transvaal. However, in the early 1870s, a large deposit of diamonds was unearthed on their farm. They then discovered that their land, previously claimed by both the Transvaal and the Orange Free State republics, was in fact, British.

Apparently it was just inside the border of the Cape Colony and they were now, actually, British.

What happened to the brothers I don't know but Cecil Rhodes attached their name to what became the world's dominant diamond trading company.

***

British ambition had been hampered by defeat in the 1880/1881 First Boer War. The resounding rout at Majuba Hill, following the disasters at Laing's Nek and Bronkhorstspruit must have hurt British pride and of course there was a desire to control the country and its gold production. Certainly they wanted to bring this upstart of a tiny white tribe into line.

Whatever the reason Lord Milner would become the manipulator (perhaps war-monger would be more accurate) to bring the change about.

Of course, a peace treaty had been signed, but the Transvaal Boers were unsophisticated and it wasn't difficult to get them to fire the first shot in 1899.

According to the rule book it would be no contest; Britain could, and did by the end of the war, field 450,000 trained solders. Not only from Britain but also recruited from Australia Canada, New Zealand and Rhodesia; five for every Boer, man, woman and child.

The problem with this enemy of farmers was that they weren't trained; and they weren't stupid. They didn't stand and shoot it out like a European army, neither would they charge headlong into battle against machine gun fire like the native tribes. Lacking the discipline and the officers of the British, they shot from cover and got out in a hurry when they had to.

Lord Kitchener soon realised that this was a different kind of war and decided to destroy their support, so he embarked on a scorched earth policy. His troops torched Transvaal and Free State farms and imprisoned the women and children in concentration camps. While these were never intended as death camps, the death toll from exposure, malnutrition and disease was horrendous.

Not surprisingly, the Boers in the field became deeply embittered and some retaliated by attacking Cape farms as well as railways and military installations.

Meanwhile many Cape Boers, who, initially, might have sympathised with their northern cousins, had no option but to defend their farms and businesses against the attackers from the Boer republics.

The British army supported any community which was prepared to fight its corner and could contribute fighting men.

My grandfather, Evert du Plessis, became recruit number 99 in his local force.

Unfortunately his group were captured by the Scheepers and van der Merwe gang of 300 or so men. They were closely guarded and their horses and footwear were taken away; their farms left undefended.

On the night of August 19th 1901[23] this gang raided Evert's farm, Keurbooms, near Oudtshoorn. They ransacked and torched the house, stole whatever they could and destroyed the rest including livestock.

Hester Helena du Plessis fled with her eight children into the freezing Karoo night. My mother, Evelyn, was not quite four, Helgard was two and Maggie, at three months, was a babe in arms.

---

[23]See page 117 *Commandant Gideon Scheepers and the search for his grave* ISBN 0 6202 4534 4.

Several of the raiders were named du Plessis; they must have been relatives.

Meanwhile, van der Merwe and Scheepers had separated. On Sept 9th Col Crabbe caught up with van der Merwe at Driefontein farm, where van der Merwe was killed in the ensuing firefight[i24], as was one of the du Plessis.

Scheepers was subsequently captured, court martialled and sentenced to death for murder. The victims were unarmed blacks and mixed-race messengers working for the British.

It would seem that Scheepers regarded them as traitors to the Boers; something which would seem to be an acknowledgement that their white blood originated from the Boer settlers.

Scheepers was executed by firing squad on 18th January 1902.
***

After the war the British Government paid compensation for the farms which had been destroyed by the British forces. It refused to compensate Cape farmers who had fought on the British side and consequently had their farms destroyed by the Boers. The result was widespread poverty.
***

When the 1914-1918 war broke out, Evert du Plessis and his two sons, my uncles, Thomas and Helgard, all volunteered. Evert was a medic/stretcher bearer, Thomas and Helgard served at the front. Helgard was fourteen.

All three survived the war but Thomas died of blackwater fever circa1927. I don't know if Helgard served in WW 2, most South African veterans did volunteer for the second time. Helgard was still alive in 1947.

All South Africans were volunteers and most fit young men seemed to be on active service. However, there were others still bitter from the Boer War who supported the Nazis. Instances where men in uniform were attacked and severely beaten were not uncommon.

In all Evert had ten daughters and three sons. The third son, Pieter, died on 9th February 1906. He was just seven months old. Evert's wife, Hester, died 24th April 1908.

Evert, my only grandparent still alive when I was born, died in 1956. I met him over Christmas in 1947/48 when we stayed with my Aunt Jo in Oudtshoorn.

I was seven

---

[24]See pages 75 and 76 *Commandos deur die Klein Karoo* for an account in English by Major Russel. ISBN 0-620-37339-9